THE
BATTLE
FOR COAL

THE
BATTLE
FOR COAL

Miners and the
Politics of Nationalization
in France,
1940–1950

Darryl Holter

 NORTHERN ILLINOIS UNIVERSITY PRESS
DeKalb 1992

© 1992 by Northern Illinois University Press
Published by the Northern Illinois University Press,
DeKalb, Illinois 60115
Manufactured in the United States using acid-free paper ∞
Design by Julia Fauci

Library of Congress Cataloging-in-Publication Data
Holter, Darryl
    The battle for coal : miners and the politics of
nationalization in France, 1940–1950 / by Darryl Holter.
        p.   cm.
    Includes bibliographical references and index.
    ISBN 0-87580-167-6
    1. Coal trade—Government ownership—France—
History—20th century.   2. Trade-unions—Coal miners—
France—History—20th century.   3. Reconstruction
(1939–1951)—France.   I. Title.
HD9552.6.H65   1992   91–28157
338.2′724′094409044—dc20   CIP

Jacket/frontispiece photograph courtesy of Houillères du
Bassin du Nord et du Pas-de-Calais.

For Oliver S. Holter and Helen Marie Holter

Contents

List of Tables

Preface

WHAT BEGAN AS A case study of a controversial, two-month labor dispute has resulted in a book on French coal miners, their unions, and the politics of nationalized coal across more than two decades. I began to explore the subject by starting with the periodical literature from the late 1940s, but I found myself pushing further and further into the past in an effort to understand the coal-mining industry and the development of the miners' movement. It seemed to me that traditional approaches to labor history, which focused on the conflict and interaction between organized labor and business elites, were unable to explain adequately why and how coal mining was nationalized. Time and again I encountered the increasingly important role of government in economic policy-making as the state expanded its influence over a wider and wider terrain. I grappled with how to fit the state's development into the ongoing conflicts between coal operators and mine workers. Gradually, I began to construct a model built upon the interaction of coal operators, mine workers, and the state.

The story of the coal miners and nationalization provided some answers to larger questions about postwar France that had long intrigued me. How did the Left and organized labor emerge as such a potent political force after the liberation? Why did their movement fall apart after a few short years? How was state intervention connected to changes in the balance of power between labor and business? What was the real story about the "big strikes" of 1947 and 1948? How did the cold war affect French politics at the local level and in the labor movement? The book offers answers to these questions that are derived from the experiences of a key industry, a large work force, and a major labor union.

Source materials presented a problem. Because my focus is on a relatively recent period, very few historical works have been published on the subject and many of the archival materials I sought were not readily available. However, I discovered a wide body of literature in economics, sociology, law, industrial relations, political science, and international relations that touched upon issues related to coal mining. In addition, I found that local newspapers and labor periodicals were very useful sources. The task then became one of pulling this material together and using it to reconstruct the story of the coal miners. I also tried to go beyond the existing literature by focusing on the miners and their unions as important actors in the shaping of coal policies.

The archives of the Charbonnages de France in Paris were very useful because their holdings include documentation from the leading mining organization as it underwent a number of changes in the transformation from a private to a public entity. This includes material from the Comité Central des Houillères de France (CCHF) (before 1940), the Comité d'Organisation des Houillères (COH) during the war years, the Office Professionnel des Houillères (OPH) for 1944 and 1945 and the Charbonnages de France for 1946 and after. The Charbonnages de France and the Houillères du Bassin of the Nord–Pas-de-Calais (HBNPC) do not allow access to the minutes of administrative council meetings, but former members had retained reports that were shared with me and proved extremely useful.

Many individuals helped to make this book possible. Research began under the direction of the late Professor Harvey Goldberg at the University of Wisconsin–Madison. He encouraged the project and discussed it with me as it progressed. I think he would have enjoyed the final results and would have been proud to see another book on French labor by one of his former graduate students. Professor Étienne Dejonghe of the Université de Lille in France steered me toward important source materials. Jolyon Howorth and Erik Olin Wright offered suggestions as the project began. A number of individuals in France were kind enough to assist me, including Léon Delfosse, Catherine François, Jean Gordon, Daniel Hemery, Diana Johnstone, Gilbert Sauchel, André Théret, and Isabelle Vellay. Gary Cross and I spent hours discussing how to conceptualize the relationship between labor and social reform in a century marked by state intervention. I benefited from comments on various parts of this work by a number of scholars, including Susan Bachrach, Jim Cronin, Patrick Fridenson, Olivier Kourchid, Richard Kuisel, George Ross, and Irwin Wall. Drafts of the manuscript were read by Professor Étienne Dejonghe.

Carole Shammas probably deserves the most credit for listening to me talk about these coal miners for so long.

Abbreviations

CCHF	Comité Central des Houillères de France (top management body in the coal-mining industry before nationalization)
CEPAG	Commission d'Études des Problèmes d'Après-Guerre (a Resistance research group)
CFTC	Confédération Française des Travailleurs Chrétiens (the Catholic trade union federation)
CGC	Confédération Générale des Cadres (a union of managerial staff)
CGT	Confédération Générale du Travail (France's largest trade union federation)
CGTU	Confédération Générale du Travail Unitaire (Communist-backed labor organization that merged with the CGT in 1936)
CNPF	Conseil Nationale du Patronat Français (France's main business organization)
COH	Comité d'Organisation des Houillères (established by the Vichy government to direct the coal industry)
COICMS	Comité d'Organisation de l'Industrie des Combustibles Minéraux Solides (official title of the COH)
CRS	Compagnies Républicaines de Sécurité (state police force)
CUSA	Comités d'Unité Syndicale et Action (clandestine labor groups formed during the Occupation period)
CVCEP	Commission de Vérification des Comptes des Entreprises Publiques (established by parliament to monitor nationalized industries)

DGEN	Délégation Générale à l'Équipement National (economic planning agency set up during the Vichy period)
ECSC	European Coal and Steel Community
FO	Force Ouvrière (anti-Communist labor federation that left CGT in 1947)
HBNPC	Houillères du Bassin Nord–Pas-de-Calais (the coal mines of the Nord and Pas-de-Calais region)
IGAME	Inspecteur Général de l'Administration en Mission Extraordinaire (special antistrike military force)
INSEE	Institut National de la Statistique et des Études Économiques (government agency that collects data on the economy)
JOC	Jeunesses Ouvrière Chrétienne (Catholic organization for young workers)
MF	Ministère des Finances (Ministry of Finance)
MRP	Mouvement Républicain et Populaire (the Christian Democratic Party)
OCRPI	Office Central de Répartition des Produits Industriels (wartime agency concerned with allocation of industrial materials)
OEEC	Office of European Economic Cooperation (postwar economic agency involving western Europe and the United States)
OPH	Office Professionnel des Houillères (the coal industry's top management body after the dissolution of the COH and prior to the establishment of the Charbonnages de France)
PCF	Parti Communiste Français (the French Communist party)
PDP	Parti Démocrate Populaire (Popular Democratic Party)
RIC	Résistants d'Inspiration Chrétienne (a Catholic Resistance group)
SFIO	Section Française de l'Internationale Ouvrière (the French Socialist party)
SIHN	Syndicat des Ingénieurs des Houillères du Nord–Pas-de-Calais (an organization of engineers affiliated with the CGC)

SNIM   Syndicat National des Ingénieurs des Mines (an
            organization of mining engineers affiliated with the CGT)

UNITEC   Union Nationale des Ingénieurs, Techniciens et Cadres
            (a Communist-backed organization of engineers)

THE
BATTLE
FOR COAL

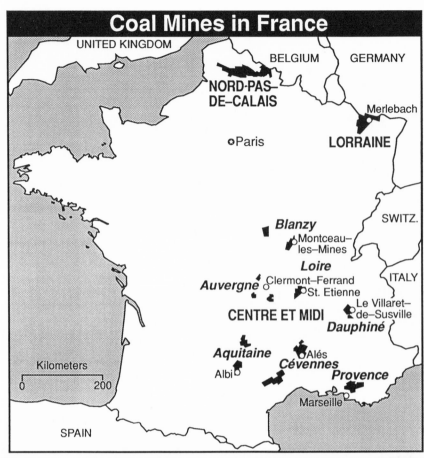

Coal Mines in France

UNITED KINGDOM

BELGIUM   GERMANY

NORD-PAS–
DE–CALAIS

Merlebach

⊕Paris

LORRAINE

SWITZ.

◗ Blanzy

◖Montceau–
les–Mines

Loire

Auvergne ○ Clermont–Ferrand

◗ St. Etienne

ITALY

Le Villaret–
◖de–Susville

CENTRE ET MIDI

Dauphiné

Aquitaine ○Alés

Albi ▢   Cévennes

Provence

Marseille

Kilometers
0   200

SPAIN

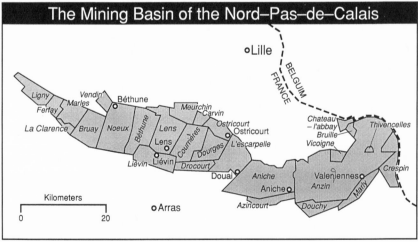

The Mining Basin of the Nord–Pas–de–Calais

○Lille

BELGIUM
FRANCE

Ligny   Vendin   Béthune
Marles
Ferfay   Meurchin
                    Carvin
La Clarence Bruay Noeux Béthune Lens Ostricourt   Chateau   Thivencelles
                                    Ostricourt   –l'abbay
                           Lens Courrières   Bruille
                                    Dourges L'escarpelle Vicoigne
                    Liévin Liévin Drocourt
             Lièvin   Drocourt   Valenciennes ○   Crespin
                    Douai ○ Aniche   Anzin
                              Aniche Marly
Kilometers   Azincourt   Douchy
0   20   ○Arras

Introduction

A s German troops retreated from France's northern coal basin in September 1944, economic recovery hinged on a desperate search for coal. Nearly 90 percent of French primary energy consumption derived from coal. However, French coal production had plummeted during the war years, and imported coal was not available in war-torn Europe. To solve the coal shortage France, traditionally the world's largest importer of coal, was forced to rely on its own troubled coal-mining industry, and especially the recently liberated coal-producing regions of the Nord and Pas-de-Calais, which provided about two-thirds of French coal output. In Paris, the new provisional government proclaimed its intention to revive the economy. But the path to economic recovery led through the northern coal mines and the tools needed to break the energy logjam were in the hands of 150,000 coal miners.

The story of labor, the coal crisis, and nationalized industry in France provides a unique lens that both magnifies and refracts the larger elements of politics and society in western Europe. As a case study in industrial policy, an examination of French coal mining can deepen our understanding of the postwar experience with government ownership, labor relations, and worker participation. It also reveals how industrial policies can secure the support of organized labor in situations of national emergency.

Nearly all the literature on the French postwar economy makes reference to the coal crisis, but the subject has rarely been explored in detail. Nor has the large body of material from economic, political, social, and historical sources been brought together and analyzed in order to reveal how France confronted and eventually overcame its coal shortage. As the story is uncovered, however, the limitations of traditional methodologies begin to emerge. Econometric literature on energy issues reveals little about how the new industrial policies helped France bridge the energy gap.[1] Business scholars who have written on French industrial policy have shown little interest in historical approaches to the subject. Economic literature rarely pays attention to worker issues and the role of labor organizations.[2] The same is true of most of the works by political scientists.[3] Some of the best historical research has been done by local historians, but their emphasis lies more with highlighting the uniqueness of their region than generalizing about the connections between economic policies and national politics.[4] Diplomatic historians have probed foreign policy issues related to the French coal crisis, but they tend to see economic issues and labor relations as secondary elements whose fates were determined by the larger international framework.[5]

The limitations of traditional approaches suggest the need for a more synthetic conceptual analysis that can transcend the boundaries separating economics, social science, and history and bring these various elements into a more coherent focus. This study is a cross-disciplinary labor history that attempts to integrate industrial conflict, politics, and the emerging cold war economy of postwar Europe. It begins by focusing on a central subject: the mine workers and their unions. In this approach, the coal miners and the labor organizations in the mining communities are treated not as obstacles to economic growth but as important "actors" or subjects in a crucial struggle to rebuild the French coal mines. The industry's key strategic location and the new politics of the liberation period produced a situation wherein the actions of the miners had an impact on the rest of the country. No wonder the posters plastered up in the mining communities exhorted "Miners: all of France is depending upon you!" The coal miners and their union leaders were vital agents in a process of industrial and social reform. They made choices and took action that affected the coal-mining industry and the French economy as a whole.

The key episodes in the story of the coal mines—the shaping of the nationalization, the battle of production, the strikes of 1947 and 1948—serve as the study's narrative framework. The transformation of the industry—from backwardness and disrepair in 1940 to record-breaking productivity in the 1950s—provides the backdrop against which labor's actions can be more clearly discerned. Within this narrative setting, various themes are explored, in a roughly chronological order, throughout the book. Since these themes come into play at various junctures in the narrative and because they often overlap, it seems appropriate to identify them briefly before reviewing the literature on each.

Nationalized Industry: A Paradox (1940–1945)

Government ownership and industrial policy provided a framework for increasing coal production and opening the way to economic recovery. A final chapter in a long history of state intervention in coal mining began in 1944 when the government took control of the northern coal mines. Yet the new structures and policies of nationalization were constructed over a three-year period and were subject to economic constraints and political pressures. Government proclamations were not sufficient to resolve the coal miners' grievances, especially when wildcat strikes threatened economic recovery.

Labor and the Battle of Production (1945–1947)

A larger role for labor organizations was necessary to restore order in the mines, foster labor-management cooperation, and promote a "battle of production." The union-led production campaign intensified in 1945 and 1946 and output increased. But controversy surrounded the actions undertaken by union leaders to increase production. In 1947, new policies reduced labor's representation in management and produced a reemergence of industrial conflict in the mines.

Labor Politics and the Cold War (1947–1950)

Union policies were closely linked to political struggles that emerged with the beginning of the cold war. Socialists and Communists competed for power within the unions, the nationalized industries, and local government. But cold war pressures deepened political conflicts within the government and inside the coal mines, leading to the big strikes of 1947 and 1948. The failure of the 1948 strike ended labor's attempt to increase its role in coal policy-making. But French coal output edged upward, American coal exports increased, and the mines were modernized. The government abandoned its emphasis on energy independence and moved toward economic integration in the European Coal and Steel Community in 1950.

NATIONALIZED INDUSTRY: A PARADOX

For more than a century, nationalization has provided a cornerstone for economic democracy for labor and the Left.[6] The business community, however, has tended to see government ownership as the first step toward a socialist economy. But although the proponents of state ownership have usually been dissatisfied with its results, some of the biggest opponents of nationalization have learned the value of state intervention, especially when failing but essential industries were revived in order to enhance overall economic growth.

The bulk of the literature on nationalized industry in France has not gone far beyond the old pro-and-con debates to shed much light on the paradoxical nature of nationalization. Enactment of nationalization measures in France led to a number of highly negative reports, usually connected to conservative political campaigns, in the late 1940s.[7] Researchers in the 1950s wrote pessimistically about the nationalizations. David Pinckney found that excessive influence of labor unions gave the nationalized industries a bad reputation.[8] A study on nationalized industries in France and Italy, published in 1955, took Pinckney's criticism further and contended that the French government, in an effort to break Communist influence, was compelled to replace a decentralized, democratized system with highly centralized state-control mechanisms.[9] Warren C. Baum's study for the Rand Corporation in 1958 argued that state ownership shielded too much of French industry from competition, thus preventing a dynamic economy.[10] Disenchantment with the results of nationalization on the part of labor unions and leftist parties in the 1950s contributed to the pessimistic consensus against nationalization.

A few writers, who focused less on the internal difficulties of nationalization and more on its impact on the rest of the economy, produced less critical assessments. Some even began to link nationalization with the economic boom of the 1960s. Buried within Herbert Luethy's pessimistic account of the French economy, written in 1953, is a description of the nationalized industries as an enclave of modernism in an old France that remained bureaucratic and backward.[11] Several economists noted that the state regulated prices in the nationalized sector in efforts to stimulate the private sector and to serve as a check against inflation. John Ardagh reported that planning mechanisms left France in a good position to make the best use of Marshall Plan funds, most of which went into rebuilding key industries, such as coal mining.[12] François Caron claimed that state-directed promotion of key sectors of the French infrastructure, especially energy, laid the foundation for true industrialization.[13] Jean-Jacques Carré, Paul Dubois, and Edmond Malinvaud found that investment in the public sector industries allowed the government to widen the extent to which the rest of the economy could develop.[14] John B. Sheahan, author of a study on "promotion and control" of French industry, revealed the value of public ownership as a support system for private enterprise.[15] Andrew Schonfield focused on the growth of public power in west European capitalism in order to explain the economic boom of the 1960s.[16] Pasquale Saracena, top economist for the

Italian state holding company, saw public enterprise as necessary to maximize the potential of the economy and society while avoiding swings toward underconsumption and stagnation that could result from implementing pure market principles.[17] Richard Kuisel's study of business and the state situated the nationalizing of French industries within a century-long evolution from economic liberalism to new forms of economic management.[18] These studies expand our understanding of planning and the role of the public sector in the French economy. Yet none of them focus on the role of workers and labor organizations, leaving the contradictory and paradoxical nature of government ownership relatively unexplored.

The best recent overview of the nationalization process in France was produced after a number of French scholars convened in 1980 to discuss historical aspects of state-owned industry. The resulting book, edited by Claire Andrieu, Lucette Le Van, and Antoine Prost, explores the ideology and origins of nationalization, how it was perceived by political parties, business, and unions, and the different ways in which government ownership was extended over various industries.[19]

A close examination of nationalized coal mining, with particular attention to the role of labor, helps to explain the paradox of nationalization. As the process of government ownership unfolded, the state mixed labor demands for social reform and worker participation with business demands for modernization and capital accumulation. The particular mix never remained constant but fluctuated in relation to changes in the economy and politics. Government intervention to overcome economic bottlenecks frequently meant reconciling conflicting concerns of industry and labor. The results could only be contradictory.

Some of the concepts elaborated by recent "state theory," especially the notion of relative autonomy of the state, can be fleshed out by focusing on the story of state intervention in nationalized coal. The French state was compelled to rescue the economy by mediating between classes to restore order in the mines.[20] By nationalizing the industry, however, the state acted against the interests of the old coal operators. Staking out a position of "autonomy" relative to the narrow interests of one employer group, the state guided the removal of the coal mines from private hands into the public sector. This process permitted (and indeed required) the introduction of new forms of worker participation and social reform that reduced conflicts in the mines and helped to increase coal output. But state intervention was also aimed at improving the business climate by holding down the price of coal, assisting the process of accumulation by coal-consuming industries, and taming a disaffected but strategically located mass of mine workers.[21]

This study of nationalized coal mining reveals how state structures and policies emerge out of a three-sided relationship between employers, organized labor, and state managers. Faced with a coal crisis in late 1944, the new government, directed by a liberation coalition of Gaullists, Communists, and Socialists, offered the miners nationalization of the mines and the promise of a sweeping new reform of employment practices in exchange for increased coal output. A few months later, when bitter conflicts between mine workers and management continued to sap the production effort, unions were given an even bigger decision-making role in the industry, including the responsibility to prevent strikes. Production increased, but changes in the political situation altered the composition of the government and forced changes in coal policies. When military forces occupied the coal-mining basin to put an end to the coal miners' strikes, the state, now governed by an anti-Communist coalition, rolled back many elements of the social reform in the mines as part of a process of modernization. Once the miners' movement was broken, the battle of production was transformed into a drive to increase productivity by increasing output while reducing the work force.

In a comparison of postwar nationalization of industries in France, Great Britain, Germany, Austria, and Italy, Claire Andrieu found that French policymakers were most willing to extend state control over entire industries, exercise strong control over the economy, and institute real power-sharing arrangements within the nationalized industries. Andrieu attributed these characteristics of the French model to the fact that the nationalization was instituted with little delay by a left-oriented government at a time when conservative forces were relatively weak.[22] This analysis seems accurate, but it partially obscures the key role played by labor organizations representing workers in the industries brought under state control. For example, the act of extending government ownership over the mining firms did not succeed in putting an end to the bitter conflicts that erupted between workers and management personnel. From the perspective of the miners, only the Confédération Générale du Travail (CGT), France's largest trade union federation, possessed the legitimacy that was required to move away from conflict and toward labor-management cooperation. The significance of labor's leverage emerges in bolder relief when we compare it with the situation after World War I. Then the government teamed up with coal operators to rebuild the industry, with no real input from organized labor. After World War II, however, the government removed the industry from the hands of the old owners and created a labor-state alliance to install a new mining regime. This is why the issue of nationalization cannot be separated from an analysis of the new role played by labor.

LABOR AND THE BATTLE OF PRODUCTION

In an effort to win the war quickly and get the economy moving again, leaders of the CGT abandoned their adversarial relation to management and traditional commitment to class struggle. Instead, they called upon workers to increase production as rapidly as possible. Nowhere was the "battle of production" waged more systematically than in coal mining. The results were quite impressive. Within months after the end of the war, French coal output edged near prewar levels, rising at a more rapid rate than most other industries.

Despite its importance to the French economy, this unique episode in labor-management relations has never been explored in detail. Most of the research that has dealt with the coal crisis has focused on the actions of government officials, politicians, and planning experts. Labor's contribution to the postwar economy is rarely discussed. When the unions are mentioned, their role has usually been seen as unimportant or negative, even though union officials headed economic ministries, authored new social policies, and performed managerial roles in industry during this period.

Conservative writers dismissed the battle of production as a tactical ploy by the Parti Communiste Français (PCF), although several publicly applauded the union's new constructive role. Socialists, the chief rivals to the Communists in the coal-mining communities, sought to prosper from the anomaly of the emphasis on production and the fact that some of the new policies were unpopular among rank-and-file workers. Critics further to the left were even more hostile, seeing the production campaign as a symptom of the PCF's capitulation to parliamentarianism and modern capitalism.[23]

More recently, however, a few scholars have begun to take another look at the battle of production. The essays by Évelyne Desbois, Yves Jeanneau, and Bruno Mattei offer some critical new insights into the production campaign. Seeking to go beyond the published record, these researchers have utilized less traditional historical sources, such as oral history, images of miners in popular literature, and the use of wall posters and other media. The result is a reinterpretation of the period in psychological and cultural terms. They conclude that although the production battle was waged in the name of a new economic system, the long-term results—mine closings, unemployment, and industrial disease—seemed merely to duplicate the old order.[24] Rolande Trempé pushed the chronological bounds of the battle back to the days of the Popular Front and the years of the German occupation. In a brilliant analysis of the internal workings of the coal industry, Trempé uncovers a surprising degree of continuity in the way the coal operators, unions, and state mining engineers interacted to create a "mystique of production" within the framework of the "national interest" in three different coal crises.[25]

A close examination of the battle of production produces a complex picture. Increasing labor's voice in the management of the industry became the starting point for transcending industrial conflict and forging an unprecedented degree of collaboration between workers and management. Union-led policies based on labor-management cooperation allowed organized labor to project a different image. By promoting cooperation at a time of national crisis, "constructive unionism" displayed a new face to an enlarged membership, including many first-time union members. The battle also offered a new public image for the miners, who in the past were sometimes considered to be overpaid and pampered with management-provided housing and free coal. Now union leaders exhorted the coal miners to put the nation's economic requirements above their own specific concerns. At the same time, management's inability to restore order and the workers' critical position at the point of production enhanced the ability of union leaders to win a larger role in determining coal policies. As output began to edge upward, CGT leaders sought to turn the coal mines, traditionally a symbol of alienation and class conflict, into a showcase for a new brand of worker participation.

This study exposes the point and counterpoint of labor-management cooperation and industrial conflict. By focusing on the action of miners, we see how shop-floor pressures and bread-and-butter economic concerns combined with national and international politics to drive the miners' union from the production battle to the picket line. The battle involved a trade-off between the unions and government. On the one hand, labor leaders assumed the tough task of convincing skeptical miners that a new era would open if they were willing to make an extraordinary effort to close the nation's energy gap. In return, the unions demanded representation in policy-making at all levels and a sweeping social reform designed to improve the coal miners' dismal living and working conditions. This study reveals how the the deal struck between union leaders and the government was created and how it fell apart. For three years, from September 1944 to November 1947, labor leaders delivered their part of the bargain, restoring order in the mines, calling upon workers to cooperate with management personnel, fighting absenteeism, and preventing strikes.

The threat of renewed conflict, however, loomed in the background even as the experiment with cooperation yielded record-breaking results in production. Workers soon saw their real wages drop precipitously due to inflation. Moreover, the creation and staffing of new organizational structures in the nationalized mines drew criticism from those who felt the union had gained too much power. The CGT leaders found themselves being pushed from the arena of policy-making. Disputes between underground miners and foremen erupted. The grievance system broke down under the weight of numerous charges and complaints. Disputes with management led to situations in which workers were slow to arrive at the coal face or mysterious equipment problems forced workers to return to the surface installations earlier than expected. By the spring of 1947, union leaders found it difficult to prevent unauthorized work stoppages, signaling the beginning of the end of cooperation.

When the coal miners walked off the job in 1947 and 1948, many government officials and political figures seemed convinced that the strikes were part of an insurrectionary movement. This interpretation has been echoed by subsequent writers. However, a close look at the strikes suggests that the miners, far from trying to overthrow the government, were trying to restore the terms of the trade-off that had provided the basis for nationalization and labor peace.

Most writers who have made reference to the strikes have relied on journalists from the Paris-based dailies, a few political commentators, or the opinions of government leaders. Few researchers bothered to interview union leaders or ask rank-and-file activists their views on the motives behind the strikes. As a result, the strikes are described in predictably similar terms: The Communists successfully exploited a poor economy and led thousands of unwitting workers into revolutionary strikes. They had dangerous objectives: to prevent economic recovery, to topple the government, to prepare for a seizure of power, to keep France out of the Marshall Plan, or all of the above. A few observers, including Alexander Werth, questioned this emphasis on politics, arguing that declining purchasing power inevitably propelled labor militancy. But such reasoning carried less influence than bombastic speeches in the Chamber of Deputies or screaming newspaper headlines.

In the mines, the discussion on whether or not the strikes were political (as critics of labor argued) or economic (as union leaders contended) was at best a false debate. The strikes were both. Economic factors, especially soaring inflation and the accompanying decline in real wages, explained the broad support for the strikes. But the strikes were political by necessity. The government could refuse any wage settlement reached without its consent. Thus, the only way for the unions to halt the slide of real wages was to convince the government to adopt policies to control prices and raise wages. This important point, missed by most contemporary writers, was rarely considered by subsequent researchers. However, in a study of strikes in France published in 1965, Robert Goetz-Girey argued against making sharp distinctions between political and professional strikes, particularly during the early postwar period.[26] The most important study, written by Edward Shorter and Charles Tilly, looked at strikes since 1830. The authors revealed how the strike was gradually transformed from an effort to maintain job control to a device for pressing working-class demands at the national level and in the political arena. While noting that the 1947 and 1948 strikes seemed more like civil war than collective bargaining, they also found that hundreds of thousands of white-collar employees and nonunion workers also walked off the job during those same years, without central orchestration and without searching for political confrontations.[27]

Close examination of the strikes reveals that a large number of coal miners viewed them as defensive actions aimed at retaining or restoring rights they had won previously, especially in the social reform that followed nationalization. The connection Tilly and Shorter saw between collective action and labor's desire for governmental intervention applied to all French workers, but it was particularly true for the coal miners, who worked for a government-directed industry. Writers who were close to the action in the coalfields noted that the miners seemed resigned to striking as the only way to force the government into action. How could it have been otherwise? Once the mines had been nationalized, workers confronted the state, not as an arbitrator in a conflict between labor and management, but as the employer. In the nationalized sector, labor action was, by necessity, a political act. And the problems that produced the strikes could be resolved only in the political arena.

LABOR POLITICS AND THE COLD WAR

Union policies were linked to political struggles, which were increasingly affected by the cold war. Researchers have been most interested in establishing the connections between the French Communist party and the Soviet Union or describing the shifting fortunes of the national political parties. Few have focused on labor politics, particularly at the regional level or in specific sectors of the economy. This study sheds light on key elements in labor politics: the relationship between the PCF and the CGT, the competition between the Socialist party and Communist party for popular support, and the influence of the cold war on coal policy and labor politics.

The strong link between the PCF and the CGT has long fascinated observers. Yet few researchers have asked why the Communists emerged as the dominant force in French labor. More specifically, why did French workers elect Communist leaders to top union posts, follow Communist union leaders into an unprecedented production campaign, and brave government opposition by participating in the big strikes of 1947 and 1948?

Georges Lefranc, a prolific writer on French labor in the 1950s and 1960s, described a "Communist conquest of the CGT."[28] That interpretation was taken up by other writers on labor and French communism, namely, Adolph Sturmthal, Val Lorwin, and Alfred Reiber. Sturmthal and Lefranc identify a conjuncture of fortuitous events that allowed the PCF to dominate the largest French union: the Soviet Union's heroic wartime reputation, the Communist role in the Resistance, the discipline of their cadres, and the purges of non-Communist competitors in organized labor.[29] Val Lorwin added detail to Lefranc's overview without departing from his findings.[30] He described how the Communist wing of the CGT mobilized its forces in the months after the liberation, taking control of the CGT apparatus and the major unions of the federation. Lorwin noted the weaknesses of the anti-Communist oppositionists and the Communists' energetic efforts to appeal to young workers. A "mystique of unity," wrote Lorwin, led workers to join the ranks of one major labor organization and to stand together as a class rather than as individuals.[31] Alfred Reiber attributed the Communist success among the unions to "Communist terror within the CGT" and the "apathy" of workers in the CGT.[32]

Widely cited in subsequent literature on postwar politics, Sturmthal, Lefranc, Lorwin, and Reiber saw an insurrectional political force leading an uninformed mass of industrial workers. These early interpretations of French labor politics underscored old generalizations about Communists: that they were dangerous revolutionaries, pliant tools of Soviet expansionism, or less than legitimate elements in the labor movement. This negative view of the Communists is connected to a portrayal of workers as docile, unwitting simpletons who understood little about political reality. In this oft-repeated viewpoint, the Communists "conquered" the labor movement after the liberation by tricking foolish workers into supporting union leaders who represented interests other than those of the workers.[33]

More recent scholars have searched for a new understanding of the appeal of French communism. Annie Kriegel saw the party as a "counter-society" that offered members and sympathizers an alternative to the dominant political culture.[34] The counter-society was aimed at replacing the old order, and when it was harnessed to the goals of the Soviet Union, it became a subversive force. Kriegel's thesis has been challenged by writers like Georges Lavau and Irwin Wall who contend that the PCF plays a functional role in a complex society by offering a voice to the "little people," factory workers, poor people, struggling farmers, alienated employees, intellectuals, and immigrants.[35]

Annie Lacroix-Riz has also examined why the PCF emerged as the leading political force in the CGT.[36] She looked at sources never explored before: private papers, internal party communications, correspondence from dozens of trade unions, recently released government archival sources, and local and regional party and trade union papers. The result is a rich treatment of party-union relations, including evidence that workers were active participants, not passive observers, in union activities. Disputing the notion that the Communists "conquered" the CGT, Lacroix-Riz suggests that "a largely generalized consensus" among workers allowed the Communists alone to lead the way in reconstituting the unions. She finds an "osmosis" between workers and Communist activists. "The Communists took over the top positions in the CGT," Lacroix-Riz wrote, "because they had obtained a dominant position within the French working class."[37]

George Ross considered the matter of how trade union concerns were squared with the party's political strategy by creating a model for analyzing the relationship between the PCF's political agenda and CGT policies. By comparing changes in the labor market with party-union relations over a half century, Ross reveals how the CGT carved out a degree of autonomy relative to PCF political goals. For Ross, the key to the Communist victory in the CGT was the organizational factor. Although the 1920s and early 1930s were poor times for union activism, they produced a new generation of labor activists with useful organizing experience, especially in the private sector. Donald Reid, in his book on the miners of Decazeville, suggested that although the pro-Communist miners did not expect to win many strikes in the 1920s and 1930s, they used the strikes to help workers understand the sources of their exploitation and to build cadres of activists committed to working against them.[38] When the CGT grew from 1.5 million in 1939 to 6 million in 1946, the Communists were carried into leadership positions. "The spoils in the CGT," wrote Ross, "went to the faction best prepared to carry out this organizational work."[39]

The rise and fall of the French Left hinged upon relations between the two parties. Most studies of that relationship have centered on national politics, election results, and foreign policy conflicts. From the perspective of the coal-mining communities, however, a different picture emerges. On the one hand, the intensity of disagreements between the parties did not always coincide with, or reflect, political events at the national level. On the other hand, several controversies that erupted in the mining basin sharpened conflicts between top leftist leaders in Paris. In the mining basin, Socialists and Communists competed for power and influence within the union movement, inside the management of the nationalized mines, and at the municipal level. Competition turned into conflict when Socialists supported an anti-Communist faction that broke away from the CGT and led a "back-to-work" movement during the strikes of 1947 and 1948. Confrontations during this period poisoned Socialist-Communist relations at the local level for many years.

Examining relations between the two parties through the prism of the coal crisis helps us to understand the origins and outcomes of these conflicts. It also allows us to discern how and why both parties shaped and reshaped their political strategies. The Communists constructed a bastion of power in the mining industry as part of a larger strategy to make their party a key player in the postwar political structure. This strategy rested on the party's influence within the structures of governance in the mines and its ability to regulate the actions of organized labor. Once the Communists were driven from their posts within these state structures, the only weapon in their arsenal was the threat of a wave of industrial unrest. A policy of power at the summit yielded to a strategy driven by rank-and-file discontent. The situation for the Socialists was the opposite. After losing out to the Communists in the unions, the Socialists sought to establish a grass-roots following by speaking out against the "Stakhanovite" production campaign. But once Socialist Prime Minister Paul Ramadier fired Communist cabinet members, Socialists found themselves responsible for administering the unpopular policies that they themselves had criticized.

The cold war was an important, but frequently misunderstood, factor in French politics. Much of the literature on French politics in the postwar period has emphasized the powerful international forces that pushed France into the Western camp.[40] Almost no literature has focused on how the cold war affected local politics and key sectors of the economy.[41] Viewed from the coal-mining basin, however, the cold war's impact on politics provides a different picture. Rather than having caused the split between Socialists and Communists, the cold war greatly intensified existing conflicts, adding depth to a widening hole in the heart of the liberation coalition and, ultimately, limiting the scope of social and economic reform. The cold war also provided party leaders with a rationale for division that split the labor movement and the liberation coalition. When Socialist union leaders left the CGT to form a new anti-Communist labor federation, Force Ouvrière (FO), they argued that the whole world was choosing sides and that France belonged outside the Soviet orbit. Likewise, when Communist leaders of the Federation of Miners launched their epic strike in 1948 they justified their actions as necessary to prevent France from losing its national economic independence. The cold war added a powerful new dimension to old rivalries.[42] Within the context of the cold war, the 1948 strike, and the government's action to repress it, more closely resembled a military campaign than a work stoppage.[43]

The failure of the 1948 miners' strike definitively ended the union's participation in management. Additionally, the wholesale dismissals of union activists afterward curbed labor's power at the base. This opened the way to a new productivity drive based on reducing the work force through layoffs, attrition, and hiring freezes. As coal production edged upward and American coal imports increased, the coal shortage eased. Modernization of the mining facilities was assisted by funds provided by the Marshall Plan, and the emphasis on energy independence was abandoned in favor of integration into the European Coal and Steel Community. France's battle for coal came to an end.

1.

French Coal Mining, Labor, and the State to 1939

The economic importance of coal encouraged early state involvement in mining. Yet the degree and nature of that intervention depended upon key variables including domestic demand, availability of imported coal, action by coal operators and mine workers, and the political orientation of the government in power. In general, coal operators sought to increase productivity, cut labor costs, and establish an individual-based payment system. Mine workers sought to maintain control over production techniques, the apprenticeship system, and methods of payment. The state aimed to ensure continuous production, limit dangerous work situations, and minimize labor conflicts.

The policies that governed French coal production were developed over time through the interaction of coal operators, mine workers, and the state and reflected shifts in the balance of power between workers and owners. Production increased during the nineteenth century but never came close to satisfying the growing demand for coal. Through its economic ministries and corps of mining engineers, the French government steadily increased its role in the industry by resolving conflicts among coal operators, mediating labor disputes, and instituting technical changes aimed at making the industry more efficient. But economic dislocations caused by World War I and the depression deepened the mining firms' reliance on government assistance. In the 1890s, after years of unsuccessful strikes and protests, mine workers began forming labor organizations and won regionally based wage agreements. During World War I the government fostered labor-management cooperation by providing for worker participation in production plans. But labor relations deteriorated during the economic downturn of the 1930s as management implemented new "scientific management" schemes to rationalize the production of coal. Strikes unleashed after the Popular Front elections in 1936 forced coal operators to settle with the miners' union in a landmark agreement. But labor's victories were short-lived as France headed toward a war that intensified the coal industry's problems and revealed the need to restructure the industry and reform its labor practices.

STATE PROMOTION OF COAL MINING

The coal basin of Nord and Pas-de-Calais forms part of a large coal bed that extends from Great Britain through Belgium, France, Germany, Poland, and ultimately to the Ural Mountains in the Soviet Union.[1] Coal was being extracted from coal mines in the neighboring town of Mons, Belgium, as early as the twelfth century. The Belgian coal deposits were located close to the surface of the ground, making exploitation relatively easy and allowing the mines to provide coal for markets in Belgium and France. Business leaders and government officials on the French side of the border became concerned about the region's dependence upon Belgian coal and the increasing shortages and high price of wood for use in heating workshops and homes. If coal could be found in Belgium, why couldn't it be mined in France?

The government offered concessions to entrepreneurs who were willing to explore for coal deposits.[2] However, as the coal bed moved south and west into the region of Nord and Pas-de-Calais, the coal deposits were situated much deeper.[3] In addition, a good deal of the coal deposits located on the French side of the border possessed characteristics— irregular-shaped coal seams cut by numerous fault·lines—that made them more difficult to exploit. Exploration was begun in the 1720s under the direction of Vicounte Jacques Desandrouins. The problem of flooding seemed insurmountable until steam-driven water pumps were developed. Nevertheless, it was not until 1734 that Desandrouins found coal deposits that yielded a type of coal that could be used for many purposes: to fuel factories and workshops and provide heat for homes.[4] Located near the town of Valenciennes, the site eventually became the home of the Anzin Coal Company.

The French government's edict of 1744 regarding coal mining was an early and important example of state intervention in the industry. Concerned about the effect of deforestation upon France's ability to maintain a strong navy, the monarchy issued new rules aimed at fostering coal production. Basing its action on traditional law, the government reasserted its power to grant coal-mining concessions to private operators.

The need to promote greater efficiency and safer working conditions provided the formal explanation for creating the concessionary system.[5] But the government's action worked to the detriment of local landowners and peasant-miners, who claimed their own rights to mine coal. The government's promotion of mining entrepreneurs encountered resistance from peasant-miners in the coalfields of the Aubin basin, the Loire, Languedoc, and Auverge. But in the Nord basin the early coal entrepreneurs had consolidated their discoveries before a class of peasant-miners could emerge with their own claims. Peasant-miners and small operators were thwarted by the depth of the coal deposits, which required sophisticated drilling and underground outlays, and the problem of flooding, which required expensive pumping equipment. Thus the mines at Anzin were developed without local interference. Equally important, in the case of the Anzin company, the government assisted by helping to resolve conflicts between private entrepreneurs who had obtained concessions from the crown and noble landowners who claimed, on the basis of feudal privilege, the exclusive rights to mine coal. In 1757 the government brought together mining entrepreneurs and local nobles in the north of France to form the Anzin Coal Company, which soon became the largest coal firm in France. By the time of the Revolution, forty years later, Anzin employed 4,000 workers, who produced one-third of the total French output.[6]

Actions taken by the revolutionary government and the Napoleonic regime also revealed how the state's promotion of industry shifted with changes in political orientation. The *cahiers de doléances* of the First and Third Estates included demands for abolition of the concession system. But a stirring speech by Honoré-Gabriel Mirabeau focused on the success of the Anzin Coal Company, emphasizing the advantages to be gained by coal operators' overcoming the parochial interests of local landowners. Compromise mining legislation by the National Assembly in 1791 maintained the concessionary system while acceding to many of the concerns of small landholders and peasant-miners in southern and central France.[7] But the Napoleonic mining law of 1810 strengthened and rationalized the concessionary system, laying the basis for increased capital development in coal mining. The new law required concessions to be granted to those best equipped to exploit them without giving preference to landowners. In exchange, the government demanded that concessionaires indemnify property holders, pay an annual production tax to the state, and maintain standards set by the state and enforced by government engineers.[8]

Throughout the nineteenth century, the government promoted coal mining by enacting tariffs to protect the industry from British and Belgian competitors and by using its power to grant concessions in ways that fostered concentration of enterprises while preventing any one company from achieving a monopoly over the industry as a whole. Coal operators consistently complained that the particular geological characteristics of the French coalfields made it more costly to mine coal in France. Responding to these concerns, tariffs were levied in 1819, 1821, and 1822.[9] They were lowered during the period of expanded coal exploration in the 1830s but were reinstated under pressure from the mining companies.[10] Until the 1870s, when railroads and canals linked Paris to the northern periphery, French firms found it hard to compete because of high transport costs. Britain used water transport, which was less expensive than rail or canal transport.[11] The neighboring Belgian mines, situated at roughly the same distance from Paris as northern France, penetrated the French market through the north in the 1830s and forced many mining companies of the region to work together to pressure the government to increase the customs tax on Belgian coal. The first organization of coal operators was formed in 1840.[12] In the 1850s, during the railroad boom, tariffs were reduced because transport costs fell. Tariffs came down further under the 1860 treaty with Britain. French coal production increased, but British imports increased even more rapidly. Napoleon III offered a sizable loan to the industry, but it was soon exhausted. French coal operators demanded, and eventually received, new tariffs in 1865.

Yet no amount of tariffs could eliminate foreign competition, because the French coal deposits were insufficient to satisfy domestic needs. Faced with this situation, French mining firms attempted to corner the local market through regional ties with industrial consumers. Rather than expand to a growing national market, the northern mining companies sought agreements with nearby textile mills and steel plants. This situation fostered a peculiarly strong sense of individualism and a "jealous particularism" that contributed to disunity among the mining firms.[13] United in their support for tariffs on foreign coal, the coal operators fought among themselves for shares of a local coal market and were unable to form a stable employers' organization until the end of the century.

The power to grant concessions afforded the government a means of intervening to enhance competition or to promote greater concentration and mergers of small firms. The growth of metallurgy increased demand for coal after 1830 and influenced the July Monarchy to foster the merger of small mining firms with the Anzin company in 1847.[14] The action reflected the concern, based on feverish and largely unsuccessful attempts to mine coal in the 1830s, that small companies launched without sufficient financial backing were doomed. The policy of concentration, however, was reversed in 1852 when the state prohibited any mergers undertaken without state authorization. The regime of Louis Napoleon initiated a policy of "regulated competition." Competition was fostered in order to lower coal prices, but restrictions on mergers or concentration prohibited the largest and most powerful mining companies from expanding unchecked. One important long-term effect of the 1852 decree on coal mining was that several minor coal-mining companies eventually emerged in northern France, all of them possessing roughly similar capacities of production. No one mining company was able to dominate, by mergers or by acquiring capital in neighboring mines, any other company.[15]

Throughout the nineteenth century, the government utilized its power to set standards for the coal-mining area, especially in the area of mining safety. A decree issued in 1813 provided that managerial control could pass from an operator to a state engineer in the event of a serious accident in the mines. Firms were required to maintain medical supplies and to cover the cost when employees were seriously injured on the job. Management could also be brought to court and tried for negligence if a worker was killed in a work accident.[16] State engineers also became involved in promoting forms of management control that enhanced production and promoted safer methods of extraction. In particular, they used regulation of mining safety to redefine the rights and responsibility of management personnel. After 1875, the state engineers attempted to standardize safety procedures. Such was the case in the introduction of the safety lamp. In an effort to keep working, miners often relit lamps underground instead of sending them to the surface for relighting—a practice that sometimes caused fires in the mines. The new safety lamp could not be opened by the miners, but only by management. "A company employee issued the lamps at the beginning of the shift and collected them when the miners left work," wrote Donald Reid, "thus enabling the company to monitor the arrival and departure of workers."[17] However, as Reid found in his study of coal mining in the Aubin basin, bureaucratization of safety measures frequently resulted in shifting some of the key skills from the most experienced miners to management personnel. In the name of safety, the use of explosives to dislodge coal was taken out of the hands of miners and given to management after dynamite was used to frighten miners who returned to work during strikes in the late 1880s.

State mining engineers began promoting schemes to rationalize the method of extracting coal in ways that further increased management's power in relation to the mine workers. During this period, the government took action to increase the number of mining engineers by establishing a new École des Mines in Douai in 1878 as a complement to the mining engineering schools already in place in Paris, Nancy, and St. Étienne.[18] The state mining engineers encouraged mining firms to move away from the traditional "crew" system of payment, whereby a lead or "chief" miner negotiated a rate for a particular site and was paid a sum that was then divided among the various workers in his crew, toward a more specialized system wherein management, not the lead miner, determined the rates paid for each individual job. Other changes weakened the traditional apprenticeship system and reduced the miners' ability to decide which workers were hired and their rate of advancement in the mines.

Toward the end of the nineteenth century, labor unrest, domestic competition, and the threat of coal imports pushed French coal operators toward cartelization and the formation of employer organizations. Seeking to open up the French economy, Napoleon III signed a free-trade agreement with Great Britain, allowed the formation of joint-stock companies, permitted unions to be formed, and made strikes legal. One result of this liberalization was a wave of strikes in the late 1860s. Strikes subsided during the depression years of the 1870s. But the long and bitter strike at the Anzin mines in 1884 foreshadowed strikes in other mining basins. It ushered in a new era of industrial conflict and provided Émile Zola with material for his novel *Germinal*. Confronted with labor militancy, dissatisfaction among many republican politicians, and the emergence of socialist politics in the working-class districts of the mining regions, the coal operators put aside many of their differences and united to defend their common interests. A new Comité des Houillères, a central committee of French coal mines, was formed in 1886.[19] Under competition from coal firms in Belgium and the Ruhr, a large group of mining companies in Nord and Pas-de-Calais formed a regional cartel in 1891 that attempted to divide markets and set prices. Despite their antipathy to many forms of government involvement in the industry, coal operators saw the value of state intervention when labor unrest appeared and strikes threatened. Rolande Trempé has noted that the mine owners favored an active role when strike situations seemed to require repression but often refused to submit to government arbitration during other labor disputes.[20] In 1901 the mining companies joined with the metals industry to form the Union of Metal and Mining Industries, one of the most powerful industrial associations. Its job was to investigate labor legislation, tariffs, and tax issues and to lobby for the mining and metals industries. Mine operators fought against mandatory retirement funds and the establishment of worker safety delegates in the mines.

French coal production during this period had increased significantly,

TABLE 1. French Coal Production and Imports, 1820–1910
(In millions of tons)

Year	Coal	Coal Imports	Year	Coal	Coal Imports
1820	1.1	—	1870	13.3	6.0
1830	1.9	.6	1880	19.4	9.9
1840	3.0	1.3	1890	26.1	11.6
1850	4.4	2.8	1900	33.4	16.2
1860	8.3	6.1	1910	38.4	19.9

Source: B. R. Mitchell, *European Historical Statistics, 1750–1970* (London, 1978), 186–89, 231–36.

TABLE 2. Top Coal-Producing Firms in France, 1912
(In millions of tons)

1. Lens	3.4		6. Béthune	2.0
2. Anzin	3.1		7. Liévin	1.9
3. Courriéres	2.8		8. Blanzy	1.8
4. Bruay	2.6		9. Vicoigne-Noeux	1.7
5. Aniche	2.0		10. Marles	1.7

Source: Marcel Gillet, *Les Charbonnages du nord de la France au XIXe siécle* (Paris, 1973), 480–83.

from 1 million tons in 1820 to 41 million tons in 1913 (see table 1). The increase in French coal production, however, was dwarfed by the output of Great Britain and Germany during the same period, mostly because the French deposits were smaller and more difficult to exploit. Coal imports also continued to climb. About two-thirds of the coal mined in France came from Nord and Pas-de-Calais.[21] Further indication of the predominate role of the northern basin is revealed by the fact that nine of the top ten coal producers in 1912 were located in the north (the exception was Blanzy) (see table 2).

Describing the French coal industry at the turn of the century, François Caron emphasized the emergence of the Nord and Pas-de-Calais region as the largest producer of French coal. But Caron also saw "a protected sector" with a cartel that fixed prices depending on where the coal was sold.[22] French coal operators never came close to filling French demand. Production increased, but growth of production and productivity had declined. Several technical advances—including the use of compressed-air jackhammers (*marteaux-picquers*), conveyor belts for moving coal, and sorting machines—were introduced, but only in a very limited way. Marcel Gillet noted a slowing in the rate of growth in production in the northern basin in the period from 1896 to 1914, attributed in part to a lack of mechanization and difficulties in recruiting workers. Gillet summed up the industry's strengths and weaknesses as "growth without development": strong quantitative growth and ability to adapt to competition but insufficient industrial, social, and cultural development.[23]

LABOR STRATEGIES

Collective action by mine workers developed in relation to changes in the industry's practices and forms of state intervention in the organization of work. The difficulties involved in extracting coal from below the surface of the earth facilitated specialization and an early division of labor. Workers who removed the coal using picks and explosives were called *abatteurs*, meaning those who "knocked down" the coal, or "hewers." Typically the hewers dislodged the coal by making a deep horizontal cut below the coal seam, placing explosives in a small hole near the top of the seam, and igniting the blasting powder. Their goal was to knock down a sizable amount of coal, preferable in large chunks (*gros*) rather than in less valuable small pieces (*menu*). The hewer was assisted by a number of *manoeuvres* or "helpers" whose job it was to remove the coal in baskets or, later, in carts pushed by other helpers or pulled by horses. Another important and highly skilled job in the larger mines was that of the *boiseurs* or "timbermen" who constructed the wooden support system used to maintain large underground tunnels.

Coal-mining *équipes* or "crews" were organized not by the coal operators but by the hewers, who often put members of their family to work as helpers. Over the course of the nineteenth century, as operators searched for a stable work force and mine workers sought ongoing work, an apprenticeship system developed in which the hewer became a *chef mineur*, or chief miner, who employed his children and others in his mining crew, teaching them the skills of the trade so that they could move up from the ranks of helpers to become hewers. Older workers who could no longer work as hewers might be kept on as helpers, timbermen, or *du jour* workers, those who worked in installations located on the surface. Typically, chief miners owned the tools needed to extract coal, including explosives and lamps. The chief miner would negotiate with an engineer to determine the amount of money to be paid for a particular job, based partly on the conditions of that particular job site. Payment was made to crews, not to individual workers, a practice that greatly enhanced the power of the chief miner over the other workers in the crew. Thus the hewer's experience and skill in knowing how to approach a particular coal seam helped to decide how much pay the crew would receive. His knowledge and experience also were important factors in the safety of crew members.[24]

The relative autonomy enjoyed by the coal miners derived from the fact that underground mining could not be regulated and supervised as in a factory or office setting. For the miners, this meant that every situation required a specific approach and a rate of pay that corresponded to the job's difficulty. While coal miners favored the flexibility of this system, management sought to reduce the mine workers' autonomy. Disagreements between engineers and chief miners over the proper rate to be paid for extracting coal from a particular site were built into the system. In addition, the organization of work and system of payment tended to create a strong sense of solidarity among the mining crews, whose members looked to the chief miner rather than the company for their livelihood.

The domination of the coal-producing regions by the mining firms and the creation of company town systems in the nineteenth century both worked against and contributed to the solidarity that became a hallmark of the miners' movement. Coal operators enjoyed a degree of social control over coal miners that was unparalleled in France. Managerial policies were rooted in a paternalistic view of the relationship between employers and workers. Although coal operators undertook the responsibility of looking after the social welfare of its employees, workers were required to remain loyal to the firm and to avoid the advice of dangerous outsiders. Management sought to build a social environment that would foster cooperation between employers and workers while limiting the ability of workers to create independent forms of expression and organization.[25] Labor policies reflected that unequal relationship inherent in managerial paternalism. The companies controlled virtually all aspects of the lives of the coal miners and their families: wages, housing, schools, churches, medical care, retirement, and distribution of food and water. They also employed the local police force. This overarching control reinforced strict lines of hierarchy and caste in the mining regions.

Company control over the mines served to isolate the large mass of workers from potential allies. Unlike more industrially and commercially diversified regions, the mining basin required fewer services, stores, and centers of exchange and distribution to serve the large number of mine workers and their families. Often a mining community possessed one doctor, one lawyer, one parish priest, and only a few stores. The small number of persons engaged in the liberal professions deprived the mine workers of the possibility of exerting their power as clients to demand better services and as consumers who could threaten to take their business elsewhere. Economic isolation combined with geographic concentration produced a mono-industrial economy in the coal-mining villages. Describing the northern mining basin, Philippe Ariès noted that "the particularism of the black country, a consequence of its specialization, has been fostered and hardened by the policies of the mining companies," which exercised a "quasi-feudal control" over the mass of mine workers.[26] The real center of the mining town was not the church or the city hall but rather the offices of the mines. Engineers formed a privileged class as the mining companies raised barriers that prevented easy access to such positions. The establishment of separate residential areas and schools for the engineers and their families further defined the difference between worker and manager. Observers noted that workers easily substituted the word *engineer* for the word *bourgeois* in the northern mining region.[27]

Mine workers began to organize at least as early as 1833, when the coal miners at the Anzin Coal Company launched a five-day strike and protest. Unhappy with wage cuts and generally miserable working and living conditions, the coal miners left their jobs and staged protests in May. The company called for the army to quell the strike, and a peaceful demonstration ended with nine arrests.[28] During the 1840s, miners refused to work in a number of mining communities along the Loire River valley, including Anzin. When coal operators and local authorities tried to uncover conspiratorial organizations behind the strikes, they found that mine workers were developing a new ideology regarding labor relations based on collective organization and action.[29] The Anzin company's position as the largest and most prosperous mining firm in Nord was threatened in the 1860s by competition from the new coal mines being exploited to the west in the Pas-de-Calais region. Seeking to cut labor costs and mine more coal, the operators initiated a new plan of reorganization in the Anzin mines. But workers initiated various forms of collective action, including mutual assistance and strikes such as the large one in 1884.[30] Other strikes erupted in other mining basins in the next few years.

Although the problems that drove the miners toward organization were rooted in conflicts between labor and management, the government's active involvement in the coal-mining industry was a key factor in shaping the type of unionism that took root among the coal miners. From its earliest days, unionism in the coal mines, unlike its counterparts in other sectors of the economy, aimed at winning key demands by means of legislative reform. This derived from the fact that the state was deeply involved in the industry, first in deciding on tariffs and other policies aimed at protecting French industry, and later in the regulation of safety standards and the reorganization of work and management. When government engineers intervened in the industry, their aim was to help coal firms improve their efficiency and increase production. But prying open the lid of management prerogative also opened the way to new practices that were beneficial to the workers. In strikes, for example, the state rarely, if ever, sided with striking miners. Yet state engineers sometimes regarded the occasion of a strike as proof that various policies, including some that dovetailed with workers' demands, were needed in order to facilitate coal production. Mine workers also found that government intervention in a strike situation could sometimes lead to a negotiated settlement with limited gains, rather than the usual dismal defeat they suffered in most strikes.

New legislation in 1890 that provided for mine safety delegates, who were elected by the workers but paid by the company, reinforced the miners' orientation toward government action to make improvements in their working conditions. In 1894 legislation that allowed the miners to win a long-contested right to control their mutual-aid and pension funds was approved. In most elections for mining delegates and representatives to manage the mutual-aid funds, the union-backed slates emerged victorious, even where only a small percentage of the mine workers, usually the hewers and other more skilled workers, actually paid dues to the union. These legislative reforms, and the ensuing protection of worker activities from interference by management, greatly solidified support for the miners' union.

Management success in reducing the chief miners' autonomy on the job may have unwittingly served to strengthen the union's image among the workers. Gradually, and often at the urgings of the state engineers, management began to break up the traditional crew system of production and payment. In doing so, the coal operators "shifted the variable element in wage-setting from the conditions of production to production itself."[31] The new organization of work compelled the hewer to concentrate all his attention on extracting coal, rather than on organizing production and instructing apprenticeships. Meanwhile, helpers and other workers were assigned to specific tasks. New categories such as *aide-boiseurs* and *aide-picquers* were created. The apprenticeship system was altered in ways that weakened the chief miner's authority. Miners complained that the new child labor laws limited the hours that could be worked by those younger than 18 years, thus making it harder for them to take on more responsibility (and earn more pay) on the job. Management assumed a greater role in hiring new employees and extended the number of years an *aide* was required to serve in one category before being able to move up in the ranks. This process of specialization, which took place over the course of several decades, weakened the power and authority of the chief miners. However, the emerging new labor organizations in the mines filled the vacuum by attempting to protect the mine workers through political pressure, reform legislation, and early forms of collective bargaining. In 1891 the first in a series of wage agreements was negotiated between union leaders and the mining firms of Nord and Pas-de-Calais. These collective bargaining agreements, or *conventions*, soon became benchmarks for the establishment of wage rates in other basins, granting further legitimacy to the miners' union and laying the basis for creating a national federation of miners' unions.[32] The terms of the conventions were later extended to the Loire but remained out of the reach of smaller mining basins in the south and west.[33] Nevertheless, some operators extended the union wages to the work force to demonstrate that the union was not needed at that particular firm. Others waited to see what rates were granted in the northern mines and set their wage rates a bit below.

The success of the miners' union in pursuing a strategy of legislative reform and collective bargaining in the 1890s set its political and economic agenda for the next 50 years—and beyond. The reformist perspective dominated the political thinking of the leaders of the miners' union of the Nord and Pas-de-Calais region and was personified by Émile Basly, the Pas-de-Calais miner who emerged as a union leader during the coal strike at Anzin in 1884 and became a Socialist deputy.[34] In turn, the political orientation of the northern mining basin was reflected in the politics of the national Federation of Miners. The reformists favored state intervention to compel the mining companies to come to terms with the miners' organizations. A history of failed strikes had taught these trade unionists to use the strike weapon only reluctantly. Born in the eastern end of the mining basin at Anzin, the union was defeated there in the strike of 1884. It resurfaced in the western part of the basin, but a failed strike in 1893 destroyed the union in Pas-de-Calais. The idea of the general strike, popular among workers in many countries, was regarded by the reformist unionists as hopeless. Rather, they favored strikes of all mine workers in a particular region for clearly specified economic goals. By striking, the mine workers sought to force local elected leaders and government officials to intervene and bring the mine owners to the bargaining table, thus opening the way to a negotiated settlement.[35] Linking localized or regionalized strike activity and political action could produce a powerful coalition when parliamentary leaders from mining areas joined with local mayors and municipal council members in sympathy with the mine workers. But when mine workers voted to strike three times in 1901, union leaders in the northern unions refused to follow suit. A year later, when the general strike was called, the unions from Nord and Pas-de-Calais signed a separate agreement that undercut the national effort.

The reformists, however, had their critics within the union movement, mostly among Socialist militants who took a more revolutionary stance but seldom remained united long enough to form a stable labor organization. Unimpressed with the strategy of municipal socialism and sometimes deeply suspicious of close ties with political parties, the various revolutionists reflected the crosscurrents of anarchism, socialism, and revolutionary syndicalism. Some of these groups remained inside the Federation of Miners, but others, including a radical minority of miners from Nord and Pas-de-Calais, formed a new miners' federation, the Union Fédérale, and affiliated it with the national Confédération Générale du Travail. Despite disagreements, which usually reflected both political and regional differences, the various miners' unions moved toward greater organizational unity at the national level. In the strikes of 1902, for example, national demands took precedence over local demands, which were laid over for settlement once the national agreement had been reached. In 1906 the Union Fédérale merged with the Federation of Miners. Two years later, the federation affiliated with the CGT.[36]

Some writers have viewed the strong reformist trend among miners as a product of the long tradition of paternalistic and autocratic control by the owners combined with geographical and social isolation. Rolande Trempé, however, locates the source of reformism in the miners' relationship to the state. Because the mines were legally a part of the national patrimony, the coal miners, unlike most wage earners, could call upon the state to resolve conflicts that affected the coal mines. Confronted with a serious coal shortage or the threat of violence, the state could intervene to force a settlement. While this arrangement carried no guarantee that the miners would win any of their demands (and although the operators refrained from officially recognizing the unions), it nevertheless offered the coal miners a strategic option that was unavailable to most workers.[37] In addition, union leaders learned how to articulate the workers' demands within a perspective of the community, the region, or the nation. Conscious of France's vulnerable energy situation as an importer of coal, the miners found it easy to connect their specific needs as workers with national interests.[38] Thus, even as they fought for better wages, miners would often support policies aimed at protecting the French mines from an influx of British and German coal.

The emphasis on political and legislative action at the national level pointed the mine workers toward government ownership of the mines as the only real way to protect mine workers and the mining communities from mass layoffs, low wages, and other problems. The elusive notion of "la mine aux mineurs" ("the mine to the miners") took root among the mine workers, mingling with early conceptions of nationalization.[39] In the 1890s Émile Basly toured the French mining basins extolling the virtues of nationalization. From the miners' perspective, the task of building a national federation of mine workers became linked with the idea of a "nationalized" industry. In 1897 Benoit Malon wrote a series of articles for *La Revue socialiste* in which he promoted the nationalization of several industries, including coal mining. During the last decade of the nineteenth century a group of Socialist luminaries—Jaurès, Guesde, and Vaillant—called for nationalization of the coal mines in parliament.[40] The demand for nationalization found its way into the labor, as well as the Socialist, agenda.

Ultimately, however, it was the economic trauma of the Great War of 1914–1918, rather than speeches on the floor of parliament, that forced the French state to intervene decisively in the industry after 1914, with important implications for labor and management.

WAR, RECOVERY, DEPRESSION

The French government's economic plans for war in 1914 were based on the assumption that the war would be a short affair, not a long battle of economic attrition. In August, German armies began their march through Belgium. By mid-November they had swept through ten *départements* in northeastern France, including some of the most important coal-mining, textile, and steel-producing centers. At one point, two-thirds of the northern coal basin was under German occupation. Wartime destruction touched the installations at numerous mining sites, and the mines were flooded at Lens and Liévin.[41] Coal production fell precipitously when 65,000 miners out of a total of about 200,000 were drafted for combat.[42] Shortages developed as bottlenecks arose in the production and distribution process. Industrial and agricultural output plummeted. Transportation systems broke down.

Seeking to stabilize the vital energy sector, the government set price levels and divided up the domestic coal market among the various coal operators. In an effort to coordinate production and allocation of coal, a national coal board was created in 1914. Trade union leaders agreed to support the war effort by encouraging increased production and opposing strikes. In addition, the Dalbiez law of August 1915 created mixed committees of engineers and a miner delegate.[43] Coal output increased as the state provided some funds to reequip the industry.

Wartime intervention by the government was accepted by the coal operators with reluctance.[44] Willing to receive government assistance to re-build the mines after the war, the operators were determined to break wartime price ceilings and to dispense with experimentations in worker participation. Union officials proposed new plans for economic reorganization, featuring an important role for organized labor in the postwar recovery process. But such initiatives were quickly shelved once the war ended. Nevertheless, government commitment to reconstructing the occupied regions of northeastern France resulted in an ambitious rebuilding program. More than 200 mines introduced some of the latest machinery, including electric power generators and other technological changes to increase productivity.[45] Eight of the eighteen firms in Nord and Pas-de-Calais produced 75 percent of the northern basin's total coal output.[46]

Most coal-mining firms never moved far beyond the modernization efforts of the early 1920s, however.[47] They continued to use steam-powered locomotives to move coal rather than switch to more efficient electrical-based transport systems. Mining engineers tended to accept the widespread opinion that mechanical coal-cutters were of little value in the French coal mines because of geological irregularities and narrow coal seams.[48] Prior to World War II, only 6 percent of the coal mined in France was extracted by mechanical coal-cutters, while 86 percent was extracted by hand-held jackhammers, and the rest was removed by hand.[49] Low prices meant leaner profits and dividends for stockholders and made coal operators less willing to invest in new machinery and equipment.

French coal operators during the 1920s experimented with new techniques in the scientific management of labor, continuing the trend toward individual payment that had destroyed the old crew system of production and payment. Some firms increased productivity in the late 1920s by applying new techniques, such as the "longwalls" extraction system. After watching productivity drop 16 percent from 1913 to 1925, the Anzin Coal Company took action to concentrate underground production, reduce the number of surface workers, and lengthen the work day.[50] The result was a decisive improvement in productivity. Under the longwalls system, management grouped hewers side by side to work on especially large coal faces. The length of the face being worked could vary between 20 and 100 meters. In Nord, the average longwalls length was 35 meters, and in other basins it was slightly less.[51] Increasing the specialization of extraction, loading, and sorting of coal allowed a smaller number of workers to produce a larger amount of coal in a given period of time. It put an end to the old system whereby the chief miners negotiated with engineers over the rate to be paid for extracting coal at a particular site. Rationalization of the process of production destroyed the crew system and allowed management to pay workers standard rates based on ever-changing occupational categories. It also permitted management to identify the least productive workers and paved the way for new management experimentation with remuneration systems aimed at individualizing as much as possible each miners' wages. During the late 1920s a new time-motion system modeled on the theories of Frederick Winslow Taylor was introduced in the French coal mines. The Bedaux system, named for a mining engineer, attempted to measure the average speed at which most workers could accomplish a specific task. It utilized a point system in which a point represented the amount of work a miner in good health could do in one minute. Thus an average worker should make 60 points an hour, a more aggressive worker could reach 80 points, and a slower worker might reach only 45 points in an hour. The value of each type of job was also determined by examining the total number of operations required to accomplish it. Typically, a worker who fell below the 60-point average for two days in a row would be reassigned to another, lower-paying, job category.[52] Initiated by the Anzin company in 1927, the Bedaux system was incorporated by other mining firms, especially during the years of economic downturn in the 1930s.

The other important development that occurred in the northern mines after World War I was the unprecedented recruitment of Polish workers. Between 1919 and 1929 more than 100,000 Polish miners were hired to work in the French coal mines.[53] They replaced the large number of French miners who never returned from the war or who left the mines for better-paying jobs in construction and other industries once the hostilities had ended. The influx of Polish miners restored the work force to its prewar levels.[54] Immigrant workers, who in 1927 accounted for one-third of the workers in the coal mines, were usually placed in the harder, underground jobs. By 1932, 86 percent of the immigrant mine workers were employed underground. By contrast, only 54 percent of French miners worked underground.[55] Because many of the Polish miners came from the more modernized mines of Westphalia, they may have proved more adaptable to the new rationalized work system than their French counterparts.[56] Another incentive for coal operators to hire Polish miners was the fact that they could be more easily terminated when production fell. That is precisely what happened during the economic downturn of 1927, when the migration of Polish mine workers tapered off. As Gary Cross noted in his important study of immigrant workers in France, the Polish miners provided coal operators with a flexible labor supply. This gave the mine owners a new advantage over the French workers by making it harder for them to demand higher wages or better working conditions when the labor market tightened.[57]

Coal production peaked in 1930, but the depression unleashed a new economic crisis. Prices dropped and profits fell. Coal consumers cut back on coal orders and reduced their stockpiles. Industrial demand fell precipitously. Seeking to stabilize the regional economies and curb cutthroat competition, the government established fixed zones for coal sales in the domestic coal market.[58] In Paris, the coal lobby won an agreement from the government to lower taxes on coal and to reduce the costs of transporting coal by rail. Anticipating a fall in prices, the operators joined together to cut production. In 1936 the government fixed prices on coal. It also provided state subsidies to keep numerous mines afloat.

Because it enjoyed government assistance, the coal-mining industry was able to maintain profit levels that were higher than most other industries in France during the depression. But government help generated little incentive to invest in new machinery and equipment. As the slump deepened and prices continued to fall, coal firms and shareholders shifted investments from coal production to auxiliary industries such as cokeries, synthesis factories that produced ammonia, methyl alcohol, and benzol. Electric plants that served the mines and related industries were also viewed as prime targets for new investment. Under pressure to cut labor costs during the economic downturn, the coal companies took the opportunity to extend the use of scientific management techniques. The labor force was reduced and reorganized. Smaller workplaces were shut down, and workers were concentrated, sometimes 40 or 50 at a time, on a large coal face. Rationalization also involved new divisions of labor in the mines. In some mines the system of work shifts was altered so that the first shift extracted coal, the second transported coal, and the third washed and loaded coal.[59] Over the miners' objections, coal managers extended individual pay systems over more categories of workers. Productivity rose to new heights.[60]

Mine workers complained that these new schemes were degrading and destroyed traditional values of solidarity among the miners. Workers were tied to the same task and cut off from their fellow workers. If a miner worked too slowly, his pay was cut. If he worked rapidly, the foreman would adjust his rate of payment downward, figuring that the job was too easy. The new Bedaux system also produced sharp conflicts between miners and lower-ranking management personnel, leading to stronger surveillance and stiffer penalties. "The supervisors watch us work, with their stopwatches in their hands, encouraging more and more output without considering the most elementary safety measures," wrote a miner for the union newspaper.[61] Statistics on injuries in the mines of the Anzin underscore the miners' criticism that scientific management had less to do with technical improvements than with higher productivity.

Between 1932 and 1935 the number of mine workers injured on the job increased from 48 to 79 per 1,000.[62] A report prepared by Pierre Parent, vice president of the Coal Mines Committee, noted that the new system had made a great impact on the "mentality of the miners, who feel that they have lost their independence and are now tied to a chain."[63]

COMPETING TENDENCIES IN THE MINERS' MOVEMENT

Socialism and communism formed the two major poles of political attraction in the mining communities of Nord and Pas-de-Calais. Although both movements derived from common origins in Marxism, they offered different political perspectives and opposing strategies for organized labor. The Socialists had established deep roots in northern France, based on the success of municipal socialism and their dominance in the CGT miners' federation. They emphasized legislative action, education, and bread-and-butter economic issues. The Communists, emerging in 1920 as an offshoot of the Socialist party, condemned labor reformism and viewed their movement as part of a worldwide effort aimed at overthrowing capitalist governments and building socialist societies. In 1922, Communist militants called upon workers to leave the CGT and join a "red union," the Confédération Générale du Travail Unitaire (CGTU). From the early 1920s on, Socialist *confédérés* and Communist *unitaires* competed for leadership of the miners' movement.[64]

At first, the Socialist tendency dominated labor politics in the mining region. The CGT miners' federation advanced economic demands but carefully avoided strikes. Socialist labor leaders used their influence in municipal government and parliament to defend the mine workers' interests. The Communist-led union, by contrast, depended upon tight internal organization and rank-and-file militancy to construct an independent labor apparatus. Frequent communiqués were issued to all mine workers by means of a shop-paper. Communist miners, or unitaires, were grouped into workshop "fractions" in order to maximize their effectiveness. The CGTU unitaires involved themselves in day-to-day economic issues, but they were also willing to call strikes and demonstrations around political demands that were not supported by their opponents. A recent survey of strikes in France revealed that about 90 percent of the strikes that erupted between 1923 and 1935 were initiated by unitaires.[65] Communist-led coal strikes in 1923 and 1926 were dismal failures. In Pas-de-Calais, only about 3,000 out of 50,000 mine workers struck in 1923. A roughly similar response occurred in 1926. Labor action, however, had the advantage of being able to attract the more militant workers. A demonstration protesting the trial of Sacco and Vanzetti, for example, drew a young mine worker, Auguste Lecoeur, into the CGTU and the Communist party in 1927. Lecoeur went on to become a top leader in both the union and the party. Brief work stoppages also occurred when Communist miners protested the firing of a union safety delegate and unfair treatment of immigrant workers. The unitaires, in conformity with their internationalist views, placed a special emphasis on defending the Polish miners. (One of the immigrant miners expelled from the northern mines during this period was Edward Gierek, who headed the Polish government in the 1970s.) While these activities rarely produced a large, stable union membership, the experience produced a tested cadre of trade union leaders with a wide network of activists in the mines.[66]

The depression brought mass unemployment to the mining region, especially among the immigrant workers, who bore the brunt of the layoffs. Hundreds of Polish workers were forced to return to Poland. Workers who were lucky enough to retain their jobs saw their hours cut. When the coal operators announced wage cuts in March 1931, the miners pushed CGT leaders to the brink of a regional strike. At the last minute the government intervened and the reformist leaders called off the action. CGTU leaders, however, continued to promote the strike effort, which was followed by about half the work force in Nord and a smaller percentage in Pas-de-Calais. The strike continued for several days.[67] The government considered the situation serious enough to require state intervention to arbitrate bitter disputes over layoffs and wage cuts.[68]

Although mass joblessness led many to call for expelling all immigrant workers, labor unions tried to minimize the effect on immigrants in the coal mines. In 1932 the CGT established the Fédération des Émigrés Polonais en France to extend pension and union rights to Polish miners. The CGTU opposed the expulsion of Polish workers and favored unemployment compensation for immigrants who had been laid off.[69] In the Pas-de-Calais town of Bully-Montigny, 4,000 miners stopped the expulsion of a Polish CGTU leader in 1932 by organizing 24-hour shifts to protect him from the authorities.[70] Polish miners recalled how their comrades who went on strike were ordered to leave the country within 48 hours. Polish families watched sadly while their belongings were seized by authorities and sold to the other miners' families.[71] In 1934 a group of Polish miners in Escarpelle (Nord) conducted a sit-in to protest being laid off.[72] Nevertheless, the weight of joblessness fell hardest on the Polish mine workers. The Coal Mines Committee reported that while 17 percent of French miners lost their jobs between 1931 and 1935, 33 percent of immigrant workers lost their jobs. The percentage of immigrant workers in coal mining fell from 42 percent in 1931 to 34 percent in 1936.[73]

By 1935, the CGT miners' federation in Nord, Pas-de-Calais, and

Anzin numbered about 29,000, while 7,000 were claimed by the CGTU.[74] Together, the two unions represented only about one-fourth of the work force in the northern mines. However, the depression experience, combined with widespread concern regarding the rise of fascism in European politics, moved French workers toward militancy and stronger bonds of unity. In December 1935 an estimated 10,000 miners from both unions demonstrated together in Lens, the capital of the mining region of Pas-de-Calais.[75] When the Communist party adopted the Popular Front strategy, the way was opened to unity between the CGT and CGTU. Negotiations for leadership positions at the regional level of the newly united Federation of Miners resulted in veteran CGT leaders winning 22 positions compared to 10 for the former CGTU members. The Communists lost their "dual union" and were held to a minority of seats on the union's administrative council. But the unitaires probably gained the most from unification. Inclusion in the top ranks of the union apparatus allowed the Communists to sit at the negotiating table with the mining companies for the first time. The unification also provided them with more legitimacy among the broad ranks of mine workers and offered them the chance to address much larger bodies of the rank and file. Already adept at putting out their party's shop paper, the pro-Communist writers now composed articles for the union newspaper, *La Tribune des mineurs*, which reached 14,000 families each week. Although the Socialist trade union leaders maintained top leadership positions in the union, the Communist unionists scored strong victories in elections for union safety delegate positions, especially as the ranks of the union swelled with new members caught up in the enthusiasm for labor action. In Pas-de-Calais, the unitaires won 32 out of 62 delegate seats; in Nord, they captured 17 of 21 seats; and in the Anzin mines, the unitaires won 16 of 23 delegate positions.[76] Membership in the newly reunified miners' union grew from about 40,000 in December 1935 to 65,000 in April 1936.[77]

Like their French coworkers, the Polish coal miners were swept up with the euphoria that followed the Popular Front victory in 1936. "The Popular Front opened our horizons," said one Polish mine worker."[78] After years of hard times, the days of 1936 represented a new liberation for Polish and French workers. They made use of unemployment insurance and participated in the first paid vacations in France. Polish miners also began to join the miners' union in large numbers. Their participation in the elections for safety delegates was felt when Léon Delfosse, the Communist activist in the Ostricourt mines, was elected delegate from a mine where 75 percent of the workers were Polish. *La Voix du mineur*, distributed in Anzin, reserved at least half a page of every issue for information printed in Polish.[79] Polish miners were appointed to more leadership positions in the local union. The new enthusiasm for the CGT by Polish mine workers was underscored by the decision of the independent Société des Ouvriers Polonais to merge with the CGT-affiliated Fédération des Émigrés Polonais en France.[80] After signing up the immigrant and surface workers, the ranks of the miners' union in northern France swelled to about 100,000.

This unity paid dividends in 1936 when miners joined with other workers in a strike wave spawned by the victory of the Popular Front. The May–June strike in 1936 displayed an unprecedented degree of unity and militancy that surprised many labor leaders and profoundly shocked the coal operators. Although most interpretations of the 1936 strikes in France have emphasized their supposedly spontaneous character, a close study of the situation in the northern mining basin reveals that rank-and-file union militants, usually from the unitaire groups, provided the organizational backbone for a broad-based strike movement that overwhelmed the union leaders. Under the threat of a general strike on May 1, the companies accepted arbitration on April 28. Then the threat of a strike in the mining basin and a general movement of strikes compelled the companies to sign an agreement limiting the use of the Bedaux system.[81] For French miners, the terms of the settlement that ended the May–June strike were impressive: a 12 percent raise, return rights for laid-off workers, and a banning of the Bedaux system. As Aimée Moutet has shown, the miners fought hard against the despised Bedaux system, which in their minds was tightly linked to the deterioration of working and living conditions in the 1930s. So deep was the workers' resistance to the system that it presented union leaders with a difficult choice: to support the economic policies of the Popular Front or to back the wishes of the newly recruited union membership.[82] In order to get workers back on the job, the Popular Front government instituted a new 40-hour work week and paid vacations. Membership in the union soared as nearly every worker in the mines, including those employed in the surface installations, enrolled in the union.[83] Interest in unions also extended to the lower-ranking supervisory and technical staff in the mines, who began to form their own unions. Even the engineers began to group together in their own organization, the Syndicat des Ingénieurs des Houillères du Nord–Pas-de-Calais (SIHN), in Lens in July 1936.[84]

In the northern mining area, however, the Popular Front was more myth than reality as the powerful upsurge of worker activism sharpened the disagreements between the two factions within the reunited CGT. Against the backdrop of deepening international crisis, Socialists and Communists found themselves locked in a struggle for control of the unions. The Communists sought to maintain the myth of Popular Front unity while reaching out to Socialist workers and undercutting the Socialist leaders. The Socialists echoed the thesis espoused by the leader of the Nord CGT, Georges Dumoulin, a veteran leader of the Federation of Miners, who warned that the Communists were trying to "colonize" the union movement.[85] Disputes arising out of contract negotiations drove a deeper wedge between the two groups in September 1938. The coal operators' organization, the Coal Mines Committee, announced that it would demand an end to the 40-hour week, pushing it up to 42 hours. This created great anger in the mining regions. However, negotiations began to make progress, and a tentative, six-month agreement was reached on September 1. The next day the agreement was ratified by union leaders from across the country, including two Communists from Nord and Anzin. However, that same day a Communist leader from Nord, Cypriot Quinet, wrote an article that was highly critical of the proposed settlement in *L'Humanité*, the PCF's daily newspaper. The northern Communist daily, *L'Enchaîné*, also attacked the proposal and called for mass meetings to criticize it. Communists who had agreed to the proposal now withdrew their support in meetings wherein angry workers charged the confédéré union leaders with selling out the miners. Elections for union safety delegates in Pas-de-Calais took place the next day, and the results revealed how successful the Communists had been in tapping into the anger of the miners. The ex-unitaires captured 42 of the 66 delegate seats.[86]

The events in Munich also polarized the two groups. The Communists argued for collective security, and their leaders in the miners' union supported a special production effort with the goal of strengthening France against the Axis powers. By contrast, many of the confédéré leaders, especially Georges Dumoulin, the CGT's top leader in Nord, favored maintaining peace above all. Then the Popular Front crumbled and the Daladier government moved to restore business confidence by eliminating the 40-hour work week in 1938. In many mines, management began reintroducing the Bedaux system, over the miners' protests. Spontaneous strikes erupted in several industries and CGT leaders called a one-day strike for November 30. But the confédérés, fearful of opening the way to further Communist gains within the labor movement, were reluctant to engage in an all-out strike effort. In the coal mines, the strike call was heeded by strong majorities of workers in mines where Communists were the dominant group and by smaller percentages of workers where the confédérés held sway.[87]

Fractured by deep political division, the miners' federation was virtually immobilized when the notorious German-Soviet nonaggression pact was signed. News of the controversial agreement spread through the mining community and sparked an acrimonious debate within the miners' union. At first, Communists denied the pact had been signed. Then they justified it on grounds that the Western allies never had any intention of joining with Soviet Russia to fight the Third Reich. But Socialist critics and conservative writers scored the Communists for slavishly following Soviet foreign policy shifts. Top CGT leaders, most of whom were not Communists, issued a directive to all unions calling upon them to remove union officials who publicly supported the pact. Non-Communist union leaders were named to replace them. Reformist union officials went to the home of Léon Delfosse and seized his union records and documents.[88] The government took steps to outlaw the Communist party, and many of its cadres went underground to escape prosecution during the period of the "phony war." Then the Nazi armies occupied northern France and the Vichy government assumed power in collaboration with Germany. One of its first steps was to dissolve all trade unions.

On the eve of war, the CGT Federation of Miners found itself in a poor position to defend its members. Union leaders pleaded with workers to retain their loyalty to the CGT, but large numbers of miners stopped paying dues and attending meetings. As war with Germany began to seem inevitable, leaders of the miners' union continued to direct their main line of attack against the Soviet Union and the internal menace of communism. The final issue of *La Tribune des mineurs*, which went to press on the day of the German invasion, attacked Communist mine workers for distributing leaflets critical of the union leadership.[89]

Although the reformist wing of the union reclaimed its former leadership role by pushing aside the Communists, the coming of war promised new uncertainties for reformist unionism.[90] But the Communists fared little better. Driven from positions of power in the unions, and internally divided over the issue of the German-Soviet pact, the Communist labor apparatus was thrown into disarray. As the Nazi military machine swept across France, the labor movement was weak and divided.

2.

Coal Politics from War to Liberation, 1940–1945

From military defeat in 1940 to liberation in 1945, France passed through five traumatic years. Global war dominated international politics as the Axis powers expanded in Europe, Africa, Asia, and the Middle East. Only in late 1943 did the tide begin to turn as the Allied forces began to retake occupied lands. When the Axis occupation armies withdrew, the various local regimes that had collaborated with them also fell, kindling popular sentiment for a new political and economic order.

A similar pattern evolved in the mining regions of Nord and Pas-de-Calais. The wrenching experiences of war, occupation, and liberation profoundly changed the lives of the residents of the mining communities. For the mining companies, occupation subjected coal policies to German military and economic demands. But the end of occupation marked the beginning of a new era that posed another danger to the coal operators: the threat of nationalization. For mine workers, the occupation brought economic hardship and political repression. But liberation offered the promise of sweeping political and economic reform once the Nazi-collaborationist yoke had been thrown off.

Management policies and labor relations in the coal mines reflected the changes created by the occupation. The major problems of the earlier period—technological backwardness, lack of capital investment, labor discontent, heavy reliance on government assistance—emerged in even bolder relief as the industry struggled to meet German and domestic demands for coal. Wartime difficulties produced renewed calls for drastic economic reform of the nation's energy sector. By the time the occupation ended, the major question was not whether or not the coal industry would be reformed but, rather, how far the reform would go in expanding state controls and bringing organized labor into the decision-making process. The answer depended in large part on how the coal miners and their labor organizations intervened once the occupation came to a close—and how that intervention was played out in the political arena.

COAL MINING: CONTINUITY AND CHANGE

During the occupation years, French coal mining was marked by continuity as well as change. Continuity was evident in the persistent problems that plagued coal mining, in the personnel directing the industry, and in management's approach to the organization of work and union activism. But elements of change were also revealed in the centralization of administrative control, new attempts at modernization, and economic planning initiatives. The state's role in the economy increased greatly. In the first two years following the armistice, a new group of "modernizers" controlled French industry while the collaborationist government under Marshal Pétain attempted to create a "national revolution" under the aegis of Nazi Europe. While the modernizers at Vichy experimented with long-range planning, alternative plans were being developed by economic advisors to the Resistance movement.

Military defeat pushed the French economy to the brink of crisis. Already a big importer of coal, France saw its imports from Germany and Belgium dry up at the same time as the Germans annexed the coal mines of Lorraine and put those of Nord and Pas-de-Calais in a "prohibited" zone under the control of German military forces in Brussels. As a result, the Vichy government directly controlled only 20 percent of the coal produced in France. Vichy's new minister of Industrial Production, a former leader of the national CGT, René Bélin, faced the job of halting the economy's deterioration. In a symbolic gesture toward cooperation between workers and management, the Vichy regime dissolved labor unions and employer organizations in 1940.[1] But while labor unions were forced underground, the employer groups were reconstituted in a slightly different form. Each branch of industry and trade set up its own directing group called the Organization Committee.[2] In the case of the coal mines, one decree dissolved the old Coal Mines Committee, but another placed the industry under the control of the state and a new Comité d'Organisation de l'Industrie des Combustibles Minéraux Solides (COICMS), also referred to as the Comité d'Organisation des Houillères, or COH.[3] The head of the dissolved Coal Mines Committee, Robert Fabre, continued in his same position within the new Organization Committee. Fabre was followed by nearly the entire cast of influential men of coal mining.[4] For example, Maxime Bucher, general director of the Lens Mining Company, was named one of the five members of the COH. During the occupation period, Bucher retained key leadership positions in the coal-mining industry: he served as the principal delegate from the COH to Nord and Pas-de-Calais, represented the COH in the government's Technical Commission, and maintained his presidency of the Chamber of Coal Mines in Nord and Pas-de-Calais as well as his presidency of the Bank of the Coal Mines of Nord and Pas-de-Calais.[5]

The organization committees were operated by private businessmen and monitored by government ministries—in the case of the mines, the Ministry of Industrial Production.[6] In February 1941, Industrial Production chief René Bélin, a former leader of the anti-Communist wing of the CGT, was replaced by Pierre Pucheu, an industrialist. Soon Pucheu was removed and François Lehideux, nephew of Louis Renault and head of the committee for the automobile industry, took over as the minister of Industrial Production. Committee leaders were appointed by the organization committees, with the approval of Vichy and the Germans, and soon the "dissolved" business groups dominated the new organization committees. The committees were further linked to the government through finance inspectors and state engineers, most of whom were already tied to the personnel of the committees through education in the École Polytechnique or the five Écoles des Mines and through family connections.[7] In 1943 a Parisian financial journal described the organization committees as the old employer organizations under a new name.[8]

Old labor practices were reestablished in the mines during the occupation period. The miners complained that the brutal policies from the period before the Popular Front strikes had returned. The situation looked different to the engineers and foremen for whom the reversal of gains won by workers in 1936 meant the restoration of order and discipline in the mines.[9] The work day was lengthened to eight hours and fifteen minutes in December 1940 and then to nine hours for many categories of workers. Miners complained that the weakening of the union safety delegate system resulted in more injuries and deaths. The dismantling of the unions also allowed the companies to bring back the Bedaux system and forms of individual payment. When the time-study approach did not work with a particular coal vein, management divided the mine workers into small groups of three or four workers with definite tasks, and the individualized wage system was reinstated.[10]

The German economic decision makers favored high coal production, but output continued to fall. The old practice of recruiting underground workers intensified. Thousands of experienced miners left the region to escape the occupation. Others were drafted in the mobilization effort and

TABLE 3.   Mine Workers and Productivity, 1929–1944
(Nord and Pas-de-Calais)

Year	Mine Workers (Underground)	Productivity (Daily output per underground worker in kgs.)	Year	Mine Workers (Underground)	Productivity (Daily output per underground worker in kgs.)
1929	133,000	966	1941	101,000	1,015
1938	104,000	1,136	1942	104,000	982
1939	—	—	1943	112,000	901
1940	—	—	1944	104,000	797

Source: INSEE, *Mouvement économique en France de 1938 à 1948* (Paris, 1950), 218.

never returned to the mines. Union leaders and political activists fled to escape repression or forced labor in Germany. Mining companies were forced to negotiate with German authorities in efforts to return French prisoners of war who were miners. The Germans, desperately seeking new sources of labor, were willing to release engineers but not workers.[11] In October 1943, they agreed to allow French workers to work in the mines rather than in German factories. The Germans pressed for a big hiring effort. About 38,000 young people, mostly from the northern cities of Lille, Tourcoing, and Roubaix, entered the mines.[12] Most of these workers were without prior experience in mine work.

The coal operators watched in dismay as both coal production and labor productivity fell (see table 3). They responded by cutting the number of paid vacations, aggressively pursuing workers suspected of faking illnesses, and demanding that workers come in to work every other Sunday.[13] But the problem of absenteeism could not be curbed even by the establishment of a good attendence bonus system.[14] Food shortages had produced a black market that pushed prices to levels that most miners could not afford. The miners then circumvented both the official market and the black market by going into the surrounding countryside to trade directly with the peasants. Frequent forays to purchase food, which continued to be a regular feature of life in the coal basin long after the wartime hostilities had ended, contributed to absenteeism in the mines.

Protests by the miners were met occasionally by the carrot but more often by the stick. Police surveillance was heightened, and as in the past lists of union activists and known Communists were maintained. In November 1943, for example, mining engineers were instructed to "make accurate lists of which miners are in which pits at all times. Also, it is important to have their addresses. In case of a strike, engineers must immediately compile a list of the workers who participate in it with their exact addresses. It is important to know, beforehand, exactly where they live." [15] In the context of the German occupation, these repressive practices drove an additional wedge between workers and management. It was bad enough that the bosses were reinstating their old practices, said the coal miners. It was worse that they were doing so to help the Nazis.

Although the industry confronted persistent problems, important elements of change also emerged during the occupation period. As Robert Paxton observed, the Vichy experience "afforded French businessmen and administrators with the most substantial lesson in planning and state management of the economy up to that time." [16] The various factions that played leading parts in directing Vichy's economic program included the new group of modernizers. Many of these individuals were outsiders for whom the death of the Third Republic opened new opportunities. As Richard Kuisel has noted, the modernizers tended to be relatively young but well trained in business or public administration. "Aggressive and elitist by temperament," wrote Kuisel, "*dirigiste* and modernizing by conviction, they soon ran the administration of the economy." [17]

Wartime dislocation dictated a strong role for the state. Even so, the goal of the organization committees was not to direct the economy but to organize it with the participation of the employers. [18] According to Henri Rousso, the committees were centers of decision making that brought together the various reins of executive and legislative power. In a more streamlined way, the committees defined policies for each industrial branch under the coordination of the government. In order to prevent the various organization committees from competing with each other for scarce primary resources, including coal, the government established the Office Central de Répartition des Produits Industriels (OCRPI). [19] By 1942, the government had begun paying the mining companies a fixed number of francs per ton in exchange for guarantees that the companies would invest a certain amount of capital into funds for modernization. [20] The industry's dependence on the state for these subsidies allowed the government to intervene in virtually all aspects of the industry. Thus, a report in 1943 noted that the coal industry "has been controlled technically and financially by the state, which determines its cost price and sale price and fixes its profit margin as well as the sums to be used for new works." [21]

Economic planning during the occupation years was undertaken by a new agency, the Délégation Générale à l'Équipement National (DGEN) under the direction of François Lehideux from the Ministry of Industrial Production. Lehideux's assistant in charge of the mines, industry veteran

Fanton d'Andon, was involved in the drafting of the first plan.[22] Although Vichy's economic plan criticized excessive state intervention and did not suggest nationalizing key industries, it was predicated on the need to break the old "Malthusian" fear of overproduction.[23] The 10-year plan did not set production targets (as the postwar Monnet Plan would do), but it did target coal mining and hydroelectric power for special priority. The movement was toward rationalization and concentration. Breaking with old patterns, the organization committees surveyed all firms in an industry, assessed stocks, closed down less efficient firms, allocated scarce resources, established fixed operational principles and product quality, and proposed price schedules. In 1943, German economic director Albert Speer concluded an agreement with the French minister of Industrial Production to increase productivity in France. Coal mining was classified as a "priority industry" and the Coal Mines Organization Committee tried to move toward energy self-sufficiency.[24]

Technical experts found new and important roles alongside the leading businessmen within the organization committees. Aimé Leperq, a distinguished mining engineer, became president of the Coal Mines Organization Committee in 1940 and continued to serve until August 1943. A report on the industry in 1943 noted that Leperq was an impartial president who served along with two directors from the mining companies.[25] Unknown to the authorities, Leperq was also a leader of the Civil and Military Organization, a group of managers and technicians who formed Resistance cells inside the organization committees.[26] Many of the technical experts in the organization committees continued to play important roles in the new government after the liberation. Leperq was relieved of his duties in August 1943, but he resurfaced as the first minister of Finance in France's postwar provisional government. Pierre Herrenschmidt, a key figure in the nationalization of the railroads in the 1930s, served as vice president of the Treasury under Vichy. After the liberation, Herrenschmidt moved to the Ministry of Finance, where he established a commission to find the best means to compensate the stockholders when the coal mines were nationalized.[27] Although many established business leaders were compromised by political identification with Vichy or economic dealings with Germany, much of the elite corps of the French civil and engineering service stood on the seemingly neutral ground of technical expertise. They moved easily from the Vichy regime to the Fourth Republic.[28] While it is useful to indicate the difference between the modernizers and the old bosses, it is also important to note that in 1942 nearly 80 percent of the organization committees were headed by presidents or staff of the old industrial groups and top executives. Engineers or other "experts" made up the other 20 percent.[29]

Despite changes in industrial organization and the rise of technical experts, French industry during the occupation period was unable to modernize its equipment or apply new forms of technology. In part, this was because occupation policies drained France of key resources. Moreover, even the most streamlined forms of industrial organization could not overcome two decades of technological stagnation. All the virtues of economic planning could not resolve the growing economic and social problems faced by the mine workers in northern France. Coal production plummeted, imports dried up, and consumption fell during the war years.[30] The result, despite the intentions of the modernizers, was a crippling coal shortage that slowly strangled the French economy.

While Vichy's technocrats were introducing changes in industrial organization, several groups of economic planners associated with the Resistance movement were fashioning plans for rebuilding France once the war had ended. Although many programs were created, several common themes were expressed in these Resistance plans, including nationalization of industry and economic planning. Some identified the coal industry as requiring particular attention, and most envisioned a large role for trade unions in economic decision making.[31] But while the think tanks were drawing up blueprints for the new France, coal miners were being crushed by the weight of occupation.

THE MINERS' MOVEMENT FROM OCCUPATION TO LIBERATION

Recalling the occupation period, a veteran miner explained, "During those days the mine workers spoke with one voice: their stomachs growled." Food shortages became part of daily life: wages fell behind the rise in prices. By 1943 the worker's buying power was only 70 percent of what it had been in 1938.[32] The situation in northern France was especially difficult. Not only were large numbers of German occupation authorities and troops competing with French consumers for goods on the black market, but their inflated German currency tended to drive up the prices.[33] Apart from that, several unique factors made the burden of occupation particularly onerous and helped to forge a broad-based movement against it.

Geographic and economic considerations led the Germans to consider annexing the entire northern region. The Nord–Pas-de-Calais region became a "prohibited zone" directed by German occupation authorities stationed in Brussels, Belgium. Refugees were not permitted to return. Telephone communications were cut, and mail service was curtailed. Travel to the free zones was limited. Isolated in a no-man's-land between Nazi Germany and collaborationist Vichy, the population of the northern region had the sense of being abandoned. "There was a feeling of isolation," said Ovide Legrand. "We were now in a 'prohibited' zone, cut off from the rest of France, tied to government in Brussels."[34] This isolation may have disoriented the populace, but it also compelled the local Resistance movement to develop its own strategies against the occupation.

The exploitation of French human and natural resources by German occupation was revealed in its starkest forms in the coal-mining areas. Workers, especially union or political activists, were arrested and transported to Germany to work in defense factories. Political repression became part of daily life. The linkages between economic exploitation and political collaboration were laid bare as the miners perceived that coal companies and occupation forces were working hand in hand. Patriotic sentiment became inextricably connected with class struggle, and labor disputes led to strikes and public protests. "When you see an army of occupation take over your community, it makes you sick," recalled Louis Lethien, a miner from Pas-de-Calais who participated in Resistance activities. "It really made me feel nauseous." "Little by little," said Jean Wrobleski, "the Resistance began to organize itself. We talked about it in the mines. 'It's our coal, but it's helping the German war machine.' We began to sabotage production, not by big actions, but by little things such as blocking the exhaust pumps so that the mines were flooded."[35]

Occupation authorities hoped that the coal operators could keep the miners on the job while the local police prevented public protests. But the local police often found it difficult to intervene. "The Resistance put the brakes on collaboration," noted Louis Lethien.[36] Mining engineers and foremen, most of whom claimed to be "above" politics, found it awkward to pursue aggressive production policies when it seemed that only the German military effort benefited. Friction developed between German overseers and French coal operators over labor policies in the mines. When labor discontent boiled over in the coal mines, the Germans agreed to permit limited representation rights to a weakened CGT miners' union run by Jules Priem and M. Legay, two members of the Dumoulin faction of the old CGT. A plan to reestablish the system of safety delegates by drawing solely from the ranks of older workers, in hopes that this would produce more conservative delegates, was abruptly scrapped. Local authorities learned that bypassing the most recently named delegates, those who had been installed after September 1939, could bring a return of the Communist delegates removed after the German-Soviet pact. Public manifestations of anti-German sentiment became more common as the occupation continued, as in May 1941, when thousands of people jammed the streets of Lille, crowding around the statue of Jean d'Arc. But such reflections of popular sentiment did not allow individuals to challenge directly the occupation power structure.[37] That role was filled by the Communists, the workers' movement, and the armed Resistance.

The growing grass-roots strength of the Communists was perceived much more clearly by unionists at the local level than by the Paris-based observers who monitored national developments. Even astute observers of organized labor underestimated the Communists' expanded base of support among workers during the occupation, partly because their activities were of a clandestine nature. Conventional wisdom held that the Communists had been gravely weakened by the shift in the party's line that followed the German-Soviet pact, the removal of its top leaders from the CGT unions, and the government's steps to outlaw the party. This misperception found its way into the analyses of historians, labor economists, and political commentators, who were puzzled by the party's resurgence once the occupation was lifted and the scope of Communist influence emerged more clearly. The situation in the northern mines reveals that party leaders gained a large following because they provided a pole of attraction for individuals and groups that were willing to take action against the occupation.

As the Nazi war machine took over the region, the Communists, like all groups, were thrown into disarray, but within several weeks they began to reorganize. Auguste Lecoeur, captured by the Germans in 1940, escaped and returned to northern France, where he obtained a mimeograph machine, started forming "comités des puits" in the mines, and began stockpiling weapons.[38] Ovide Legrand, recalling the early days of the occupation, suggested that because the party was prohibited in 1939, it had already learned how to work in an illegal and clandestine capacity.[39] In particular, the party's use of "democratic centralism," the internal system of organization and communication that was the hallmark of all Communist parties, served well during this period. Because lines of communication flowed vertically rather than horizontally, the system did not require large numbers of members to meet together at the same time, where they could be apprehended en masse. Tight internal discipline, unusual in non-Communist groups, made good sense in the occupation atmosphere. The Communists further refined their internal organization by forming, at various levels of the party hierarchy, triads or "triangles" of three members ("P" represented the party's political bureau, "O" referred to organization, and "M" meant mass organizations, such as unions, women's groups, and other popular groupings).[40] Each member of the triangle also headed another subordinate triangle, and only that member knew the identities of members in both triangles. The triangle system made it difficult for authorities to infiltrate and destroy the party.

Communist activists and sympathizers also established party-led factions called Comités d'Unité Syndicale et Action (CUSA) in order secretly to rebuild the unions. "There was always a lot to do," said Louis Lethien. "We sabotaged the railroad cars by cutting the brake lines and by putting sand in the wheel bearings. We made leaflets and distributed them. We sold 'solidarity coupons' to raise funds to help families of those who had been arrested by the Germans, and furnished phony identification papers."[41] Party members soon found that non-Communist rank and filers, often Socialist and Catholic workers, were willing to work with them on some of these activities. Although many of the protest actions were believed by the authorities to be spontaneous in nature, militants contended that their activities were planned in advance and well organized. The Communists' high degree of organization and their boldness attracted many young workers who had never been involved in political activities. The party even made a special point of advancing young workers without prewar party experience into positions of leadership.[42]

Within this context, a remarkable number of strikes and other protests took place in the mining communities. The French government signed the armistice agreement on 25 June 1940. Between August and October, eight work stoppages took place in the coal mines, involving a total of about 20,000 mine workers. Initiated because of wage disputes and attempts to receive pay for vacation days, most of these strikes lasted for one or two days. On 11 November 1940 (World War I Armistice Day), 35 percent of the miners in Pas-de-Calais, apparently without any organization by political groups or unions, refused to descend into the mines, perhaps motivated by BBC radio broadcasts. In the first five months of 1941, workers refused to descend in about 25 coal pits in Nord and Pas-de-Calais. These strikes were usually launched to protest food shortages and most lasted for a day or two. The Germans arrested about 80 strikers in the wake of these work stoppages.[43]

Toward the end of May 1941, another strike was launched in the northern mines. Unlike the previous work stoppages, this job action, sometimes referred to as "the 10-day strike," swept through the entire mining basin from east to west and was the first large-scale strike launched under the German occupation. Although it was motivated by demands for better food and a wage increase, the action took a decidedly patriotic tone. A leaflet distributed in May emphasized the economic plight of the miners: they were forced to go into the country to find food. The engineers and foremen seemed to care little about the fact that the miners were underfed and tired. Safety precautions had become lax, and machinery and equipment had fallen into neglect, leading to more work-related accidents.[44] Recalling the events, Louis Caron emphasized that shortages of soap made the miners particularly angry; they could not wash up after work. Forced overtime and Sunday work were other grievances. But, Caron added, these demands really provided the excuse for launching the strikes against the German occupation.[45]

The discussion surrounding the causes of the 1941 strike may have significance in determining the exact role of the Communist party during the period before the German invasion of the Soviet Union. Although it remains unclear whether or not the party's top leadership in Paris approved of the strike, it is evident that an independent center of Communist-led resistance had grown in the northern region.[46] Aware of the fact that the party's official line did not call for anti-German demonstrations, local leaders and militants easily cloaked their patriotic sentiments in bread-and-butter demands, purposely obscuring the question of whether the strike sprang from economic or patriotic grievances.[47]

The 1941 strike began on May 27 at pit number seven in the Dourges mines, a Communist stronghold and the place where the first CUSA had been formed.[48] The following day the strikers from number seven were joined by miners from four other pits in the Dourges concession. At a hastily called meeting of the "central committee of the CUSA" that same day, a decision was made to expand the strike. On May 29, the strike spread west to Courrières and north to Ostricourt. In the Ostricourt mines, 240 miners (out of 670) showed up for work but refused to pick up their lamps and descend into the mine. Questioned by the foremen, they refused to speak. No one came forward with a set of demands. No one claimed to represent the 400 miners who had not shown up for work. The mine workers stood mute and then simply left the pithead.[49] The next day the strike spread east to Anzin and west to Lens. On June 4, 80 percent of the coal miners in the region were off the job.

Key elements of the occupation experience in the northern mines were underscored during the 1941 strike. The region's isolation may have played a role in the fact that the management at Dourges did not report the strike to the German authorities until it was several hours old. Later, when the movement had spread to all the mines, the coal operators let the Germans take over the job of quelling the strikes. This event had an important effect on the coal miners. What started as a dispute over the payment system in pit seven of the Dourges mines had grown into a general strike that drew its strength from powerful reservoirs of patriotic sentiment and class consciousness. "From now on," wrote Etienne Dejonghe, "it seemed crystal clear that the companies were in the service of the Germans and not the reverse. It gave to patriotic hopes a revolutionary content."[50] National liberation merged with social liberation. Communists were the chief initiators and the main political beneficiaries of this new alchemy during the 1941 strike. "Never have we seen such a popular strike," claimed the Communist leaflets. Raising donations for the strikers proved to be unusually easy, reported strike activists.

The French police were not prepared to contain such a social explosion. Given the job of halting strikes, keeping track of all the ringleaders, and containing popular demonstrations, the local police were outnumbered and overwhelmed. They found it difficult to maintain order without being branded as unpatriotic brutes by the hostile populace. Most of the mayors of mining towns were reluctant to take action against citizens for passing out leaflets or putting up posters to support the strikes. When the German military commanders took over the repression of the strike, they established their headquarters within the main offices of the Lens Mining Company. Here the military briefings took place, a fact that, in the public mind, further cemented the connection between the mining companies and the Germans.

Once the troops had occupied the areas around the mines, the strikers could not congregate there for fear of arrest. So the wives and sisters of the miners took their places. The German troops and local police went to the homes of Polish workers and forced them to return to work. But as the German military forces marched reluctant Polish workers toward the mines, they encountered large groups of angry women that left them paralyzed for a time.[51] In the mining towns the women formed cortèges of 200 or more to demand that imprisoned miners be freed.[52]

The officially recognized union leaders found themselves in an awkward, no-win position. Representing the strongly anti-Communist, pro-pacifist tendency of the old CGT, they had little interest in supporting the strike and falling into line behind the Communists. On the other hand, openly opposing the strike risked alienation from the workers they claimed to represent. Immobilized, Priem and Legay described the strike as a futile effort, but they could do little to prevent it from spreading. Writing to the national union leaders, Priem said the authorities had asked the union to help put an end to the strike. But for the union to take such an action would amount to suicide. "If we had done that, we would have been branded as the strikebreakers and all other epithets," wrote Priem. "The union would be dead. Officially, we did not take a position on the strike, but even this was considered by most workers as a condemnation of the movement."[53] A new generation of strike-inspired handbills and illegal newspapers chastized the reformist union leaders as traitors and wreckers. Among the miners, the credibility of the official union was greatly diminished during the 1941 strike.

The repression was severe. More than 200 strikers had been arrested as of June 5. The Germans ordered cafés, restaurants, and movie theaters closed. Special rations were detained. Distribution of food by the mining canteens was halted, and merchants were ordered to avoid extending credit to strikers. In order to prevent women from gathering in front of the mines to make it difficult for scabs to descend, a new rule prohibited women from going into the streets for half an hour before and half an hour after each shift started.[54] Food shortages and repression forced many miners to begin returning to work. The regional leadership of the Communist party called for a return to work on June 9. The final tally of repression in the months that followed the strike, according to miners' union leader Roger Pannequin, was 325 miners arrested, 231 sent to German work camps, 94 imprisoned, and 9 shot as hostages.[55]

Attempts by the Vichy government to recreate new relations between labor and management by means of a new labor charter received a poor reception among the mine workers. Leaders of the government-recognized unions were disappointed by the charter. Meeting in December 1941, they agreed to seek a charter that would provide permanent and mandatory collaboration between labor and management along the lines of co-management (*co-gestion*), similar to the American system of bargaining. They favored some worker participation in managing the industry, union control of union funds, and exclusive jurisdiction to represent workers in the extractive industries. But what they received from the charter was a system that merely permitted workers to make requests and suggestions.[56]

Sharp criticism also emerged at the local level. Jules Priem contended that the charter's vague language failed to appeal to workers and that rank-and-file workers were simply overwhelmed by the more vocal opponents. Formal "parity" meetings between labor and management helped to resolve some individual disagreements, but since this format found its biggest success handling problems on a case-by-case basis, it did not prove to be a useful vehicle in dealing with larger issues faced by virtually all mine workers. In the Lens area, elections to select union administrators became a fiasco when in most mines only 1 percent to 3 percent of the miners bothered to vote. The legal unions had called for workers to participate, but the clandestine groups had been active in encouraging workers to boycott the election.[57] Most miners failed to identify with the legal union. A report on the coal industry produced in 1943 by a leading research group of the Resistance noted that the old trade union leaders were not popular because they worked with the Germans. The report added: "The unions are now seen as a facade. Most of the miners of Nord are now anti-German, Communists, and Gaullists. It is certain that Communist cells have gained predominance."[58]

In February 1943 two leaders from the Federation of Miners, Victorin

Duguet, a Communist, and Noel Sinot, a Socialist, headed a labor unity committee.[59] Two months later, the CGT was reunited once more at the national level. The Communists buried many of their old criticisms of the non-Communist wing of the union and urged all anti-Vichy political tendencies to unite. Meanwhile, reformist unionists were drawn toward closer relations with the Communists, partly because the government-approved unions lacked credibility.

Another work stoppage in October 1943 exposed the strength of the union movement and the weakness of the coal-mining companies. The strike was based on economic issues, such as a pay raise that had been delayed, the ever-present food shortages, and antipathy to Sunday work. The illegal union distributed leaflets calling for a strike committee to present demands to management: better safety measures, return to normal practices of pit-propping, election of union stewards, and an end to unfair disciplinary action and firings. The strike began on Sunday, 10 October 1943. Some engineers charged that "young kids and foreign workers" were the most active in striking. Indeed, of the 43 strikers to be arrested, 19 were 20 years old or younger.[60] After four days, only 10 percent of the miners were entering the mines. They started trickling back in the next few days, but after a week about 40 percent were still off the job.

Management's response to the 1943 strike revealed how the German military officials and the French government were tightening their control over matters traditionally handled by the local coal operators. German authorities complained that the mining companies were partly to blame for the strike.[61] They demanded that the police take more vigorous action. A large number of arrests were made, and many workers were sent to labor camps in Germany. In November, amid rumors of another strike to protest Sunday work, German military authorities summoned the mining engineers to an emergency meeting. The engineers were warned to take tough action against any strikers.[62] To bolster their demands, the Germans promised they would take action against middle management personnel as well as workers. In several cases, German military forces took up positions inside the offices of the mining companies in order to guarantee that miners were going into the mine on Sunday and that engineers were not shirking their duties. Again, the repression was severe, and there were about 500 arrests. A month later 202 were still imprisoned.[63]

To the extent that the strike in 1943 tightened the hold by the French government and the Germans over labor policies in the coal mines, it undermined the prestige and legitimacy of the coal-mining executives. Meanwhile, the clandestine Federation of Miners was growing quickly as a wide network of pit committees implanted themselves in the mines. By the end of 1943 the CGT miners' union in the Nord–Pas-de-Calais region claimed 80,000 members, certainly an inflated figure in terms of actual dues-paying members, but probably not far off the mark considering that the region was nearly 100 percent organized in 1938 and that 157,000 mine workers were employed in the northern mines in 1943.[64] With union machinery developed over the course of several years of struggle, leaders of the federation positioned themselves for the long-awaited liberation.

Paris was liberated in the last week of August 1944. Henri Martel and Jacques Seine, representing both wings of the labor movement, took over the offices of the Federation of Miners. They delegated Nestor Calonne, a Communist, to reconstitute the union in Nord and Pas-de-Calais. Within a few days, the Germans began to retreat from the occupied north, opening the way to a reconstitution of power in local institutions, including labor organizations. Calonne, Martel, and other labor leaders, backed by armed militants from the union unity committee, seized the union offices and expelled officials who had served during the occupation.[65]

As the liberation swept through the coal basin, work in the mines came to a halt. Arriving at the pithead, the miners refused to descend. Committees of workers drew up lists of demands: better food, the firing of wartime management, reimbursement for unfair fines, and the right to nominate supervisors. They complained of a lack of soap, a serious problem because coal dust imbedded in the skin of their faces, arms, backs, and chests could not be removed by water alone. They asked for work clothing and shoes. Union leaders met with officials of the mining companies, but no agreement could be negotiated until the government determined the status of the mines. Meanwhile the workers demanded action against management personnel who, in their view, were guilty of collaboration. Large numbers of engineers, supervisors, and foremen, fearful of retaliation, stayed away from the mines. Old hierarchical relationships between workers and managers were uprooted in this new context.

On the eve of the liberation, the miners' union resurfaced in a new and exciting era. But important new challenges pulled the union in opposite directions. On the one hand, mine workers were nearly unanimous in their demands for a sweeping change in the mines and in their support for the strong and militant union that had been built within the tough environment of occupation. This important factor pushed the union in the direction of militancy and class struggle. On the other hand, the collapse of traditional political power, the weaknesses of the mining companies, and the breakdown of managerial authority left the union in the unlikely position of being the only force capable of restoring order in the

mines. This reality pulled the union toward labor-management cooperation. As a wave of euphoria swept across the mining basin, it is not likely
that many workers fully considered the tension that would emerge once
the union attempted to square the demands of its members with the needs
of the nation.

LABOR AND LIBERATION POLITICS

"Who will replace the liberal bourgeoisie?" asked the daily paper in Lille,
Voix du Nord, on 29 November 1944. It was a good question. In the
weeks and months that followed the liberation, the old elite of the region
found itself cut off from traditional channels of political power, threatened by purges, and paralyzed by the specter of social revolution.

The local press reflected this change. The most important regional
daily, *Le Grand Écho*, faithful representative of the local establishment
for many years, was suppressed in the first days of the liberation. Likewise the important business weekly, *Nord-Industriel*, dominated by mining, steel, and textile interests, disappeared in September 1944. It would
not reappear until the summer of 1946. Leftist publications filled the
void. Their headlines spoke of the need to nationalize industry, purge
economic collaborators, and crush "the trusts." Nationalization was a
popular word in France in the months following the liberation.[66]

Traditional forms of political power were uprooted. Municipal elections were several months away. In the meantime, the political arm of the
Resistance, the local liberation committees, dominated by Resistance parties and individuals, designated local administrators and outlined the
purge process.[67] Local officials installed by the Germans were replaced
by councils, of which at least half the members were representatives of
Resistance groups. Incumbent council members retained their posts only
if they had participated in Resistance activity dating back to 1941. No
person who had voted full powers to Marshal Pétain in July 1940 was
eligible to participate in local councils.[68] In the first few weeks following
the liberation, nearly 3,000 persons were detained, partly to ease the
tense situation, partly to protect some of the detainees from summary
executions.[69]

"The industrial world," wrote an editorialist in *Voix du Nord*, "is
mired in pessimism."[70] Employers faced suspicion everywhere. They
were paralyzed by the rapid growth of communism and were shocked
to learn that workers were demanding to know how management operated and how company profits were divided. Liberation politics were
dominated by the relative isolation of traditional conservative forces and
the revival of leftist parties. In Paris, political leaders debated plans to

nationalize the coal mines and other industries. In the mines, however, activists focused on more immediate and concrete goals such as replacing unpopular foremen and engineers, winning a wage hike, and rooting out the Bedaux system. Across France, but especially in the coal-mining region, a new era had dawned. Arguing for a deep purge of collaborators and widespread nationalization of industry, the editors of the Socialist daily *Nord-Matin* predicted, "The Fourth Republic will either defeat the trusts or it will be defeated by them." *Liberté* added, "We cannot make deals with the trusts; we must suppress them."[71]

With the liberation providing a dramatic new opening, political parties began to reassert themselves at the national and local levels, taking into account the new realities. High on each party's agenda in Nord and Pas-de-Calais were the disposition of the coal mines and the role of unions within the industry's reform. Politics in northern France were dominated by three political forces: Christian Democracy, Communism, and Socialism.

The Christian Democrats traditionally drew their most solid support from the middle classes, but they also could depend upon a small minority of devout workers to participate in their labor organization, the Confédération Française des Travailleurs Chrétiens (CFTC). The Mouvement Républicain et Populaire (MRP), France's new Christian Democrat party, acquired instant success and became one of France's three major parties. Northern France, with old Catholic traditions, became a stronghold for the MRP, especially in the cities of Lille, Roubaix, and Tourcoing. MRP support in northern France came from several sources. The Popular Democratic Party (PDP) was a small political group of the interwar period that had fought the ruling hierarchy of the church and affirmed democracy and social justice. The CFTC was established in the 1920s as an alternative to the CGT and the CGTU among textile workers in Roubaix. The Jeunesses Ouvrière Chrétienne (JOC) had recruited young activists into the CFTC during the war years.[72] The CFTC maintained a distinct entity as a small but stable minority among workers. A group called the Résistants d'Inspiration Chrétienne (RIC) was formed in Roubaix. In October 1944, a month after the liberation, the PDP and the RIC merged to form the MRP in northern France.

Despite its left-of-center origins, the MRP soon established itself as a moderate, and then conservative, organization. The party leaders called for purges but opposed vengeance as incompatible with Christian teachings. The MRP lent its name to support for nationalization of the coal mines, but it also opposed excessive state control and spearheaded the stockholders' calls for generous compensation. While condemning the "proletarian condition," the MRP equally opposed the notion of class struggle. People were attracted to the MRP for different, even contradictory, reasons: because of its connections with the CFTC and its Resistance role, because of its Gaullism, and for its moderate political character. As long as the traditional conservative parties remained dormant and de Gaulle remained in office, the MRP could fill the large political space of the center and right.

The French Communist Party (PCF) emerged from the liberation with unparalleled prestige, a remarkable growth in membership, and prominent positions in the new organs of local political power. It was an astonishing reversal of political fortune. Five years earlier, the government had dissolved the party, and the German-Soviet pact had confused and demoralized the rank and file. Yet, within the space of a few years, the PCF had put itself at the head of organized labor, become a major party, and earned some grudging acceptance from many former critics. In fact, the stunning success contributed to the "Communist mystique." So too did the party's self-description as the *"parti des fusilés,"* the party of those who were shot, a reference to the many Communist militants who were killed, jailed, or sent to German work camps during the occupation. The party learned to wrap itself in the bloody flag of the Resistance and to champion the strategy of the *front national.* Party leaders also cited the dissolution of the Communist International in 1943 as proof of the distinctly national and patriotic character of the party.

An internal Communist document distributed in northern France noted in June 1943: "Our influence and prestige grows among the people. Many who were critical of us or even were our adversaries are now enlightened by the examples and sacrifices of our militants and are close to joining our party."[73] Membership doubled from 20,000 to 40,000 in Nord between December 1944 and December 1945 and grew from 18,000 to 38,000 in Pas-de-Calais during the same period.[74] For the first time Communist unionists were in the majority in several unions, including the coal mines of both departments, the metals industry in Lille, the chemical industry in Nord, the local transit system, and the construction industry.[75]

This success in the labor movement, however, created a new situation for the Communists. The self-defined revolutionary vanguard now became a significant force in government at the national and local level. Veterans of the turbulent years of the 1930s kept alive the dream of socialist revolution, but they also remembered their political isolation during the period of the German-Soviet pact. The last thing these new leaders wanted was to see their party confined once more to the margins of political life. Communist labor leaders headed many CGT unions, giving them new duties and imposing new responsibilities. Once the mines were nationalized, a group of Communists would hold important positions within the mining management and, in some cases, would be compelled to implement policies they had once condemned. Many Communists who had expected to see the social revolution emerge out of the patriotic struggle against Germany voiced support for higher production quotas while quietly harboring revolutionary pretensions.

The Socialist party, Section Française de l'Internationale Ouvrière (SFIO), stood politically between the MRP and the Communists. This swing position defined the Socialists' dilemma; they faced a choice between two unsatisfactory alternatives: allying with the Communists against the MRP or with the MRP against the Communists. Each option was fraught with its own set of dangers. Most northern Socialists sought to avoid the necessity for choosing, however, preferring to participate energetically in the new government while trying to carve out a distinct Socialist identity and a solid electoral base.

The party gained members in the north and was well represented in all local organs of political power. In the euphoric liberation atmosphere, Socialist trade unionists, like their most famous leader, Léon Blum, believed that socialism had become the master of the hour. "The liberation seemed to open an immense chance for us," wrote Pierre Maurroy, "to participate in the reconstruction of a new political system, and to enter a world that was free, egalitarian, and fraternal."[76] Socialists with experience in the labor movement headed important ministries and began to implement plans for nationalization and other structural reforms. Younger and more active members assumed leadership roles, and many Socialists who had left the party in the 1930s returned to the fold. In Pas-de-Calais a group of Socialists sought to rebuild their party on Marxist ideology and to restore its role as a true party of the working class.

But the rapid Communist resurgence confronted Socialist trade unionists with a thorny dilemma. Hostile behavior toward their rivals would earn them the labels of "anti-union" and "anti-Communist." However, a close alliance with the Communists would relegate the Socialists to a satellite status in the trade unions, leading to a loss of identity. Older Socialist labor leaders, strongly anti-Communist and based mainly in the three cities of Nord, chafed inside the new coalition with the Communists. But others, especially the groups in the mining towns of Pas-de-Calais or in the working class districts of Nord, feared isolation from the mass of workers. They sought to retain working relations with the Communists while building a new Socialist identity.

The first regional meeting of the CGT Federation of Miners revealed the problem facing the Socialists. It was the first large gathering since 1939, and the Communist activists were well organized. Resolutions to expel union officials and remove stewards who had replaced Communist stewards in 1939 passed after a number of patriotic speeches. Surprised and isolated, the expelled stewards, many of whom were Socialists, were unable to muster any visible support. The Socialist weekly from Lens, *L'Espoir*, belatedly took up their cause and opened its pages to the dissident militants.[77] This small group formed an anti-Communist focal point in the mines, but other Socialist union leaders were unwilling to support them openly.

The two parties of the Left also competed for electoral support from workers in the mining region. As always, the Socialists ran Socialist candidates. But the Communists formed a broader, "patriotic and anti-fascist" coalition slate that captured the mayoral posts in more than a dozen towns that had been traditionally governed by the Socialists. In Lens, the "capital" of the mining basin, voters elected a young Communist leader of the miners' union, Auguste Lecoeur.

Socialists and Communists also competed for influence in the regional food-and-clothing outlet that served tens of thousands of mine workers and their families. The CGT, along with the much smaller CFTC, had taken over the operation in 1945 and turned it into a cooperative run by the unions and the community. But the Socialists found themselves in a minority on the cooperative's board of directors. Some charged that the Communists had used their power in the cooperative to strengthen the party's influence among mine workers.

The pressures of occupation and war had brought the Left parties together against the Germans and local elites, but the liberation and the collapse of traditional power unleashed new forces that drove them apart. Competition between Socialists and Communists for power at the local level and in the unions intensified as the process of nationalizing the coal mines began to unfold.

3.

Nationalizing Coal, Organizing Labor

I t was easy to extend state control over the mines. It was harder to reshape the industry to satisfy the diverse needs of industry, labor, and energy consumers. Likewise, it was a simple matter to promise the miners a new beginning but a tougher job to solve the problems that had necessitated state intervention in the first place. Thus the two tasks of nationalizing coal and organizing the labor force in the mines were inextricably linked. "Without the nationalization," recalled Léon Delfosse, "there would never have been a battle of production." [1]

The coal crisis blocked the path of economic recovery, but attempts to increase production faltered in the poisoned social climate in the mines. The miners supported nationalization, but their most immediate concerns centered on the purges of management personnel and food shortages. Discontent grew in 1945, leading to angry protests during the summer months. The Federation of Miners was the only organization that, from the miners' perspective, possessed the credibility needed to restore order in the mines. But the union leaders' defense of unpopular decisions created an angry backlash from rank-and-file miners, who initiated unauthorized work stoppages.

Thus, while politicians struggled to enact legislation to nationalize coal mining, union leaders sought to end wildcat strikes and organize labor in order to meet the miners' demands and the economic needs of the nation.

SHAPING THE PROVISIONAL NATIONALIZATION

Political, economic, and social factors provided the rationale for nationalizing the coal industry. The National Council of the Resistance, in its charter, called for a "return to the nation of sources of energy and underground wealth."[2] De Gaulle, in his important speech of 12 September 1944, stated that "the great sources of common wealth should be exploited and directed no longer for the profit of some, but rather for the advantage of all." The general repeated the same opinion in a speech delivered in Lille on 1 October 1944.[3] De Gaulle's position reflected the political orientation of the provisional government: the influence of the Left, the isolation of most business groups, and the commitment to structural economic reforms. Newspaper editorialists attacked the old vested interests and the "men of the trusts." Nationalization could extricate key industries from the grip of special interests and guide them into the service of the national interest. In the popular mind, nationalization implied a chastisement of the old order and the birth of a new political system.[4] In the coal mines, it meant overthrowing the old mining companies.

Economic factors offered even more compelling reasons for government intervention. The coal crisis threatened to derail the war effort and weaken France's hand at the postwar negotiation table. Coal was needed to move railroads, generate electricity, turn textile and paper mills, and heat homes and workshops. Without energy, industrial recovery would remain an elusive goal. Underground work areas were often small, scattered, and underequipped. Methods of transporting miners underground, loading coal, and bringing it to the surface were old and inefficient. A shortage of conveyor belts meant that coal was often moved by hand. Horse-pulled coal wagons were generally small, and chronic shortages of rails contributed to underground transport problems. Shortages of wooden pit-props held up advancement into unexploited coal seams. Small engines used in moving coal were in disrepair due to lack of spare parts. Loading machines in the surface installations of Pas-de-Calais had an average age of 27 years.[5] Cokeries, which might have had a life span of 25 years, were already 20 years old and suffering from insufficient upkeep during the war years. Given the alarmingly sharp demand for domestic coal (foreign coal was not available), this combination of primitive infrastructure, technological retardation, and wartime damage made it imperative for the state to intervene in coal mining.

Yet economic and political factors do not fully explain the nationalization. A somewhat similar situation had presented itself after World War I. The state provided subsidies but did not impinge upon the managerial power of the mining companies. In 1944, however, the industry's leaders proved incapable of putting the industry back on its feet, in large part because of the deep chasm that separated labor from management. The impasse emerged clearly during the initial negotiations that took place between the union and the companies. Union leaders had instructed the miners to discuss their concerns and to list their demands. But when labor representatives sat down with management, there seemed to be little basis for meaningful dialogue. Union representatives found it hard to conceal their contempt for the coal operators. In one early session in September 1944, a union representative boldly charged that the hands of the coal barons dripped with the blood of patriotic mine workers. Apart from basic economic concerns, the unionists demanded a "severe purge" of management, dissolving of "the trusts," and confiscation of the property of the mining companies.[6] From their side, the coal companies argued that financial insolvency made it impossible for them to negotiate anything. They refused to entertain any plan to diminish their traditional authority and resolutely refused to discuss a proposal to rehire union workers who had been fired between 1936 and 1939.[7] As talk of impending nationalization and rumors of a purge of management swept across the mining basin, many supervisors and foremen abandoned their posts. Engineers requested immediate transfers to other coalfields.[8] Thus a stalemate ensued. From the top executives of the coal companies to the lowest foreman at the bottom of the mine, order and traditional hierarchy had collapsed. Both labor and management waited for government to intervene.

Robert Lacoste, the new minister of Industrial Production in the first postliberation government, was a Socialist, a CGT unionist, and a longtime advocate of nationalization. Faced with the coal shortage and the social crisis in the mines, Lacoste quickly installed a new administration. In September he chose veteran coal operator M. Duhameau to direct the Coal Mines Organization Committee in the northern coalfields.[9] Ten days later, Lacoste appointed M. Blum-Picard secretary general of the Ministry of Industrial Production, charging him with the coordination of the mines, electricity, steel, and chemicals. In October, Lacoste issued a decree regulating the organization committees. These economic bodies would be dissolved on an individual basis in the near future but would be directed in the interim by provisional administrators.[10] Two weeks later Lacoste suspended the council presidents and general directors of the mining companies and named a set of replacements.[11]

The northern mines were officially nationalized by decree in December 1944. Lacoste indicated that this was a provisional act. The definitive nationalization would follow once the question of compensation to the mine owners and stockholders had been settled. Lacoste suggested that this would take a year to accomplish. In fact, seventeen months passed before the definitive nationalization was approved unanimously by the Constituent Assembly in May 1946.

The provisional nationalization attempted to strike a balance between representational governance and tight state control. A consultative committee was named to advise the industry. This body consisted of twenty-four members: eight from the personnel, five from the consumers, two from the old owners, and nine from the government. Five of the eight personnel representatives were workers; the rest were engineers and foremen. The committee did not make policy but was an advisory body that met monthly. A smaller steering committee called the Permanent Section met weekly. This body was composed of eight members representing consumers, personnel, and government. In the initial phase of the nationalization, two members of the section were workers. In describing the provisional nationalization, Lacoste pointed proudly to the fact that workers were represented in management.[12] For the first time workers were allowed a voice in coal policy, even if the committee was purely consultative. However, the language defining personnel members of the Permanent Section read "workers or employees," which eliminated any guarantee that mine workers, as opposed to foremen, supervisors, or technical personnel, would always be represented on the committee.[13]

State officials maintained a strong role in the provisional nationalization. The minister of Industrial Production appointed three of the four consumer representatives, all members of the old mining companies, and four of the nine representatives of various state agencies. The five remaining state representatives were selected by the Ministries of National Economy, Finance, Public Works, and Labor.[14] Although the general director was given extended powers, he remained responsible to the minister of Mines, an undersecretary to the minister of Industrial Production. Disputes between the general director and the consultative committee were to be arbitrated by Lacoste.[15] Although the nationalized mines were granted financial autonomy, a decree issued in November 1944 created a body of state controllers whose exact role was left undefined.[16]

The provisional nationalization formula unveiled by Lacoste was criticized as too liberal by the Left and too restrictive by the Right. CGT leader Benoit Frachon criticized the fact that government pronouncements related to nationalization were often accompanied by homages to the men of the old Coal Mines Committee. Nationalization without requisition and confiscation of all the wealth of the mining companies was insufficient. "Did the companies help in the repression and arrests of miners who organized strikes and sabotage?" asked Frachon. "Do the mining companies bear some responsibility for the death of some of our patriots? Yes or no?"[17] Other CGT leaders repeated the miners' demands for a sweeping purge of management in the mines.[18]

Socialist Jules Moch, in a celebrated pamphlet entitled *Guerre aux trusts*, criticized the inadequacy of provisional nationalization. "The order of 13 December 1944 hardly suppressed the old companies," wrote Moch. "Their financial power remains intact and the mine trusts continue to hold immense means by which they hope to recover the wealth that has temporarily escaped them." Moch argued that the old companies should have no representatives in the consultative committee: "These owners have nothing in common with the mines and should not participate in their management."[19] On 2 March 1945 a joint Socialist-Communist communiqué pertaining to economic issues was published in all Socialist and Communist newspapers.[20]

Criticism of nationalization from the Right emanated from the old mining companies, among conservative leaders of the MRP, and inside the Ministry of Finance. Around the issue of compensation, mining executives launched an antinationalization campaign among stockholders in an effort to pressure government to increase its compensation package. They chose their old leader Robert Fabre for this task. Fabre had served as secretary general of the Coal Mines Committee since 1931. During the Vichy period, he assumed the same post in the Coal Mines Organization Committee. With the liberation and the impending nationalization, Fabre left the organization committee to form a new organization, the Chambre Syndicale des Houillères, or Chamber of Coal Mines.[21] In one of its first acts, the new group organized a letter-writing campaign by individuals holding stocks in the mines to protest the nationalization. While it is difficult to gauge the true impact of this action, a note from Robert Lacoste to the Ministry of Finance reveals that within a week after he issued the decree on nationalization, Lacoste was overwhelmed with letters from presumably frightened stockholders.[22]

Lacoste turned aside an attempt by the Ministry of Finance to annul the nationalization decree.[23] Seeking to resolve the compensation issue, he named a commission to study the methods of compensation. Organized in December 1944, the commission initially comprised representatives from the Ministries of Finance and Treasury, various mining engineers, and some civil service specialists. But soon others were added to the compensation commission, including longtime leaders of the old Coal Mines Committee: Robert Fabre, Pierre Parent, and Émile Martérer. Within the commission they lobbied for the highest possible level of compensation.[24]

The Ministry of Finance also argued with Lacoste over the disposition of the "annex industries." At issue were the numerous factories and refineries that manufactured various coal by-products and the electric power plants in the mining basin. Finance urged that these industries not be turned over to the state, at least until a "definitive statute and organization of the nationalized mines has been determined." The order of December 1944 had specified that the ownership of the annex industries would be settled within eight months by decrees issued and signed by the Ministry of National Economy and the Ministry of Mines. But the Finance Ministry pressed Lacoste to have all decrees relative to the annex industries countersigned by the Ministry of Finance, warning Lacoste of "extremely important financial repercussions."[25] The crux of the matter was that some of the annex industries were more profitable enterprises than the coal mines themselves. Many felt that the nationalization would be considerably compromised if it did not extend to the annex industries. The matter was not resolved during Robert Lacoste's first term in the Ministry of Industrial Production, but most of the annex industries were soon brought under the nationalization.

The political forces opposed to nationalization were grouped in the MRP. De Gaulle, who had backed state ownership in 1943 and 1944, began to shift in 1945. Addressing the Consultative Assembly on 2 March 1945—the same day as the joint Socialist-Communist statement favoring nationalization was issued—the general contended that "nothing would be more foolish than to make sweeping structural reforms. . . . It is the task of a nationally representative body either to make these transitional actions definitive or to alter them."[26] De Gaulle hoped that these reforms would be undertaken not by the Consultative Assembly but by the National Assembly, which had not yet been elected but which observers felt would bear a more conservative imprint than the Consultative Assembly.

Supporting these efforts to limit further nationalization were criticisms voiced in various business journals and conservative newspapers. Some claimed that nationalization was an impractical measure and that the old owners had done everything in their power to develop the industry.[27] Yet only a fraction of the business community, the old mine operators, and a small group of conservative diehards sought to reverse the provisional nationalization.[28] However, a broader spectrum of individuals and groups argued that the experiment with nationalization would be undermined by excessive "politicization" in the mines. Industry leaders warned that the Communists were building a power base in the new state-directed sector of the economy. Management personnel frequently viewed the social crisis and the breakdown of authority in the mines as a product of this politicization. Ironically, from the point of the view of the union leaders, the situation seemed precisely the opposite: the miners' discontent fueled their interest in political solutions, including nationalization, the Miners' Statute, and the purges.

MINE WORKERS AND NATIONALIZATION

The subject of nationalization provoked wide discussion among the miners.[29] Everyone knew that the government would take over the mines, but no one had a clear picture of what the new structure would look like. The coal miners, like the general public, assumed that workers would be granted some type of representation in the new arrangement. Local newspapers speculated on what the nationalizations would bring. Socialists hoped for tripartite management in nationalized industry. The more conservative *Voix du Nord* suggested some degree of worker participation in management. Communists, not fully certain of their attitude toward government ownership, hesitated to use the term "nationalization." Wary of playing the role of the doctor that saved the "sick" capitalist system, the Communists refrained from expressing formal support for nationalization until March 1945, when the joint communiqué with the Socialists had been issued. But Communist union leaders had urged confiscation of the mines and opposed compensation to the old owners.

Virtually every problem facing the miners related to unresolved questions about nationalization, but the legislative wheels moved slowly—indeed, the new postwar political machinery of the Fourth Republic had not yet been put into place. Many of the government's actions were viewed by the miners as too little and too late. Although the old directors had been replaced, most of the management personnel had retained their positions. Moreover, the provisional nationalization failed to contain provisions regarding working conditions, wages, powers of the stewards, retirement, and other benefits. Lacoste promised a new Miners' Statute to address these issues, but its implementation remained a long way off. "For four years we have lost all taste for the job, for our work. Now many comrades do not see much of a change," wrote a rank-and-file miner in January 1945. "We still have the same leaders in the mines . . . many of the same ones who pushed production for the Germans."[30]

Union leaders criticized the shortcomings of the provisional nationalization, but they also defended it against detractors. "Remember that a social experiment is being attempted," counseled Léon Delfosse in January 1945, "and if it succeeds it will spell death to the big trusts." Nestor Calonne described the union's position on the nationalization: "The state requisitioned the mines and issued the nationalization decree. We accepted it for lack of anything better, but we denounced what we did not like in it. When we raised these criticisms, however, many comrades thought that the old bosses were back in power. But we would be imbeciles to abandon the fruits of so much struggle. That is why we are doing what we can to try to make the nationalizations succeed."[31] While the miners gave the nationalization a reserved and cautious welcome, they waited to see how the new regime would handle the explosive issue of the purges and the problem of food shortages.

PURGING MANAGEMENT

The miners asked why they should return to work under the direction of the same managers who had reduced their pay rates, penalized them for absenteeism, and turned in their names to the authorities who sent them to work camps in Germany. What kind of nationalization plan would leave these bosses in their old positions of authority? For the miners, these questions were rooted in long-standing class consciousness and deeply seated patriotism, a powerful combination that ensured that the issue of the purges posed a direct challenge to the chain of command in the mines.

Once the occupation had been lifted, the miners turned with a vengeance on their bosses. Several directors and engineers were arrested and others were taken into custody in order to protect them from groups of angry mine workers. Yet it was the lower level of management, the foremen and supervisors, who bore the brunt of the attacks. Arriving at the mining gates in the early morning, they were turned away by threats of violence from the miners, although there were few reports of direct physical harm. Sometimes the miners let management personnel descend into the mine but then refused to follow them. A report written for the Coal Mines Committee on the situation in the northern mines on September 11, a day in which the situation had "considerably improved," indicated a genuine "crise d'autorité" in the mines. At Noeux the miners demanded that most of the supervisors and the engineer be thrown off the job. In pit number seven of Lens, the workers told two foremen to leave the work site. As a result, the remaining management personnel, perhaps out of fear, abandoned the mine. (The miners went back to work, without supervision.) At Liévin, a high-ranking engineer and all the foremen who worked under him were refused entrance to the mines. The director of La Clarence Mine Company was arrested. In the Marles area the workers stopped two engineers and three lower-management personnel and put them at the head of a column of German prisoners who were being marched off to jail. At Drocourt the miners refused to descend, but after gaining the promise of a full inquest they went to work as usual. At pit number six in Liévin a miner proclaimed himself the new head foreman.[32]

Pressed by agitation in the mining basin, regional authorities set up a procedure for purging the management personnel. Miners filed complaints with the union, and the complaints were turned over to a purge commission, which compiled dossiers on those personnel who were alleged to be collaborators. According to Commissaire de la République François Closon, 3,000 complaints were filed. Eight hundred dossiers were compiled in Nord alone.[33]

However, relatively few of the dossiers examined by the purge committee were judged sufficient for a successful legal prosecution. Most of the charges were eventually dismissed. The dossiers contained little specific information regarding actual acts of political and economic collaboration; rather, they recorded the miners' descriptions of how a foreman had demanded more production, threatened workers with being sent to Germany, or penalized an employee for working too slowly. As far as many miners were concerned, such acts by management were a form of collaboration, even though it was obvious that these charges grew directly out of class conflict and work-related tension inside the mines. Unfortunately for the miners, the legal definition of collaboration did not incorporate aspects of "social collaboration." Delfosse recognized the legal insufficiency of the complaints when he wrote in November 1944 that the information in the dossiers was often too vague.[34]

Given the weakness of the complaints, the union persuaded authorities to allow miners to come before the purge commission to present their cases verbally. But the miners were unaccustomed to speaking in such a formal setting. Ill at ease, they found it difficult to stick to the facts of actual collaboration; instead they tended to describe their own feelings toward the alleged collaborators. "This foreman was brutal to the miners," was a common complaint. "We no longer want him to be the boss. All the workers agree on this."[35]

The authorities and the union faced a dilemma. On the one hand, miners were demanding a sweeping change of management. On the other hand, most of the charges of collaboration would not stick legally. Moreover, even if a sweeping change in management could be accomplished, would such an action be justified on technical and economic grounds? Where would the new managers come from? Administrators were obsessed with this question after dozens of engineers requested to leave the northern basin or simply left on their own accord. In the meantime, many of the engineers, supervisors, and foremen refused to work in the mines, fearing for their safety at the hands of the miners. On October 12, a large group of miners marched to Béthune and demonstrated because some old leaders of the mining companies, who were thought to have been in jail, were seen walking on the streets of Lille.[36]

Closon and the provisional mine directors refused to purge anyone on what was considered "social" grounds because they feared that miners would next strike out at the engineers and directors through the foremen and supervisors.[37] Delfosse wrote in November 1944 that a weakness in the dossiers was that they "do not get to the top often enough, but go after the foreman, the immediate boss in the mines."[38] The miners had little contact with top management. They could not file a complaint, which required cosigning by other workers, for acts that they did not actually witness. Thus the high-ranking managers were relatively insulated. The new mine directors, fearing a total breakdown in hierarchy, sought to limit the purge to the lowest ranks of management. They expressed the view that most foremen were expendable and could be re-placed by "good" workers. The Federation of Miners urged lower management to step forward and implicate their supervisors. But the foremen were reluctant to participate in a purge of their superiors. Caught between top management and the miners, foremen and supervisors were immobilized and in disarray. *Voix du Nord* defended the management personnel and sharply denounced the "sabotage of management authority in the mines" that made it impossible to restore "social order and business as usual."[39] Some foremen redeemed themselves by returning to the ranks of the workers and volunteering for underground assignments.

Unable to reintegrate members of management or to find sufficient legal grounds to terminate them, authorities moved engineers to other coal areas. They assigned controversial foremen and supervisors to pits where they were not known by the workers. This tactic worked until the news spread among miners that the new managers had had dossiers compiled against them and merely had been moved to other work sites. Miners wrote letters to *La Tribune des mineurs* complaining of the slow and ineffective purges. Some leaders of the miners' federation criticized the "pseudo-nationalization" for not being effective.[40]

The purge process took months to complete. Meanwhile, miners continued to oppose the return of some management personnel. In May, 20 head foremen, 9 assistant head foremen, 106 foremen, and 9 supervisors had not been reintegrated into the mines. The cases of 7 or 8 engineers remained undecided.[41] The purge commission examined 800 of the 1,000 dossiers. Decisions were made on 600 cases but fell far short of the miners' expectations. Nearly all charges were dismissed. Sanctions were taken in only 42 cases: 18 temporary suspensions, 11 replacements, 11 demotions, and 2 layoffs.[42] A sullen and angry mood developed as many miners claimed they had been tricked.

FOOD SHORTAGES

Few in France had escaped the food shortages of the occupation period, but working people suffered the most. The black market best served those who were able to pay inflated prices. Wealthy individuals therefore did not often face starvation conditions. Likewise, the farmers did not go hungry during the long years of food shortages. Some even prospered from inflated black market prices. Shopkeepers in food-related operations could consume a portion of what they had to sell. But workers found it nearly impossible to pay for food sold at black market prices.

The causes of the food shortage were not difficult to identify. Part of the problem derived from the systematic plunder of French agriculture by Germany. Thousands of tons of wheat, fish, vegetables, sugar, and other commodities were shipped to Germany during the occupation. In addition, the German retreat and Allied advance disrupted the production and transport of agricultural goods. But, more important, the policy of artificially fixed prices, combined with wartime shortages, produced a situation in which the black market thrived. In effect, two prices existed: one set by the government, the other established on the black market. Food prices rose to their "natural level" on the black market, creating a hidden inflation that eradicated wage increases won by workers and encouraged agricultural producers to avoid the open market. A peasant in northern France could sell a cow for 25,000 francs on the black market, but the official price stood at 5,000 francs. The farmer had three options: sell at a big loss, clandestinely ship the cow to another region where prices were higher, or slaughter the cow, eat part of it, and sell the rest on the local black market.

Once the postwar inflationary spiral began to move upward, food producers, like their counterparts in the production of other basic necessities such as shoes and clothing, preferred to hold on to their stocks. Despite exhortations from the Liberation Committees, deliveries of butter continued to drop between July and November 1944. Rations of meat and butter were cut in October, prompting a protest by the city council of Lille, which threatened to take the food problem into its own hands if the authorities failed to remedy the situation. Confounding public expectations, the food crisis actually deepened after the liberation. Throughout 1945 regional authorities pressed the government to transport more food into the region and made sporadic attempts to crack down on rings of *trafiquers*. But the results were disappointing. In March 1945 reports compiled for the regional authorities in the north noted: "The food situation is less and less sufficient. Six months after the liberation we still hope for some improvement."[43]

In the mining communities, the food shortage was complicated by the abrupt collapse of the mining companies. For decades the companies had controlled nearly every aspect of life in the mining basin, including the distribution and sale of food. Some food was traditionally distributed to workers on the job. Thus, the sacks of potatoes and other food staples allotted to miners on payday had become a permanent feature of the mining occupation. Other food, as well as clothing and other necessities, was sold by the company-owned stores located in the towns and cities of the black country. During the occupation the company system began to falter. Following the miners' strike of 1941, the Germans pushed mining companies to set up a regionally centralized agency for the provisioning of food and clothing, the Société d'Approvisionnement des Houillères de

Beaumont.[44] The liberation threw the old system into even further disarray because the future of the mining companies had been called into question. The government assumed responsibility but soon turned the matter over to the mining personnel and local community representatives, who took over the agency in January 1945 and transformed it into the Central Cooperative for Mining Personnel.

Anxiety over the food situation, combined with anger over the way the purges were handled, added up to a formula for trouble for the authorities and the union leadership. "Work first, then make our demands," said the union newspaper on 30 December 1944. But a few weeks later the union leaders admitted that workers weren't following them.[45]

WILDCAT STRIKES

Seldom recognized by historians, the wildcat strikes of 1945 offer a rare glimpse into the difficulty union leaders faced in trying to square their seemingly contradictory roles as promoters of production and representatives of the working class. "Unleashed outside of the union, these strikes usually occurred spontaneously without revealing any leaders," wrote Bruno Mattei, "but others involved safety delegates who remained motivated by Resistance aspirations and opposed the strategy adopted by the CGT." About half of the miners refused to show up on the first Sunday of the year (to make up for New Years' Day).[46] In March, a strike to protest shortages of food erupted in the mines of Lens. The action spread to Bruay and soon enveloped the western end of the mining basin. Leaders of the union reacted quickly by assuming direction of the strike and turning it into a peaceful, one-day affair. A month later, new strikes erupted near Valenciennes and in the mines of Drocourt, Crespin, and Anzin—this time without the knowledge of the union.

In May, miners began to link food protests with demands for completing the purges. A drumfire of strikes swept across the mining basin. At Anzin the striking miners demanded that a supervisor be fired. At Bruay an engineer was ejected from his post. In a nearby pit, the head foreman and eight other foremen were chased from the mines. An engineer in the annexed Carbolux factory reported that he had been menaced by workers.[47] Miners also struck in Escarpelle and Aniche. At Valenciennes the miners won their demands to suspend a foreman and return a bonus that had been withdrawn by management. At Béthune they struck over lack of decent food and clothing.[48]

The Federation of Miners fought on two fronts. From the government the union demanded rapid improvement in the food situation. To disgruntled miners, they called for patience and more production as the best way to solve the food shortage. Union leaders worked closely with General Director Duhameau, Commissaire Closon, and the minister of Industrial Production, Robert Lacoste, who suddenly found himself shuttling between Paris and northern France. In May during a strike wave, Lacoste remained in the mining basin for an entire week, moving from meeting to meeting. In a radio message aired in the mining basin, Lacoste painted a somber picture of economic dislocation and the "crise du charbon." He urged miners to stay on the job. Delfosse outlined a set of demands the union considered necessary for an improvement of production: better food, including red meat, a wage increase, equal rights for Polish miners, and a "real nationalization that proves to the miners that something has changed."[49] These efforts produced some results. Following the strikes in May, Lacoste discussed the miners' demands at a meeting of the cabinet. A few days later the government decided to upgrade the mining profession.[50] On June 1 Lacoste announced a wage increase for miners—fixing their wages at a level slightly higher than that of the metalworkers of the Paris region.[51] A new "good attendance" bonus was offered to the miners in an effort to curb absenteeism. In a further nod in the direction of worker participation, Lacoste also added another worker to the consultative committee.[52]

Government leaders and local authorities had to depend upon union leaders to contain the upsurge of worker militancy. Leaders of the union worked feverishly to end the strikes. "I had the task of trying to settle these conflicts," recalled Léon Delfosse. "Often they were settled quickly after a discussion of the need to win the battle of production. But sometimes things went too far, such as the incident at pit number seven of Escarpelle when an angry worker locked an engineer in his office."[53] Closon rushed from one mine to the next, attempting to convince the miners to return to work. In order to gain the confidence of the miners, Closon often descended with them in order to speak to them underground. They generally listened to Closon speak for a long time before responding, and usually they were willing to return to work. Closon echoed the sentiments of other officials when he wrote that the situation had the marks of a mass uprising.[54] Mine directors claimed to be helpless before this upsurge.[55] According to Closon, the situation was so tense that any type of government repression would have backfired and served to deepen the militancy of the miners. In his report to de Gaulle, Closon emphasized that many of the miners were armed. The use of police against the strikers, according to the Commissaire de la République, would invite an "open and very grave conflict between the miners and the government." The "crisis of authority in the mines" became the subject of various editorials in *Voix du Nord* and Parisian papers such as *Figaro* and *Le Monde*.[56]

Protests and wildcat strikes continued sporadically throughout the summer of 1945. Union leaders worked to prevent strikes and maintain discipline on the job. Following every strike, the union called meetings in the mining towns. Union officials and stewards outlined the various demands of the miners, spelled out the actions being taken by the union, and explained why strikes were harmful. But the miners did not always follow the advice of the union leaders. On May 29, several groups of miners came to the headquarters of the miners' federation and demanded soap. Nestor Calonne drove to the co-op and left orders for soap to be delivered. A few hours later, the workers walked off the job in Drocourt to protest the lack of soap. Parent went to Drocourt to convince the miners that soap was coming and to go back to work, but a number of workers, especially the younger miners, refused to do so. Articles written for *La Tribune des mineurs* during the summer of 1945 reflected the frustration and uneasiness of union leaders before the undisciplined and angry strikers. Young miners, often the most intransigent and least experienced with union practices, were told to "reflect upon your actions."[57] In July 1945, when miners at one pit at Béthune protested the reentry of a particular foreman, Closon backed up the manager and suspended two CGT stewards. The next day a strike spread through the pits of Béthune. The federation protested and appealed to Lacoste. He lifted the suspensions. Calonne and Foulon then organized a referendum in which the miners voted overwhelmingly to return to work. Although the federation rarely alluded to its weaknesses and difficulties, *La Tribune des mineurs* admitted that the situation had become tenuous: "We are well aware that calumny and criticism has been heaped upon our militants. We also know that the rank-and-file militants are submerged by the mass of miners who, fooled by the slogans of splitters and egoists, do not really understand why, since the liberation, the CGT is compelled not only to obtain the best possible advantages for the workers, but also to consider the national situation and to safeguard the interests of France."[58]

At a time when wildcat strikes in the region under his command threatened the nation's economy, Closon relied a great deal on the disciplined Communist labor leaders. But union leaders, formerly the militant firebrands, found themselves in strange and uncomfortable new postures, working with management to quell strikes. Given the situation, probably no individual helped Closon and the local union leaders more than did Maurice Thorez, the top leader of the Communist party, when he made a dramatic appearance in the small northern mining town of Waziers in July 1945.

THOREZ IN WAZIERS

As a young man, Maurice Thorez had worked for about a year as an underground worker at the Dourges Mining Company. But his homecoming in July 1945 was no celebration. As *Liberté* explained on July 19, "the meeting is open to leaders of party sections and cells, to trade union cadres, and to miners who are party members." Thorez's audience was not the general public but the Communist trade union leaders and the delegates and activists. Obstensibly, Thorez had come to Waziers to brief party members on the recent party convention. But the turmoil in the region and the Communists' new role as a party of the government led Thorez to make a major and controversial pronouncement. What made Thorez's speech different from previous appeals to produce was the manner in which Thorez addressed the miners.[59] Thorez began by elaborating on the obstacles to higher production: large numbers of miners who had left the mines for other work, poor mining equipment, and attempts to sabotage the union-led production campaign by some managers. Up to this point, the speech echoed the basic themes of the Communist press and the line of the Communist unionists. But then Thorez moved in a new direction. Avoiding the obligatory praise usually heaped on the "brave miners" by most Communist speakers, Thorez directed his criticisms at the workers themselves, claiming they were not doing enough to produce more coal.

To a stunned audience of nearly 2,000 workers, Thorez drew out the major complaints raised by the miners and polemicized against them. Did some engineers and foremen hold back the production campaign? All the more reason for the miners to work even harder. Did some workers hesitate to work too hard because the piece-rate system could be altered to their disadvantage? Such individual concerns should not be allowed to block the liberation agenda. Was it true that producing more coal only benefited the rich stockholders who received eight francs for each ton of coal produced? No, argued Thorez. The workers should produce coal in the interests of the nation as a whole. To be certain, there were some militants, conditioned by years of on-the-job resistance to the bosses' appeals for more production, who felt like "macas" (short for "macaronis," the derogatory name used for Italian immigrants who, the miners claimed, had worked during strikes in the 1920s and 1930s) or "scabs" for working too hard. But the real scabs were those who extracted coal when such production harmed the workers, as in a strike situation. The task in 1945, Thorez argued, was to produce more coal for the working class and for the nation.

Turning to the problem of absenteeism, which had reached 30 percent in some mines, Thorez suggested that some of the medical officials of the mines may have been too lenient. Doctors who gave illness slips too easily were not true friends of the miners. "If you are sick," exclaimed Thorez, "you should have a sick day. But if you are not sick, you should work." Thorez next scolded a group of young miners who wanted to leave work early in order to go to a dance: "A scandal, inadmissible, impossible!" declared the Communist leader. Then Thorez addressed the biggest controversy in the mining basin: the purge of management personnel. He admitted that the purges were too little and too late and criticized the fact it was the lower-ranking management who were usually purged, while real responsibility lay with the "higher-ups." But Thorez added, "We can't keep purging forever."

Responding to rumors of an impending work stoppage, Thorez contended that such an action would put thousands of workers out of work. The production effort was part of class solidarity. "To produce, produce, and produce still more; this today is the most elevated form of duty to class and to nation." The production effort, explained Thorez, would also cement the alliance of the working class to sections of the middle classes and the peasantry. Predicting a winter worse than the bitter winter of 1944–1945, Thorez raised the specter of factory closings due to coal shortages. Women and children would freeze to death in their heatless homes. "All of France has its eyes on you, all of France waits for the miners—and especially the miners of Nord and Pas-de-Calais—to make a new and great effort."

Thorez's talk has come to be known as the "historic speech of Waziers." *L'Humanité* reprinted the full text of the speech. Portions of the speech were promoted ceaselessly in the regional party and labor press. Indeed, there was something bold and dramatic in Thorez's speech, which, even his detractors had to admit, demonstrated a good deal of political courage.[60] Against a background of deep social crisis, the Communist leader returned to his native soil. But rather than urge his fellow revolutionaries to the picket lines or the ballot box, Thorez counseled the miners to return to work and to toil with even greater intensity and self-abnegation. Focusing on the Communist union leaders, safety delegates, union stewards, and party members, Thorez reached out to those who were expected to rally the rest of the work force behind the line of the party, the "shock troops" in the battle of production.

Estimates of the number of miners attending Thorez's speech varied from 1,200 to 2,000. The miners were not particularly enthusiastic. After an opening round of applause, the miners responded in a much more restrained manner. Many were shocked by the bluntness of the speech and by Thorez's statement that "those who are lazy and halfhearted at work can never be good revolutionaries." The tone of the speech ran directly counter to the usual laudatory rhetoric toward those who were sometimes described as the "number one" workers in France. Miners who had expected that Thorez's journey to the north marked the beginning of a new struggle to complete the purges were deeply disappointed. Recounting the event several years later, Auguste Lecoeur wrote: "At Waziers I stood in the center of the hall. I was astonished by the very restrained welcome Thorez received from this very select group of Communist cadres from the region. Only those in the first four or five rows applauded, and the applause quickly died away. At the back of the hall, they pretended to clap."[61]

Roger Pannequin, another participant at Waziers, later described the meeting as a French version of the "Stalinist cult in action." The great leader was surrounded by an aura of authority and prestige, which rank-and-file militants were unwilling to question. Moreover, he appealed directly to the rank and file over the heads of the local leadership. Pannequin noted that many lower-level union officials and stewards felt personally rebuked by Thorez's speech, which criticized them for yielding to the miners' demands in some pits. In particular, the PCF leaders of Nord chimed in with Thorez in leveling attacks against the leaders of Pas-de-Calais, the center of the spontaneous wildcat strikes in 1945. Even Lecoeur was not immune to these criticisms. Two days earlier he had written an article in *Liberté* defending two Communist stewards who had been suspended by Closon for allegedly leading a strike against a Vichyite foreman. Indeed, in Pannequin's observation, "Thorez came to show Lecoeur that this time (unlike 1941 when Lecoeur pushed for a strike against the orders of Jacques Duclos), he could not be right against the party . . . that Thorez had returned and had taken in hand the leadership, and that he would not allow Lecoeur to build his own base of power among the mining proletariat."[62]

Perhaps, as J. P. Hirsch suggested, the light applause was to be expected. The speech was not a celebration but rather a sort of "great didactic effort."[63] The prestige Thorez carried in the mining basin, the cult built around the so-called *fils du peuple*, and Thorez's ability to combine criticism with a certain logic made his message all the more palatable to the miners. Perhaps it was true, as Jacques Fauvet wrote, that "no one but Thorez could have made such a speech."[64] Many Communists disagreed with the policy, but they did not raise those disagreements publicly. Recalling the Waziers speech, Delfosse noted that he had disagreed with Thorez's blanket condemnation of all strikes. "Some of the strikes were justified," he contended.[65] On the surface, at least, the discipline of the PCF held firm and extended into the ranks of the miners' union. Years later Lecoeur recalled that after the Waziers speech many militants stopped attending cell meetings in 1945 only to reappear during the big strikes in 1947.[66]

THE SEPTEMBER STRIKES

When Thorez left Waziers to meet with top mining officials, local union leaders focused their efforts on mobilizing workers to produce more coal. Instead, they found themselves confronted with another wave of wildcat strikes. Protesting food shortages and high prices, the miners of pit number two of Lens walked off the job without informing the union on September 13. The CGT quickly repudiated the strike and expelled some delegates who had been involved for lack of union discipline. The strike quickly spread to Bruay, Courrières, Liévin, Drocourt, Oignies, and Valenciennes.[67] Union leaders instructed the stewards to tell the strikers that their demands were in the process of being met. They warned that the miners were being exploited by provocateurs and demagogues who sought to undermine the union and sabotage the nationalization. Yet their advice was not followed and the strike continued for several days. The CGT leaders perceived a mass movement developing outside their control. Worse, from the point of view of the Communists, opposition currents inside the union appeared to be the source of these undisciplined strikes.

Throughout the month of August 1945, Socialists of Pas-de-Calais criticized the role of the Communists in the miners' union. These polemics had their own sources, but they also dovetailed with a souring of relations between the two Left parties. At the national level the Socialists, Communists, and Christian Democrats were the three major parties. Conservative parties and groupings fared poorly while the Communists made solid gains. A number of "unity" initiatives launched by the PCF failed to move Socialist leaders like Léon Blum, whose anti-Communist sentiments were deeply rooted. Communist proposals to merge the two parties sounded like political suicide to most Socialist leaders, and it is not surprising that such proposals were dismissed out of hand by the Socialists. At the Socialists' convention in August 1945, Jules Moch authored the motion that rejected Communist "unity" proposals.[68] The Communists next proposed the idea of rebuilding the Popular Front. Such a proposal made some sense given the recent election results. But Socialist leaders were deeply opposed, fearing it would lead to domination of them by the Communists. At no time did the Socialist party consider either unity with the Communists or a new Popular Front coalition. Political commentators who detected a Socialist "inferiority complex" in relation to the Communists were probably quite close to the mark.

In the mining basin, Socialist leaders viewed with alarm the surging Communist electoral strength and its power in the labor movement. "Union democracy has given way to union autocracy," wrote a union member for *L'Espoir*, and the union leaders had established a "dictatorship over the union." Other policies were singled out for criticism: the "stakhanovism" of the production drive, the union's support for extra days and hours of work in the mines, and the fact that union leaders cooperated so closely with the management of the nationalized mines. The Socialists criticized Communist exhortations to work hard. "It is impossible for the miners to work hard," claimed one writer, "because they are tired and underfed."[69] An anonymous writer called "Jean-le-mineur" charged that the co-op was controlled by Communist bureaucrats who helped themselves to the best provisions while the miners went hungry. The CFTC raised similar criticisms. According to *Nord-Éclair*, the strikes were protesting high food prices and the particularly high prices at the co-op.[70] Although both the engineers and the CFTC were represented in the administrative council of the co-op, pro-Communist elements had become dominant. *Nord-Éclair* soon began to refer to the co-op as a "new trust."

As far as the Communists were concerned, the strikes were provoked by a handful of "collaborationist" Socialists who had been driven from their union posts nine months earlier. The charges were not totally groundless. Indeed, the strikes of September were stronger in those areas where Socialist labor elements were the strongest.[71] Begun at pit number two in Lens, the strike quickly turned into a march of 200 to the union headquarters at Lens. Once inside the union hall, the miners heard a speech from Henri Lemaire, a former union official who had been ousted at the Miners Congress of December 1944. Lemaire urged the miners to spread the strike to the rest of the region. According to *La Tribune des mineurs*, another strike leader, Fleuret, was a former union leader who had removed eight of the twelve stewards from his section of the union in 1939 for being Communists.[72]

Nothing better underscored the dangers of the situation to Communist union leaders than the meeting of union delegates in Lens to select representatives to present their demands in Paris: they chose the Socialist Paul Sion rather than Auguste Lecoeur, the Communist mayor of Lens and a top leader of the Federation of Miners.[73] Reports written for the local authorities claimed that the angry miners were unwilling to follow

Communist directives condemning strikes and extolling the virtues of production.[74]

Union leaders like Léon Delfosse were concerned that opposition elements had linked up with opponents of nationalization in an effort to undermine an elaborately planned mass meeting scheduled for September 17. The union had worked very closely with the mine directors to plan this "monster meeting" in order to launch a campaign to produce "100,000 tons of coal per day." Featured speakers included Minister of Industrial Production Robert Lacoste, miners' union leader Henri Martel, and CGT leader Benoit Frachon. Special trains had been organized in order to transport 25,000 miners to the meeting place in Lens. Despite fears that the event would be disrupted, the meeting took place without serious incidents. The miners' response to Frachon, Lacoste, and Martel, according to some reports, was relatively subdued. Speeches were interrupted with chants demanding, "Purge!" "Food!" "Soap!" and "Bread!" But the wildcat strikes had abated. On the day before the rally, the miners returned to the job.[75] After September 1945, 18 months passed before another strike erupted in the mining basin.

The end of the September strikes closed an uncertain period in the history of the mining basin. Despite their alarm at being "submerged by the mass" and their fear of losing ground to oppositional currents inside the Federation of Miners, postwar union leaders survived the crisis. No formal opposition emerged to challenge the Communists inside the labor movement, and the union's democratic centralist structure kept anti-Communist unionists from positions of power. Summing up the September strikes, editorialists for *La Tribune des mineurs* exclaimed: "There can be certain periods when the strike is not the weapon of the working class, contrary to what has been said in the course of the last strike."[76] The Communists' rapid consolidation of power within the union, combined with its prohibition of strikes and other job actions, raised new questions about the party's strategy. A skeptical, sometimes angry mood continued to be expressed in the mines. Order had been restored, not by force, but by persuasion and promises. Yet old grievances remained unresolved.

After the end of the wildcat strikes, however, tension in the mining area eased somewhat. A commission was set up by Lacoste to examine the Miners' Statute. New agreements with the Ministry of Labor provided 25 percent wage increases for Sunday work, and a labor-management parity commission resolved the issue of pay for women workers.[77] Discussions on the legislation that would permanently nationalize the entire coal-mining industry were intensified. In national elections in October, the PCF emerged as the nation's largest vote-getter. The new cabinet named by de Gaulle included five Communists, and while the general withheld the key ministries of Foreign Affairs, War, and Interior from the Communists, the PCF leaders found themselves heading most of the "economic" ministries. Marcel Paul, leader of the CGT electrical workers' union, took over Industrial Production from Robert Lacoste. Paul pledged to the miners that he would enact the nationalization and the Miners' Statute within months. François Billoux headed up the Ministry of National Economy, and Ambroise Croizat was named to Labor. Charles Tillon was put in charge of Armaments. Thorez became one of four ministers of State.

"Below the surface of 'national unity,'" wrote Alexander Werth, "the struggle grew in intensity during that spring and summer of 1945 between the elements hoping to build a 'new France' and those hankering for a 'return to normal.'"[78] At the national level, this struggle was reflected in the breakup of the old Resistance coalition and the four-cornered battle to reshape the economy that was waged by the three major parties and de Gaulle. In the coal-mining region, the conflict between the old and the new took place within the attempt to establish new structures for the coal-mining industry and the struggle to restore order in the mines. While it may not have been visible at the time, either to state managers or union leaders, the twin tasks of nationalizing coal and organizing labor were well along the way to being accomplished by the end of 1945. The provisional nationalization had been strong enough to dislodge the old owners and prevent them from returning to power. And the miners' upsurge from below resulted in the institution of a power-sharing arrangement that gave workers a voice and went beyond a purely statist nationalization. The public consensus for state intervention remained broad. De Gaulle needed Communists in the government, especially because they were so useful in dampening worker discontent and promoting higher production. But in January 1946, de Gaulle, in one of the many abrupt, enigmatic moves that would baffle observers, suddenly resigned as president. His departure led to the creation of a "tripartite" government of Socialists, Communists, and Christian Democrats, which, for many, rekindled hopes for a new France. The wildcat strikes ended, the protests over the purges subsided, and coal production slowly began to inch its way upward. The battle of production was under way.

4.

The Battle of Production
in the Mines

Much has been written about labor conflict in postwar France. Less is known about the two-year period of labor-management cooperation known as the "battle of production." From 1945 to 1947 leaders of the CGT broke with long-standing union traditions by repudiating strikes and calling upon workers to collaborate with management in efforts to increase coal production. The result was a steady increase in coal output and a decline in work stoppages. But the production drive sparked controversy among the miners because it institutionalized individual payment systems and because cooperating with management sometimes appeared to put production concerns ahead of the needs of the mine workers.

Although the battle of production in the mines has been referred to on many occasions, it has only recently been examined in detail.[1] A wide spectrum of observers, from conservatives to Socialists, tended to view the production campaign as a tactical ploy by the Communists to maintain their party's position in the government. Some unionists were critical of the way the CGT leaders promoted production while abandoning old union dicta such as the right to strike. Critics to the left of the Communists were even more hostile, viewing the production campaign as symptomatic of the PCF's inability to chart a revolutionary strategy.

Close examination, however, reveals a more complex picture. At its core, the production campaign represented an informal trade-off between organized labor and the government. Labor assumed the tough tasks of convincing the miners to return to work, smoothing out conflicts between workers and managers, and urging the miners to break production records. In exchange for this unprecedented new role, the unions demanded nationalization of the industry, representation in management, and improvements in wages and benefits.

The story of the production campaign, from its origins in the war against the Nazis to its demise in the early days of the cold war, sheds new light on why French unions initially led the battle but later retreated to traditional adversarial relations between labor and management.

THE POLITICS OF PRODUCTION

The CGT's promotion of the battle of production upset traditional relations between labor and management. Labor seemed to be playing the role reserved for management. PCF leaders contended that increasing production was the highest form of class consciousness. Union leaders urged miners to work longer hours and to report for work on Sundays and holidays. They demanded discipline in the workplace and energetically condemned absenteeism and sloppy work habits. The union also condemned strikes as counterproductive. So successful was the union-backed strike ban that France, alone among Western countries, remained nearly strike-free in the first three years following the liberation. In the mines, once the wildcat strikes of September 1945 had ended, another work stoppage did not occur until June 1947.

This new "constructive unionism" was more than a means of controlling the workers. It was also aimed at positioning the union in a highly visible role of leadership at a time when management was in disarray. The crisis of authority caused by the suspension of the old mining leaders and the issue of the purges left a management vacuum. The union, emphasizing its patriotic duty and a mature attitude toward economic reconstruction, took upon itself the role of serving as the critical agent for restoring order and discipline in the mines.

In order to rally the miners to produce coal while waiting for important new reforms to be instituted, union leaders wove together three themes: patriotism, solidarity, and voluntarism. The battle of production originated in a context of war. The miners began their "liberation strike" on 21 August 1944. By the time the Germans had withdrawn, the strike had already closed down all the coal mines. Yet the pressing need for coal to produce steel for armaments and to get industry rolling once again convinced union officials to urge an immediate return to work. "In the liberated coal areas, the miners were in the first ranks of the victorious fighters," reported Henri Martel, a Communist leader of the miners' union in Nord, in a radio appeal addressed to the miners from London. "They guarded the mining installations, guns in hand, to make sure they would not be destroyed by the enemy. Today they are descending once again into the mines to intensify war production and quicken the pace of liberation."[2] But while the miners were willing to return to work, they also met with the coal companies and demanded new agreements on wages and working conditions as well as sweeping changes in management personnel. Paralyzed by rumors of impending nationalization and widespread purges, the mining companies claimed financial insolvency and waited for the new government to intervene. Management's reluctance to negotiate in the face of a critical coal shortage that crippled the war effort led union leaders to charge, in what would become a familiar refrain, that the "men of the trusts" were sabotaging the fight to increase coal production. "The war was still going on and we said, 'Every minute of lost work prolongs the war,'" recalled André Théret. "For us, the idea of producing coal was linked to the fight against fascism."[3] On September 10, Benoit Frachon, secretary general of the CGT, addressed the Communist cadres involved in union work at a big meeting in Paris. Looking beyond the termination of wartime hostilities, Frachon endorsed the production campaign so that France could return to its former position as an independent nation. "Political independence," declared Frachon, "requires economic independence." The national leadership of the Federation of Miners pledged its union to "a maximum productive effort" in order to win the war.[4]

The battle of production was also cast in terms of solidarity between workers and other sectors of French society. It no longer sufficed to raise the mine workers' concerns. Demands were now to be shaped within the larger framework of the gradually improving economy. With this in mind, Victor Foulon authored an article in the union newspaper in December 1944 entitled "Work First, Make Demands Later."[5] Citing the desperate need to provide industry and consumers with coal, union leaders condemned strikes. Victorin Duguet, writing in November 1944, attacked "ringleaders" and "provocateurs" who talked about strikes. Writing during the last-ditch German offensive that penetrated into the eastern part of the mining basin in December 1944, André Théret raised the possibility that those who agitated for strikes were helping the Nazis: "Don't listen to them when they tell you to strike."[6] The emphasis on solidarity and willingness to consider not only the miners' demands but also the larger concerns of the economy as a whole allowed the union to project a new public image of the miners.

The Communists also injected a strong dose of voluntarism into the production campaign. Union leaders conveyed the impression that the miners, by determined will and unyielding effort, could reverse 15 years of stagnation of coal production. Again and again the miners were described as "soldiers" in the fight to close the energy gap. "In the battle of production, as on the war front," said Frachon, "in order to guarantee victory, it is necessary to block the route of the traitors and pessimists."[7] "The miners want to produce more coal," said Duguet, "and they can do it!"[8] Union publications referred to the coal miners as France's "first workers," implying that they were the most important workers in France. The Communist writers contributed to this myth building that turned coal miners into "superproletarians." The union produced a special appeal to the young workers, urging them to "rally to win the battle for coal."[9] In March 1945, Frachon exhorted the national committee of the CGT to generate support for the campaign. "We call upon the workers once again," said Frachon, "to work everywhere and with ardour and abnegation."[10]

Patriotism, exhortations to produce, and condemnations of strikes added up to an astounding program for Communist militants. The party searched for a doctrinal road map for its plunge into the battle of production. Billoux unearthed an obscure paragraph from Engels arguing that some strikes were not in the interests of the working class. Thorez lectured on why it had been necessary to end the Popular Front strikes in 1936. Lecoeur advanced the simplistic argument that if the employers opposed the production battle, then the workers should back it. In reality, the Communists were sailing in waters uncharted by historical precedent, Marxist theory, or practical experience.

Critics were quick to point to the contradictions inherent in this strategy. Conservatives scoffed at the notion that "the trusts" were sabotaging the war effort, but they were glad to see the Communists busy preventing strikes. Socialists supported the concept of the battle but opposed the Communists' use of "stakhanovite" methods. Old-line unionists argued against the Communist party's political influence in union activities and supported the right to strike as labor's ultimate weapon. Small left-wing groups condemned the production strategy as the price workers were being forced to pay so that the PCF could become a party of the government. Although one could guess at the PCF's motives, considering the matter from the point of view of the Communists themselves, the rationale for the battle of production is not hard to identify. Within the new political and economic context, the campaign could be seen as a rational, pragmatic approach for a party that was becoming a part of the government for the first time. The war continued, the economy needed to be jump-started, and the nation looked to the new leaders to help France get to its feet. Instead of attempting to turn the war into a revolution, the PCF had fully committed itself to a bourgeois, democratic system of government. The new government was committed to the National Council of the Resistance charter and the Left was well represented within its ranks. The new situation required new tasks of the Communists. Indeed, the production campaign could be viewed as a new form of class struggle wherein revolutionaries demonstrated their competence and discipline for the benefit of the entire nation. The coal mines could be a showcase for proving that the Communists were mature enough to govern wisely and efficiently.

The battle of production also dovetailed with the PCF's "national front" strategy, which aimed to expand and broaden the party's influence among broad sectors of the populace. Promotion of production offered concrete proof of the party's patriotism, and the Communist militants, anxious to bury forever old criticisms leveled during the 1939–1941 period, capitalized on this situation. Increasingly conscious of the Communists' new role as a major party, the militants easily cast themselves as the driving force in a "New French Renaissance." The battle of production bridged the gap between the patriotism of the Resistance and the postwar desire to rebuild the economy. It also served to consolidate the PCF's new predominance in organized labor. No longer a marginal force outside the CGT or a minority opposition within, Communist militants now assumed key posts in France's largest federation. From the national level to the regional level, among union stewards and in pit committees, they bent the trade union apparatus to conform to the goals of the production campaign. At the same time, the installation of Communists and CGT officials in top governmental posts allowed the Communists to merge the prestige of the CGT with the authority vested in the state. Mine workers Léon Delfosse and Victorin Duguet accepted important positions in the management of the nationalized mines while maintaining leadership posts in their unions. The battle of production also facilitated the Communist objective of drawing engineers and technicians to the side of the working class and into the CGT; it placed a premium on precisely those attitudes that were valued most by mining engineers: efficiency, technique, and collaboration.

Labor-management cooperation, however, had its price. An important political consequence of this new collaboration was that it served as an unwritten and limited guarantee that Communist militants could retain their new posts in the pit committees, as safety delegates and union stewards, and as union-backed representatives inside the management team. The campaign allowed union activists to penetrate areas of the industry that they could not touch in the past. And because the PCF was a party of militants, as opposed to professional politicians or intellectuals, party members followed the battle-of-production line by "filling vacuums," stepping in to provide leadership not only in the coal mines but in the newly emerging union apparatus, the lower ranks of coal-mining management, and even among the engineers. By wrapping themselves in the flag of production, militants also made it difficult for their critics to attack them. Long after the war had ended, the political slogan of the Resistance—"The best way to keep from being isolated is to become indispensable"—continued to apply.[11] An unstated corollary, that no government could rule without the Communists, reflected the same perspective. As long as Communists shouldered the responsibility for mobilizing workers to produce and for maintaining workplace discipline, the party's political opponents would find it difficult to dislodge them. Moreover, purging Communists from positions of importance ran the risk that they might abandon the production campaign and use their influence inside organized labor to unleash industrial conflicts.

Yet the political leverage afforded the PCF by the battle of production could not fully offset the dangers it posed. Chief among these was the reaction of workers and union activists. If support among workers for the production drive waned, the Communists would see their popularity and credibility reduced. This could lead to halfhearted efforts in the workplace and, worse, to the emergence of organized opposition inside the union. Fear of being outflanked on the Left also conditioned the Communists' approach to the production campaign. For most union leaders, the possibility of losing the party's working-class support loomed as a greater threat than losing positions of power in the government or in the ranks of management. Further, if a Communist bastion of power could be erected in the mines, it could also be dismantled by enemies. In the north, where the party was particularly influential, the potentialities and risks of the production campaign emerged in sharpest relief. Here the party was positioned to put the line into practice and to reap the greatest possible rewards. But failure in the northern mines could prefigure defeat in other sectors of the economy.

The battle of production produced politics that made incremental, not revolutionary, changes. The campaign lent itself to a strategy of position rather than movement. It was a pragmatic approach that grew out of a new situation, with none of the theoretical underpinnings that framed many Communist strategies. The battle introduced the revolutionary unionists to new opportunities and challenges. Among the most pressing was the need to improve the mine workers' economic situation.

BONUSES AND BICYCLES

To win worker support for the production effort, significant improvements in wages were needed. Attempting to bring wages into line with prices, the government offered mine workers a 40 percent wage increase following the liberation. Additional wage settlements were made in the summer of 1945 in the parity commissions established by the OPH and the CGT. The wage package for miners featured a new minimum hourly wage that was tied, at a slightly higher rate (112.5 for surface workers and 125 for underground workers), to the wages of the metals industry.[12] The minimum wage provided a floor, not a ceiling, because the piece-rate system, already in use in many mines, was expanded so that a hardworking miner could earn 60 percent more than the minimum wage.

Implementing this system, however, meant that payment would be on an individual basis rather than by the crew. It also refocused attention on the controversial piecework system. Miners complained that individual pay systems tended to break up the solidarity of the workplace. Chief hewers ended up competing with each other to extract the most coal. Conflicts between hewers and lower-ranking mine workers sometimes erupted when hewers felt the extracted coal was not being loaded or moved quickly enough. Although the Bedaux system of rationalization had been prohibited in 1936, it had been reinstated gradually in 1939 and under the occupation regime. When miners drew up their first post-liberation list of grievances in Lens in September 1944, prohibiting the piece-rate system ranked at the top of the list.[13] Management favored individual rather than team pay, arguing that it was more adaptable to the natural irregularities of the coal seams. Besides, it allowed management to reward those who worked the hardest with higher pay directly, without having to pass through the miners' collectively structured distribution system. In a parity commission meeting in August 1944, Vial, the vice president of the northern mines' provisional management, spelled out management's position on individual pay rates by reference to what a "stakhanovite worker in the Soviet Union" would earn.[14] Despite some rank-and-file antipathy to piecework and individual pay and opposition among the union leaders (Nestor Calonne, secretary general of the union, opposed it, but Delfosse favored it), the miners' union eventually agreed to permit a system to make payments to small crews or to individual workers.[15]

Pay to mine workers was soon supplemented by rewards for high productivity. A plan to provide special bonuses for output was introduced in January 1945, despite misgivings by the CGT, and in the fall, the personnel and social service director of the mines, M. Silvain, developed a new plan for prizes and bonuses. After gaining the support of union leaders, Silvain requested the necessary funds from Lacoste, the minister of Industrial Production.[16] The plan was quickly put into effect. The mine directors worked with the union to support the new campaign. Prizes included radios, shoes, bottles of *genièvre* (a popular drink in northern France), small pigs, and extra rations of butter and soap. Among the most coveted prizes were bicycles, in short supply in postwar France and valuable as a means of traveling to the countryside to purchase food from farmers. An estimated 25,000 miners who attended a rally in Lens on 17 September 1945 heard CGT leader Benoit Frachon publicly endorse the new plan.[17]

But the question of whether the bonuses and prizes should be distributed to individuals or to groups of miners threatened the new incentive plan. Management favored individual over collective rewards. However, after the campaign had been in operation for a month, the directors reported that "the miners are still reticent to accept individual prizes and seem to favor a more collective system." A week later, they reported that the campaign had received a lukewarm welcome that varied by region. In the eastern part of the coal basin, the miners were generally more receptive. But in Pas-de-Calais, there was strong resistance to the campaign. The directors attributed these problems to differences within the local units of the miners' federation. In Pas-de-Calais many stewards contended that they had not been fully consulted or really involved in the discussions surrounding the new campaign. The director of the mines at Marles described opposition to the prize campaign as "intransigent."[18] In September 1945, in line with Silvain's production campaign, management began to install large production "thermometers" at the entrances to the mines. But in several mines, the workers protested. Union stewards and members of the pit committees claimed that management had not won their approval before installing the thermometers.[19]

Some miners favored the collective methods because they saw in individual payment the return of the hated Bedaux system. Several miners in 1945 wrote letters that voiced this suspicion to *La Tribune des mineurs*. Louis Caboche, a shop steward, complained in May 1945 about the great anomalies in this system of payment. "The technicians make the pay schedules inside their offices," he wrote, "and don't know the real situation, although they pretend to know what they are doing. I see it as the Bedaux system, camouflaged."[20] Others argued that individual payment, bonuses, and prizes generated discord among the miners and destroyed worker solidarity. Such criticisms were raised most frequently in the pages of the Socialist weekly *L'Espoir*, where several veteran CGT miners expressed their disagreements with the new system.

The mine directors attempted to regularize the payment system in November 1945 with new instructions to management: "There are two forms of payment: collective, paid by the wagonload of coal, and individual payment with bonuses. Do not allow any other form of payment.

This should become 'the method.' The Federation of Miners is in agreement with us on this. However, if the workers are agreeable, we can introduce, in some pits, a system of payment by small teams of two or three workers. We would consider this as a transition from one form of payment to another." [21] Leaders of the union supported the individual payment system, reasoning that every worker should be paid according to the work performed. Thorez, who had defended individual payment in his speech at Waziers, reiterated his support for the new system at a large gathering of miners in Valenciennes in December 1945. In March 1946 the union in Pas-de-Calais proposed that individual payment be extended to the surface installations. In the summer of 1946, Marcel Paul, who had replaced Lacoste as head of the Ministry of Industrial Production, established a commission to study the possibilities of generalizing the individual payment system. [22]

While some miners opposed individual payment, management personnel were concerned about disputes that frequently arose when rates had to be renegotiated because of unforeseen changes in the coal vein or the work situation. Engineers, supervisors, and foremen complained that the politically charged atmosphere in the mines gave workers an opening to challenge management's authority. In management's view, the balance of power between the mine workers and management had swung so far to the side of the worker that it was difficult for management to always act decisively. The engineers, supervisors, and foremen saw themselves on the defensive while the miners, armed with new rights, were more prone to disagree and argue, especially around the setting of pay rates. Managers contended that this situation also contributed to a general swelling of the rate of payment for certain tasks. Although the cadres examined the work site and determined the rate of payment, mine workers could dispute management's assessment. If the matter could not be settled between a union steward and management, it could go before a locally based parity commission. But under the conditions that existed in the mining communities, many managers sought to avoid becoming embroiled in heated debates with the miners. Thus, while critics complained about a crisis of authority in the mines, many of the disputes derived from the controversial payment system and the fact that management personnel were sometimes reluctant to take a hard stand when such disputes arose.

EMULATION CAMPAIGNS

Although material incentives such as bonuses and bicycles were important features of the battle of production, Communist union leaders also tried to use moral and political incentives to increase production. Their newspapers and speeches depicted the production campaign in terms of the miners' voluntarism, patriotism, and class consciousness. Miners were described as heroes who had battled the Nazis during the occupation, produced enough coal to win the war, and now fought in the front lines to rebuild the economy. In September 1945 tricolor posters plastered on the walls of the mines proclaimed: "To reconstruct France, we must have coal." Soon another poster appeared: "France needs coal, France needs you."[23] In order to honor the values of voluntarism, patriotism, and class consciousness and to harness them to a productionist strategy, special recognition was given to individual miners and groups of miners who had displayed exemplary zeal in the battle of production.

Liberté, the region's Communist daily newspaper, ran a special daily column entitled "On the Front of the Battle of Production." It contained two parts: a salute to a particular group of miners for their efforts and a public denunciation of those workers, foremen, or engineers who allegedly held back production. The young miners of Sabatier became "a team to emulate" when they extracted 167 tons of coal in one morning shift in Bruay-sur-Escaut. The miners of pits number four and seven at Liévin increased their individual output to 1,200 kilograms in February 1946 and were rewarded with a special food bonus.[24] The union also encouraged the miners to work Sundays and holidays. They asked miners to work on 15 August 1945, a national holiday, in order to produce coal for factories that made materials for rebuilding war-damaged housing.[25] Seeking to put into practice the Communist notion that "leaders lead by example," officials of the miners' federation sometimes descended to work a shift in the mines to show their support for the production campaign. Maurice Thorez, probably the most famous (honorary) member of the union, donned a helmet and descended at pit eight in Escarpelle and in the mines at d'Auby.[26] It is doubtful that Thorez knocked down much coal, but his many visits to the mining basin during his period as a government minister show the priority the PCF placed on the battle for coal.

The emulation drive took more innovative forms as well. In 1946 Louis Daquin and a crew of political filmmakers close to the CGT and the Communist party celebrated the patriotism and productivity of coal miners in a film, *We're Building France*. The film described the battle for coal as the latest episode in a long struggle for national independence. A second film, *Miners of France*, was produced by the Charbonnages de France. It emphasized the improved working conditions for miners and explained that modernization would transform the miners from laborers to technicians. No longer would they be industrial slaves. The film also lauded the miners for their courage, tenacity, and abnegation.[27] A miner from Oignes invented a more efficient jackhammer—living proof of the creativity and intelligence of the working class.[28] A targeted appeal was made to youth. When Lecoeur was named minister in charge of the mines in 1946, he ordered management to allow boys as young as fourteen to work underground if they seemed strong enough. Women were hired in the surface installations. Against the criticisms of the CFTC and the MRP, the Communists maintained that the notion that women should not work in the mines was a "bourgeois idea." Most of the women were employed in such jobs as sorting and washing coal. Descriptions of how women were contributing to the production effort were given a regular place in the CGT and Communist press.

Union leaders sought to stimulate the "professional consciousness" of miners by increasing their involvement in and understanding of the production process as a whole. They emphasized the idea that mine work was a skilled trade, or métier. The union set up "education centers" in Douai, Somain, Dénain, Carvin, Lens, and Hénin. Courses dealt with such subjects as how pit and production committees should work, administering the security and pension funds, running the miners' cooperative, and, after its enactment in May 1946, interpretation and enforcement of the Miners' Statute.[29] A monthly magazine called *Mineurs* was published for mining personnel under the editorship of Léon Delfosse and Louis Thiébaut. *Mineurs* attempted to explain the technical and social aspects involved in coal mining in ways that made sense to the miners, avoiding overly technical jargon and long-winded explanations. Union leaders referred to these educational and training efforts as examples of a new "pédagogie de masse."[30]

Not everyone, however, was enamored with the mass pedagogy. Socialists were quick to point out their opposition to stakhanovism and the attempts by Communists to import it into the mines. Some Communist party members voiced criticisms inside the party against the overwhelming emphasis on production at any cost. Veteran unionists remained sensitive to most miners' criticism that not much had changed in terms of the mining management. Militants who went to work every day knew how seriously the miners took the calls for "more coal for France" once the war had ended. There is evidence that worker activists dropped away from labor activities because they lacked the desire to promote more coal production. Lecoeur recalled that militants stopped coming to party cell meetings after the speech at Waziers. For Roger Pannequin, a union leader and assistant to Lecoeur, the speech by Thorez and the campaign surrounding it represented "the burial of all my childhood dreams" and the end of political illusions. Reports from local authorities and mining management provide indications that the party line was not always followed by the miners.[31] Nor is it possible to know, on the basis of documents, to what extent rank-and-file mine workers supported or opposed the battle of production. Hostility to the campaign is rarely found in the written record.

Incisive criticism, however, has come from recent studies. Bruno Mattei was critical of the Communists' attempts to create a "mythology of the miners" based upon two elements: the miners' love for their work and the coal miners as the "vanguard of the working class." Constant use of these themes created images of the miners, for the public and for the miners themselves, that failed to reflect reality.[32] The miners were supposed to live up to these characteristics that had been created by revolutionaries turned productionists. Yves Jeanneau contends that the images of the battle of production—the coal miners as heroes, the nation's need for coal, and the campaign to extract 100,000 tons per day—dominated not only the posters that appeared on the walls of the mining regions, but also the newspapers and the radio of the time. "The propaganda only convinced those who were willing to believe," wrote Jeanneau, "it reduced to silence the dissident voices."[33]

Despite the shortcomings of the battle for coal, these projects involving some degree of "worker participation" represented a decisive break with old labor-management relations. Indeed, the campaign surrounding the battle for coal suggested the capacity of the working class to play a key role in running a major industry. The CGT championed this idea when it demanded worker representation in management, pushed for production committees in the mines, and took charge of the cooperative and the social security and retirement funds. Raising coal output became connected with a strategy for empowering the miners. While critics attacked the union for building a bastion of power in the mines, the CGT argued that such steps were part of a process of democratization of the industry. A significant role for the miners' union distinguished a real nationalization from a false nationalization. Through the lens of the battle of production, the miners personified the characteristics of a working class "for itself": a highly developed professional outlook, commitment to their métier, an understanding that the people were in dire need of coal. Such an image was cultivated by the rhetoric and literature of the campaign. No doubt André Ribaud had this image in mind when he wrote that the miners represented "an anticipation of that which will be the future socialist *volonté*; the attachment to work, conscious participation in technique, and unity among the workers."[34]

MOBILIZING MANAGEMENT

A successful battle of production also required a much higher level of collaboration between mine workers and management, but establishing effective working relations between them ran up against a long history of mutual mistrust.[35] Antagonism derived from the fundamentally different (sometimes contradictory) objectives of those who were wage earners and those with the responsibility to manage them. Even before the advent of longwalls and the Bedaux system, relations between workers and cadres were always strained. Rationalization schemes seem to have made the situation even worse. On the one hand, the miners felt helpless before an authoritarian system of command and what seemed to be a capricious form of compensation. Management, especially the foremen, bore the brunt of the miners' anger over job assignments and pay rates. On the other hand, the engineers complained that the Bedaux system limited their prerogatives and options in dealing with the workers. Time-study specialists and efficiency experts took over responsibilities that had belonged to the engineers.[36]

Economic and political factors also came into play. Sharp class differences separated the engineers from the workers. Engineers lived in different areas of the mining basin. Their children attended special schools and usually did not play with the children of the mine workers. Engineers had usually been educated in the most elite and conservative schools in France. They were not trained to be particularly sensitive to the problems facing the miners and were taught to use their authority with vigor.[37] In addition, many engineers and technicians who entered the mines during the war years came from other areas of France and thus lacked any real understanding of the culture and history of the northern mining basin. The politically charged strikes of the Popular Front period and the long years of management repression of militant unionists also contributed to negative relations between workers and managers. Four years of occupation created additional obstacles to developing an understanding between labor and management. From the miners' view, many in management had collaborated with the enemy. But the vast majority of engineers and other cadres saw the situation quite differently. "The engineers could not comprehend the motives behind the miners' anger toward them," wrote Etienne Dejonghe.[38] While there may have been some management personnel who had actually collaborated with the Nazis, the engineers claimed that most of them had always separated their management duties from their political activities. They viewed the Nazi occupation as an affront to their national pride, although they considered strikes and sabotage as inappropriate tactics. Most of the cadres identified themselves as Gaullists, and some had even worked with the Resistance movement. Aimé Leperq, for example, worked with the Civil and Military Organization, and Blum-Piquart was part of the Free French in London. Others were associated with the movement Jeunes Patrons, or Young Employers.[39] But although some management personnel may have participated in the Resistance, their activities were largely invisible to the miners, who had engaged in their own fight for survival during the war years.

Once the miners' union declared war on the coal shortage, they confronted the contradictions inherent in trying to pursue the purges at the same time. Management personnel found themselves in a paradoxical situation wherein the union mistrusted them but needed them in order to win the battle of production.[40] For the engineers, the liberation meant a breakdown of authority. The top coal operators were suspended, engineers abandoned their posts for fear of reprisals, and foremen stayed away from the mines. Meanwhile, the workers demanded new rights, and from the engineers' perspective it seemed as if the union had set up a system of parallel power. In the mine, engineers could give only orders that were backed up by the union delegate.[41] "The Germans left and at least one thing had changed, even if there still were food shortages: the workers were no longer afraid," wrote Évelyne Desbois. "Now it was the turn of the management personnel to be afraid of reprisals and denunciations."[42]

Engineers found themselves locked between a virtual absence of authority above and a hostile mass of mine workers below. But the liberation also opened a new era for management and new opportunities for pursuing labor-management cooperation. The nationalization released engineers from the control of the old coal companies, allowing them to implement policies based solely on efficiency and technical expertise. It also led engineers to reconsider the possibility of collaborating with the workers' unions and, in some cases, creating organizations of cadres that were affiliated with the CGT and CFTC.[43] The SIHN, affiliated with the CGC, remained largely dormant during the war years but reemerged in September 1944. Meanwhile the CGT began its first serious attempt to organize engineers and other cadres by setting up industry-wide cadres groups and by inviting independent unions within the industry to affiliate with the CGT.[44] A Cartel Confédération des Cadres was formed at the end of December 1944 in order to bring more cadres into the CGT.[45] The cartel was represented in the top bodies of the CGT and was instructed to create a federation for cadres.[46] These efforts first bore fruit in those industries dominated by the CGT: 150 cadres from the metals industry met in February 1945. Cadres from the nationalized mines organized the Syndicat National des Ingénieurs des Mines (SNIM) in May 1945.[47]

Jean Armanet was a key figure in the CGT's early success with mining cadres. A head engineer in the nationalized mines and a dynamic former professor at L'École des Mines in St. Étienne and in Paris, Armanet served as the first president of the SNIM. Many of Armanet's former students who would not otherwise have been prone to join the CGT followed him into the SNIM. "One day Armanet announced that a number of engineers were proposing the creation of a new union of mining engineers that would be affiliated with the CGT," recalled an engineer. "I knew that our miners were in the CGT, but I would never have had the idea that we should go and join them."[48] About 40 engineers met in Paris in May 1945 to form the SNIM. At that meeting Armanet, Pierre Lebrun, and Victor Duguet were assigned to call informational meetings for engineers and other cadres in the mining basin.

The SNIM grew during the battle of production, undoubtedly aided by the emphasis on productive effort, the social peace cultivated by the PCF, and the Resistance legacy of the CGT. The miners' federation did its best to promote an image of collaboration between the two unions. No rally or meeting was complete without speakers from the federation and SNIM. Each issue of *La Tribune des mineurs* contained articles on the role of cadres and the activities of SNIM. Every big name leader who came to the region to speak at one of the rallies paid a special tribute to the cadres who had allied with the labor movement. Drawings of white-coated engineers and helmeted miners holding hands and standing in front of overflowing coal wagons appeared in *La Tribune des mineurs*, promoting an image of cooperation. Many young engineers who followed Jean Armanet into the CGT were motivated by the idea of collaborating with the workers to bridge the energy gap and rebuild the economy. "Armanet was someone we considered to be very serious," recalled one engineer. "This was a very troubled time. Disorder was everywhere. Everyone was trying to find out how to increase production in order to reach the famous goal of a hundred million tons. Armanet said to us: 'to solve this problem we must shake hands with the workers and go to the CGT.'"[49]

In December 1945 *La Tribune des mineurs* claimed that half of the engineers in the mines of Bruay had joined the SNIM. Three months later, the same union stated that the SNIM represented 50 percent of the engineers and cadres in the mining industry.[50] The figures were subject to dispute. The Syndicat des Ingénieurs des Houillères du Nord—Pas-de-Calais (SIHN), affiliated with the Confédération Générale des Cadres (CGC), had revived after the liberation and also claimed to be the main union among the mining cadres. Although no figures were ever made public, *Nord-Industriel* claimed in December 1945 that the majority actually belonged to the CGC-affiliated group.[51] The question of which union was the "most representative" was not an esoteric issue. Under the nationalization plan of December 1944, only one organization would represent the cadres on administrative councils and in dealings with the government. In 1946, the CGT's SNIM was named the most representative union, and its leaders, including Armanet, assumed new positions in the nationalized mines. Yet the SIHN protested that it, not the SNIM, was the larger group of mining engineers. While debate swirled over which labor organization was most representative, the miners' federation searched for an organizational framework to coordinate the actions of workers and management personnel.

FROM PIT COMMITTEES TO PRODUCTION COMMITTEES

The miners' union served as a critical agent for restoring order and discipline, but CGT leaders lacked a blueprint for internal reorganization in the mines. Some Socialist writers advocated direct worker participation without spelling out how such an arrangement would function. The CFTC supported active collaboration of workers and management, but their formula for the partnership remained vague. The Communists criticized concepts such as "socialization" and "the mine to the miners" as unrealistic slogans, but they too failed to elaborate an alternative structure capable of bringing together workers and managers inside the nationalized industry. Eventually, the CGT settled on a pragmatic strategy aimed at improving conditions and consolidating union power inside the mines while acquiring positions inside management that could help defend those gains. At the top levels of management, the union favored a governance structure based on the old CGT formula of 1918: a tripartite committee of representatives from personnel, consumers, and the state. The strategy "from above" was a high-profile activity that generated a good deal of controversy and was the subject of much public scrutiny. By contrast, the strategy "from below" developed in a much less public way as labor leaders, administrators, and local and state officials hammered out a new internal regime for the nationalized mines.

During the occupation period, miners had formed illegal "pit committees." In the chaotic weeks following the liberation, these committees were enlarged and used to air grievances, pursue the purge process, and recruit more miners into the union. Once the union was reorganized and put into place, however, the pit committees lost much of their raison d'être. During the battle of production union leaders transformed pit committees into "production committees" of engineers, technicians, foremen, and mine workers.

The pit committees lacked any formal power, but they often provided the union with an informal veto power. For example, an engineer who lacked union support for a plan of exploitation might find himself unable to execute the plan. During the prize campaign in September 1945, engineers were instructed to get the agreement of "two or three influential workers in the pit committees" before deciding which miners should receive a bicycle as the top producer in that pit.[52] When *Le Monde* attacked the "crisis of authority in the mines" during the wildcat strikes in March 1945, CGT leader Henri Martel suggested that the mine directors "listen to the suggestions of the miners in the pit committees rather than laugh at them." Articles written for *La Tribune des mineurs* in the summer of 1945 often ended with an appeal to "make the pit committees work."[53] The union claimed that management was too reluctant to apply suggestions emanating from the pit committees. "It's your job to establish the production plans and determine the methods of exploitation," said Frachon to the members of management who attended a large meeting in Lens in September 1945. "But you will wield more authority if it is based on respect and not simply concerned with technical factors, but with human factors as well. Examine the plan for each pit with the miners themselves. Open up the plans to more collective criticism."[54]

One miner recalled that although the pit committees had no formal power, many miners were interested in them because they could play an important role in the planning and execution of coal production.[55] Representatives of the miners inside the pit committees often doubled as safety delegates or union stewards. If a dispute arose, they had the authority to call upon the miners to halt production. However, once the battle of production was endorsed, the Federation of Miners refrained from using the pit committees as a trade unionist arm in the mines. For example, in September 1945, when Martel met with the mine directors, he told them that "individual demands should not be dealt with by the pit committees, which should be concerned solely with questions relating to the development of production and the organization of work." In January 1946 the mine directors reported that CGT leader "Frachon estimates that the functioning of these committees is too unwieldy and interferes with the direct action of the director over the personnel. Each pit committee should designate among its members a small group of three or four that the engineer will consult with to establish the program of production."[56] Under the system established by Auguste Lecoeur in 1946, the role of the committees was strictly limited to matters of production. Union activities, for example, were not supposed to be discussed. There is little evidence to indicate the degree to which workers were involved in the production committees. It is unlikely that their participation approached the level desired by some of the most fervent advocates of nationalization. Nevertheless, production plans required approval by the production committee. Since mine workers held three of five positions, including the delegate, they could nullify plans they felt would not be accepted by rank-and-file miners. Although the production committees were tolerated by management, many engineers felt that they reduced management's authority, turned technical problems into partisan debates, and broke the chain of command in the mines.

The CGT's attempt to increase the role of workers in the planning and execution of coal production marked its farthest extension in the direction of worker participation. Yet the limitations of the production committees were obvious. They functioned only within the framework of an extraordinary drive to produce more coal. Hence, their existence was contingent upon the union's unswerving commitment to increasing production and management's willingness to collaborate with the committees.

AUGUSTE LECOEUR, LABOR'S MINISTER OF MINES

In January 1946 Auguste Lecoeur was surprised one morning when his postman addressed him with the title "Monsieur le ministre." [57] It was, according to Lecoeur, his first indication that he had been named to a cabinet position in the French government. From February to December 1946 Lecoeur served as the undersecretary to the minister of Industrial Production, Marcel Paul. Lecoeur's responsibility was to oversee the ministry's relations with the coal industry. Thus the leader of the miners' union became the minister of Mines.

The political career of Auguste Lecoeur from 1927 to 1954 reads like a rags-to-riches novel set in the world of French communism. Born to a family of miners in Lille, Lecoeur entered the mines at the age of twelve. A few years later, in Paris, he participated in a demonstration in support of Sacco and Vanzetti. That night he joined the PCF. Returning to Lens, Lecoeur worked in the mines and then in a metal-fabricating plant, where he became active in the metalworkers' union. When the Spanish civil war erupted, Lecoeur volunteered for action and served as a battalion leader under André Marty in the International Brigades. When he returned to France, Lecoeur became secretary of the PCF federation in Pas-de-Calais. He was arrested by the police and jailed for six months in 1939. On his release, Lecoeur entered the army and saw action on the front in 1940. Captured by the Germans, Lecoeur managed to escape and return to Lens, where he organized clandestine trade union work. The famous miners' strike of 1941—celebrated as the first strike against the Nazi occupation—was unique because Lecoeur and others in the northern basin advanced anti-German political themes months before the Nazi invasion of the Soviet Union. Although it was regarded as a political deviation at the time (apparently Duclos reprimanded Lecoeur for launching the strike without orders from party leaders), the strike paid off in the long run because it demonstrated the party's patriotism and independence from Moscow. Soon the miners' strike of 1941 found a hallowed position in the mythology of the PCF. In 1942 Duclos summoned Lecoeur to Paris and put him in charge of reorganizing the party's clandestine work. It was a dangerous task and one that had taken its toll of Communist cadres. But Lecoeur managed to put together a solid apparatus of underground political leaders. After the liberation, Lecoeur asked to be sent back to Lens. He was elected mayor of Lens in the municipal elections in 1945.[58]

Lecoeur's background as a labor organizer, soldier, and clandestine *résistant* made him a unique member of the French cabinet. Although he was only 34 years old, the new mayor of Lens had nearly twenty years of militant organizing experience. Beginning as a *galibot* in the mines, Lecoeur rose to become one of the top PCF leaders in the early 1950s. Tall, broad shouldered, square jawed, and curly haired, the minister of Mines looked more like a football player than a government official. He made full use of his prestige in the coal basin, his clout inside the PCF, and his oratorical skill to mobilize the miners for the battle of production.

Lecoeur wasted no time. He began by calling a meeting of 300 miners who were union stewards at the CGT headquarters in Lens. Lecoeur took the podium and claimed that those who said that "nothing had changed" were flat wrong. "Whatever its shortcomings," exclaimed Lecoeur, "we cannot equate the nationalized mines with the old companies." He sharply criticized those who advocated work stoppages. "We cannot say that the way to win our demands is to strike," said Lecoeur. "In fact, the opposite is true." Exhorting the miners to smash all obstacles to increased production, Lecoeur punctuated his speech with a story of Charles DeBarge, a well-known militant from the region who had been killed by the Nazis: "One night we had a meeting and Charles was late," recalled Lecoeur. "We asked him why he was late and he said, 'I was late because I had to stop and shoot a Nazi on the way.' If Charles was alive today he would say, 'I know it's time to punch out, but I want to load another 100 kilos before I leave.'"[59]

Lecoeur next brought together the management personnel. Standing beside Duhameau, the president–general director of the mines, and Jean Armanet, the leader of the SNIM, Lecoeur explained that he had already instructed the miners not to blame the management for all the problems. But Lecoeur demanded that management "should work with the pit committees to develop a plan for production and then try to apply that plan with intelligence, initiative, and a frank spirit of emulation."[60]

Similar meetings were held throughout the mining basin in Lecoeur's first few weeks as minister of Mines. The format for these meetings was

usually the same: exhortations to produce, a call for greater collaboration between workers and management, and the other themes of
the battle of production. The emphasis on production intensified after
Lecoeur became minister in part due to changes in national politics.
De Gaulle had suddenly resigned in January 1946, and the new tripartite
government was beginning its first hopeful months. For union activists,
the increasingly prominent presence of Communists in the government
seemed to indicate that the wheels of reform were turning again. The
miners' federation pointed to the new government as a reason to produce
more coal. "Some people still say that nothing has changed," wrote *La
Tribune des mineurs*, "but the miners know better. Now there are two
militants from our region who are in the government—Thorez and Lecoeur."[61] In March 1946 coal production in Nord and Pas-de-Calais surpassed the 1938 level.[62]

However, Lecoeur faced formidable obstacles. Skilled underground
workers were in short supply. This problem was aggravated by the departure of several thousand Polish workers, mostly experienced underground miners, who left the region to return to their recently liberated
homeland. There was also a serious shortage of experienced management
personnel. Absenteeism continued to be a problem. Plans for modernization and building new works had not yet been drawn up. The future of
the annex industries, left outside state control by the provisional nationalization, remained to be determined.

Once in office, Lecoeur quickly understood that solving these problems required more than recruiting a few more engineers or sending more
workers underground. In an attempt to demonstrate to the miners that
he took his new job seriously, Lecoeur utilized his power as a government
official to move against the old elite in the top levels of management.
Lecoeur suggested the idea of installing a worker as a vice president in
the mines and apparently received the support for Director Duhameau.
"A new stage in the battle of production has begun," wrote *Liberté* on
February 27. On March 5, Lecoeur dismissed all three vice presidents of
the mines, Bucher, Laffite-Laplace, and Vial, all longtime leaders of the
coal industry. In their places, Lecoeur named Léon Delfosse, secretary of
the Federation of Miners; Dumez, an engineer; and Armanet, the leader
of the SNIM. For some of Lecoeur's followers, his bold action seemed to
resemble the purge that had never really been accomplished. The old-line
bosses were being replaced by CGT leaders. *La Tribune des mineurs*
commended Lecoeur for his action, which "shows more confidence in
the working class than ever before." "The significance of this action,"
wrote *Liberté*, "escapes no one."[63]

Least of all did Lecoeur's actions escape Duhameau, the president–

general director of the northern mines. He threatened to resign and headed for Paris to complain to the government. But Marcel Paul, the minister of Industrial Production, backed his comrade Lecoeur and ordered Duhameau to carry out his instructions. According to the MRP newspaper *Nord-Éclair*, Lecoeur and Duhameau were in "open conflict." The CGC threatened to call upon its members to halt work in protest against Lecoeur's appointments. The Socialists waited a week before taking a position on the matter, and when they did, the writers for *Le Populaire*, the party's national daily, had a different view of the matter than their counterparts in the north. *Le Populaire* suggested that Duhameau should have some input into such a decision but basically downplayed the conflict and criticized the Right for making a big fuss over nothing. For the Socialists of Nord, however, Lecoeur's apppointments were strongly criticized. "By law, nominations should be made by the minister of Industrial Production after being proposed by the general director." [64] The northern Socialists published statements previously issued by Thorez, Frachon, and Lecoeur himself that commended Duhameau for his good work. The Socialist daily *Nord-Matin* complained that Dumez, who had been an engineer in Ostricourt, had been pro-Vichy during the occupation and had joined the Communist party only after the liberation. "Is it necessary to be a card-carrying Communist in order to make a career in the mines?" asked *Nord-Matin*. Meanwhile *Liberté* decided that Duhameau had "openly joined the ranks of the trusts and the old mining magnates." [65]

The president of the government, Socialist Félix Gouin, was called upon to arbitrate the matter. But then Delfosse and Armanet decided to step aside. "Our enemies have tried to draw us into a political battle, but we have thwarted their maneuvers," wrote *La Tribune des mineurs*. In a confidential letter to Duhameau that was never made public, Lecoeur scored the president–general director for having a "disloyal attitude." According to Lecoeur, Duhameau's actions were aimed at preventing the CGT from penetrating top management positions in the nationalized mines. He criticized Duhameau for demanding that Armanet resign his post as an elected leader of the SNIM in order to take a post in the mines. [66]

The 24th congress of the CGT Federation of Miners in Pas-de-Calais in March 1946 provided a forum for heightened attacks on the old mining managers and problems with the provisional nationalization. "Duhameau is a dictator of the mines," Delfosse told the miners. "He has all the powers." Analyzing the role of the pit committees, Victor Foulon ended his report by expressing hope that they "would become, in the near future, the administrative councils of the nationalized mines." [67] The congress ended on a note of unanimity. Critics of the Communist role in the CGT had been reduced to a small minority. All resolutions passed unanimously as a large number of mine workers lined up to speak in support of Delfosse's report.

The long-awaited legislation to permanently nationalize the coal mines was approved by the National Assembly in May 1946. After replacing Robert Lacoste as minister of Industrial Production, Marcel Paul had attempted to speed up the legislative process. A bill extending national-ization to all French coal mines was introduced by Henri Martel, a PCF deputy who was a leader in the Federation of Miners, in December 1945. The measure was reworked by the Council of Ministers, signed by Mar-cel Paul, and sent to the assembly for debate.[68] Enactment of the bill, however, was not accomplished without overcoming some problems. The assembly almost adjourned without taking it up. On the last day of the legislative session, Communist deputies noticed that the bill had not been placed on the list of bills to be considered. They gathered fifty signatures and appealed to the assembly president, Vincent Auriol, to put the item before the assembly. Auriol complied and the measure came up for de-bate. One deputy contended that the older owners would not receive suf-ficient compensation, but no serious opposition emerged. The bill was unanimously approved with an anticlimactic voice vote.[69]

Ten days later the Council of Ministers gave their approval to the Min-ers' Statute. It was enacted into law on 14 June 1946. The statute defined the terms of employment in the mines, labor and management rights, and procedures for setting wages, resolving grievances, and taking discipli-nary action. It was basically an agreement reached between the top man-agers (*directeurs-généreaux*), the miners' union and the ministries con-cerned. The Miners' Statute conformed to the national Labor Code drawn up by another Communist cabinet member, Ambroise Croizat, who served as the minister of Labor in 1946, but it also contained pro-visions specific to the mine workers. Like the Labor Code, the statute provided for free exercise of union rights and freedom of workers' opin-ions. It specified the conditions for hiring and layoffs and set up concilia-tion procedures to handle labor disputes. It provided for a minimum wage, bonuses for dirty or dangerous jobs, and mechanisms to apply equal pay for equal work for women and young workers and to run the apprenticeship programs.[70] In addition to provisions similar to those of the national Labor Code, the Miners' Statute set up parity commissions at the local, regional, and national levels to resolve grievances and settle differences involving hiring, promotion, and layoffs. It established wages for surface workers at 112 percent and underground workers at 132 percent of the wages paid to metalworkers in the Paris region. The piece-rate system allowed miners working at an "average rate" to earn 20 percent more than the minimum wage. Those who worked at a higher rate would earn 60 percent more than the minimum wage. The rate of 60 percent was not considered a wage ceiling, and a particularly industrious worker could earn even more. Moreover, earnings above this rate would not automatically entail a revision of the rate normally set. Eighteen-year-olds were paid adult wages. Paid vacation days were based on number of years served, the maximum being 24 days for ten years of service. Mine workers and retired miners received some coal for domestic use, free housing or compensation for housing costs, and free transportation to work in the mines. Silicosis was declared to be a job-related illness. Safety delegates, both underground and surface, were made full-time employees.[71]

The Federation of Miners was proud of what the miners had won in the statute. Going far beyond any previous agreement, the statute established many of the most basic elements sought by the union for decades. Also, by folding into the statute many of the conditions and terms of the agreement already forged in Nord and Pas-de-Calais to the coal mines of central and southern France, it helped miners in those areas, which traditionally had lagged behind the north. Both Robert Lacoste and Marcel Paul viewed themselves as the "father of the Miners' Statute." The union treated it almost as if it were a sacred document.

Efforts to change the statute were usually opposed by the miners' union. Perhaps the most important criticism raised against it was that it institutionalized the controversial individual payment systems.[72] But by the spring of 1946, the fight over this issue had probably been lost. Removing the ceiling on piece-rate pay and liberalizing the rate-setting mechanism so that miners were not penalized for extracting too much coal probably increased the number of mine workers, especially hewers, who, like Léon Delfosse, favored individual pay. The federation made a great deal out of the nationalization law and the Miners' Statute. "It was an important document," said Jean Wrobleski. "We carried a copy of the statute in our pockets because we had to learn the provisions and know them by heart."[73] The union viewed the statute as a concrete manifestation of the correctness of their leadership in the battle of production.

Although Lecoeur had been thwarted in his efforts to make big changes in management personnel, he received another chance when the new law on nationalization took effect. It established a more decentralized and democratized system. A central organism at the national level, the Charbonnages de France, was set up to guide and coordinate the work of the nine regional basins. Within that overall framework, various regional administrative councils (Houillères des Bassins) established production and investment policies. The administrative councils for the Charbonnages de France and the regional mines, based on the old CGT tripartite management plan, were made up of representatives drawn from personnel, consumers, and the state. However, despite the role given to the regional mines and the structure of the councils, the new nationalized system put a great deal of power in the hands of the state. The Charbonnages de France initiated proposals setting the price of coal and the distribution of production targets, but the government made the final decisions. The same held true in the naming of directors. The state, in effect, wielded a veto over nominations from the administrative councils of the Charbonnages de France and the regional houillères.[74] And Lecoeur, as a good Communist, was not loathe to use the state's power once it resided in his hands.

On 27 May 1946 Lecoeur announced his choices for the councils. Of eighteen positions, twelve were given to CGT members or supporters. Ten of the CGT members were from the Communist wing of the union. The CFTC was given two positions, but the CGC was shunned in favor of the SNIM, judged "most representative" among cadres. *Nord-Éclair* complained that three-fourths of the council were "members of a particular political party" and editorialized that politics had no place in managing an industry as important as coal. Jules Catoire spoke at the CFTC congress and contended that the Charbonnages de France was "under the virtual dictatorship of a political party."[75] The CGC, left with no representatives in the councils, appealed Lecoeur's appointments to the Conseil d'État. In Douai, its affiliate denounced CGT attempts to "colonize the engineers."[76] Duhameau used the May meeting of the outgoing consultative committee to charge that the CGT was trying to control the coal mines.[77]

The CGT defended Lecoeur's apppointments. Martel wrote that the real question was not the "politicization" of the mines but the need to democratize them. The system before nationalization, argued Martel, was certainly politicized, but it favored the mining barons. They refused to allow workers representation in management and declined to promote engineers who were close to the working class. Martel added his opinion that the forces most opposed to Lecoeur's appointments, the CFTC and the MRP, were the same forces that undermined the battle of production by issuing "demagogic demands" for wage hikes, opposing the emulation campaign, and supporting strikes.[78]

Again the government intervened. A decree issued in August reduced the CGT representatives by five. Members of the metalworkers' union and the electricity and gas workers' union, named as "consumer" representatives by Lecoeur, were removed and replaced by the director of the

Longwy Steel Works and the president of Éléctricité de France.[79] Louis Delaby, a CFTC leader, was named to replace another CGT representative. The miners' union answered with an unusual tactic. Breaking its own strike ban, the union called a five-minute work stoppage at the shift change. The job action also sparked a brief demonstration at the offices of the CFTC.[80]

In naming the administrative council of the Houillères du Bassin Nord—Pas-de-Calais (HBNPC), Lecoeur acted with less fanfare. Nevertheless, a behind-the-scenes struggle must have taken place between Lecoeur, the mine directors, and the various ministries. As Lecoeur noted in the speech at the council's installation ceremony on 30 August 1946, it had taken nearly three months to name the general director and the members of the administrative council. President Georges Bidault personally intervened in support of MRP leader Catoire and Sauty of the CFTC.[81] In turn, Catoire and Delaby pushed for the appointment of a CFTC engineer named Legrande, over the objections of the CGT. Legrande was installed. The appointments required Bidault's signature, but even with these changes, Bidault waited for more than a month to confirm the nominations.[82]

Another month was spent in heated debate over who would be general director of the northern mines and who would serve as president of the administrative council. Lecoeur's choice for general director, Jony Thomas, an engineer from Libercourt, drew fire from the Socialists. Auguste Laurent, a top Socialist leader from Nord, crisscrossed the mining basin speaking against Thomas. He charged that Thomas had been sympathetic to the Germans during the war but had decided to work closely with the Communists.[83] Delfosse countered that Thomas was married to a German woman from the Saar. He added that the Germans who stayed at Thomas's house were her parents, who were not Nazi sympathizers. Thomas's nomination was withdrawn when the CFTC and the MRP joined in the attack. SNIM leader Armanet was named to the post.[84]

At its initial meeting, the administrative council elected André Parent, a Communist leader in the miners' federation, as president. However, the vote was very close. At the last minute Catoire and Sauty tried to cast their votes for Duhameau, even though he was not a candidate. At the next meeting, the non-CGT council members demanded another vote. Only after three weeks of debate was a president installed: Thiébaut, an engineer with SNIM.[85]

In September 1946, two years after the government had deposed the old mining companies, the new administrative structures were finally installed. Opponents of nationalization tried to slow the process and narrow the scope of power given to labor organizations. They pushed for more compensation to the old owners and tried to keep the annex industries in private hands. The Socialists sought to preserve the nationalization while reducing the number of Communists in key management posts. Considering nationalization to be a Socialist, not a Communist, reform, the Socialists were appalled by Lecoeur's willingness to pack the councils with CGT members. They were prone to view the Communists' actions as the main threat to nationalization. The Communists sought to push nationalization forward and to maximize their influence in every corner of the nationalized industry from the boardrooms to the bottom of the pits. Critics argued that the Communists were trying to take over the mines, but from the perspective of union leaders like Lecoeur, putting workers into key management posts was part of the process of democratization. There was nothing clandestine or subversive about these actions, which the CGT argued conformed to the National Council of the Resistance charter. Labor leaders also felt a strong element of worker representation was justified by the union's leadership role in the battle of production. With this in mind, Lecoeur utilized his ministerial power to the fullest in an effort to create a pro-union majority in the management of the mines. He succeeded in placing an unprecedented number of union representatives into positions of power. But his attempts to fashion a solid CGT majority in the administrative councils fell short. Lecoeur's successes and failures mirrored, in some ways, the battle of production as the year 1946 came to an end.

VICTORIES AND OBSTACLES

By the end of 1946 union leaders could announce that the battle of production was finally being won. Coal production increased steadily (see table 4). More workers were recruited into the mines to close the energy gap. Remarkably, the upswing in output was accompanied by a rise in productivity from 814 kilograms per man hour in January 1946 to 890 kilograms in May 1947. The work week in the mines was set at 48 hours, in contrast to the 44 hours worked on average in all groups of activity.[86] A comparison of "activity" (number of workers and length of work week) in various sectors reveals that coal miners outstripped their counterparts in all French industries in 1946 and 1947 (see table 5). The upswing in coal production began to fill the energy gap caused by the lack of coal imports. In 1945 and 1946 more than 80 percent of coal consumption was provided by French coal mines (see table 6). In addition, workplace discipline had been restored after the tumultuous weeks following the liberation and during the wildcat strikes in the summer of

TABLE 4.   French Coal Production, 1945–1946

Month/Year	Output (thous. tons)	Index (1938 = 100)	Month/Year	Output (thous. tons)	Index (1938 = 100)
Jan. 1945	2,734	69	Jan. 1946	3,966	100
Apr. 1945	2,403	61	Apr. 1946	4,036	102
Jul. 1945	2,694	68	Jul. 1946	4,110	104
Oct. 1945	3,752	95	Oct. 1946	4,682	118

Source: INSEE, *Bulletin de la statistique générale de la France, 1947–1948.*

TABLE 5.   Indexes of Activity in Various Industries
(1938 = 100)

	April 1946	April 1947
Coal	153	161
Petrol	99	109
Metals	103	118
Glass	104	124
Chemical	111	124
Textiles	85	104

Source: INSEE, *Mouvement économique en France de 1944 à 1957,* 61.

TABLE 6.   French Coal Production and Consumption, 1944–1949

	Consumption	Production	Production as Percentage of Consumption
	(In million tons)		
1938	68	48	71
1944	30	27	90
1945	41	35	85
1946	60	49	82
1947	64	47	73
1948	66	45	68
1949	73	53	73

Source: A. Chabert, *Les Salaires dans l'industrie française: Les charbonnages* (Paris, 1957), 163.

TABLE 7.   Underground Mine Workers, Nord–Pas-de-Calais, 1938–1949
(Monthly average in thousands)

1938	103.8	1947	134.4
1944	103.6	1948	126.8
1945	111.4	1949	111.7
1946	134.6		

Source: INSEE, *Mouvement économique en France de 1938 à 1948*, 218.

1945. It was no coincidence that coal production began to approach prewar levels in September and October 1945 at the same time that the miners' union increased its commitment to the battle for coal. Victory could be proclaimed in another sense: while coal miners in Britain, Belgium, America, and most industrialized countries had engaged in work stoppages, the French miners had remained on the job. In all of these "victories," the unions had played a central and necessary role as promotors of the production drive, which aimed at powering an industrial resurgence in France.

Production figures, however, obscured fundamental problems facing the industry and the labor movement. For one thing, increasing production by sending more and more workers into the mines was not a long-term solution. Between 1944 and 1946 the number of underground miners increased from about 100,000 to 130,000 (see table 7). Even so, the new management confronted the persistent problem that had plagued the old mining bosses: the shortage of workers.

The Charbonnages de France reported that the number of French mine workers increased 25 percent from 1945 to the end of 1946.[87] But the figures fail to convey the desperate efforts undertaken to get more workers underground. The number of prisoners of war sent into the mines jumped from 7,600 in May 1945 to 56,000 in August 1946.[88] Attempts were made to find workers among the unemployed in Paris and Britanny and to recruit immigrant workers from Italy and North Africa. In the mines of Nord and Pas-de-Calais, underground miners numbered 91,000 in December 1944. One year later 129,000 workers toiled underground. In December 1946 the number of underground miners increased to 134,000.[89] As minister of Mines, Lecoeur made every effort to close the coal gap by recruiting more underground workers. He pushed for and received a new shipment of German POWs to replace the nearly 6,000 Polish underground workers that returned to Poland in 1945. In 1946 54,000 German POWs toiled in the French mines (see table 8). In memoranda to the mine directors, Lecoeur urged management to forget about

TABLE 8.   Prisoners of War as Mine Workers, 1945–1948

1945	Jan.	—	1947	Jan.	53,128
	Apr.	6,662		Apr.	51,237
	Jul.	14,721		Jul.	53,303
	Oct.	34,023		Oct.	45,626
1946	Jan.	40,205	1948	Jan.	34,712
	Apr.	45,818		Apr.	22,261
	Jul.	54,032		Jul.	19,536
	Oct.	54,222		Oct.	10,785

Source: INSEE, *Mouvement économique en France de 1938 à 1948*, 308.

output-per-worker statistics and to send many surface workers underground to mine coal.[90] Yet heavy reliance on immigrant workers and POWs had certain limitations. A deal with the Italian government to bring 9,000 unemployed workers to France was only partly fulfilled as the mine directors decided that the "Mediterranean workers" did not adapt well to the mines, and their output remained consistently low. The same held true for the German POWs. Lacking much incentive for the production campaign, the POWs even waged a brief strike in December 1946 to claim that management had violated certain statutes of the Geneva Convention on POW issues.[91] While management sought to increase the number of miners working underground, many workers were trying to move to jobs in the surface installations. Although underground workers earned higher wages, their work was harder, dirtier, and more dangerous. In a speech to the Chamber of Deputies in 1947, Lecoeur estimated that 40 percent to 50 percent of the miners in France were inexperienced.[92] Thiébaut, president of the administrative council of the northern mines noted that the work force of 1947 was very different from that of 1938: "In 1938 the miners included neither young nor old workers . . . and hence, the mines possessed a work force that was entirely composed of experienced and healthy adult workers. [By] 1944 the men were aged and very tired after years of deprivation. They were hungry and very badly clothed."[93]

Poor equipment was another obstacle to higher production. Reports of the mining directors constantly refer to the dire shortages of machinery, conveyor belts, fans, replacement parts, and other equipment. Lack of mechanization necessitated a greater use of manual labor. When coal wagons came to a place in the mine where rails were in disrepair, several workers had to guide the wagon by hand. Most of the sorting was done by hand. Lack of adequate elevators and cages meant that miners spent more time waiting to descend and ascend. In many cases, miners were forced to walk underground for nearly an hour to reach their work site. When old machinery broke down, production was held up for hours.

The combination of poor equipment, inexperienced workers, and excessive need for manual labor in tasks better performed with machines may have been factors in a large number of fatal accidents that occurred in 1946. Figures are not available for 1945, but more fatalities occurred in 1946 (154) than in 1947 (132) and 1948 (128).[94] Some complained that the production effort resulted in raising more coal dust, which caused silicosis, although it is hard to prove by available statistics. The number of illnesses in the mines showed a dramatic increase in 1946, but part of the reason was the fact that the Miners' Statute considerably liberalized medical care in the mines.[95] A number of explosions occurred in 1946, focusing attention on the state of equipment in the mines. At funerals Lecoeur and other CGT leaders blamed the old bosses for failing to keep the mines in good working shape.

As the production campaign began its second year, the old slogans failed to sustain great enthusiasm among the coal miners. Socialist mine workers attacked the Communists for stressing "production at any cost": "This [emphasis on production] is exactly what the old bosses used to say," complained one worker. "They used the same formula: longwalls, bonuses for good attendance, individual pay for individual work, the Bedaux system, and other so-called 'modern methods.'"[96] Some Socialists charged that accidents might have occurred because stewards spent too much time on political activities and recruiting new workers into the CGT.[97] Responding to claims that miners were being injured because of the union's emphasis on production, Lecoeur exclaimed that even if 100 miners were killed, the price would be worth it if the battle of production was won. This was too much for the CFTC leaders, who upbraided the minister of Mines. "Production, yes, but first, humanity" was the slogan adopted by a meeting of CFTC mine workers in July 1946.[98]

Union leaders clearly recognized these obstacles, but they hoped that the miners' support for the new regime could help to overcome them. For this reason, they sought to demonstrate to the miners that a real change had taken place. At the ceremony held to celebrate the naming of the new administrative council for the northern mines, Lecoeur spoke of the need for the mines to be less secretive than in the past. "The headquarters of the mines will be a *maison de verre*," exclaimed the minister of Mines. "We must make it so that a miner can actually become a president of the administrative council."[99] From that point on, *La Tribune des mineurs* took the "glass house" seriously by publicizing the events that transpired behind the closed doors of the administrative council.

ORDERLY RETREAT

Labor support for the battle of production rested upon two conditions: governmental participation by the parties of the Left and union representation within the management of the nationalized industries. In 1945 and for most of 1946 these conditions prevailed. In the last month of 1946, however, the situation began to change, paving the way for a retreat from the battle by the labor movement.

A cabinet crisis in December 1946 ended Marcel Paul's cabinet role. Paul and other cabinet members were replaced by a transitional all-Socialist government, which was set up to last only a few weeks until the formal installation of the new Fourth Republic in January 1947. But when the new cabinet was formed, Marcel Paul was not brought back. Instead, Robert Lacoste returned to his old job as minister of Industrial Production. It is not clear why Paul was dropped while other Communist ministers resumed their former posts. However, Paul had taken a high profile in fighting shortages of coal and electricity. He had boldly demanded increased deliveries of coal from the Ruhr. His forceful promotion of the nationalization of electricity and gas also drew fire from conservative political forces. Seeking to circumvent the black market, Paul also established a program to work with small producers to manufacture badly needed basic goods such as shoes, shirts, and textiles that were to be distributed through retailers that cooperated with the program. Critics charged that the Communist party was moving into the production and retailing of goods that properly belonged to firms in the private sector.[100]

The fall of Marcel Paul brought an end to Lecoeur's role as minister of Mines. The change was hardly noticed at the national level, but it was felt immediately in the northern mining region. When the government called upon miners to work the Sundays following Christmas and New Year's Day, the union abandoned its previous policy and allowed a referendum on the issue. Predictably, the miners voted against Sunday work by a 7 to 1 margin.[101] Lecoeur stepped easily from his role as administrator to that of union leader when he summoned the stewards for meeting. "The nationalization is far from perfect," said Lecoeur. "I think if we had a majority in the administrative council we would be producing 120,000 tons of coal daily. But we don't have a majority. I say this especially to those comrades who address themselves to the union in the same way as they would address themselves to management."[102] Indeed, the *maison de verre* celebrated earlier by Lecoeur was increasingly shrouded by management. On September 11 the administrative council voted, by a one-vote majority, to abolish the obligation of voting with raised hands. This seemingly insignificant change drew the curtains on the glass house by making it impossible for the union to inform its members as to how council members had voted on issues. Key trade union leaders were removed from management posts and the CGT's power inside decision-making bodies was reduced, putting an end to the old CGT dream of labor participation along tripartite lines.

Under these circumstances, the willingness of labor leaders to continue the calls for more production waned considerably. While mine workers continued to back changes in the mines, more than two years had passed since the initial proclamation of nationalization. Appeals to produce invoked little enthusiasm among the miners. Indeed, the Socialists had learned how to score points among the rank and file by arguing that the Communists had simply replaced the old bosses and reestablished old unpopular policies. The ability of union leaders to prevent job actions diminished as the social peace that had marked the first two years of the nationalization evaporated. Faced with rising inflation, mine workers pressed constantly for upward revisions in piece rates and wrangled with management over task rates and bonuses. Parity commissions were flooded with unresolved grievances. Mine workers absented themselves from work in order to travel to the countryside to buy provisions. An inquiry led by the prefect of Pas-de-Calais in August 1946 noted that "with the return of 'freedom in pricing' most prices are rising at a dizzying pace. While the producers and shopkeepers rejoice, the wage earners complain bitterly that their wage increases are devoured quickly by inflated prices." [103] Addressing itself to the sense of malaise that appeared to have gripped the mining basin, the CFTC's monthly journal for mine workers, *Écho des Mines*, complained that "one out of six mine workers is absent each day; sometimes one out of four. Each day about 80,000 miners fail to come to work, although only about 11 percent of them are really sick or injured." [104]

Yet the CGT refrained from breaking with management, even when isolated work stoppages began to occur. Duguet, president of the Charbonnages de France and a longtime leader of the CGT, came to Bruay in March 1947 with a pessimistic prognostication: "It is difficult to say this, but it is necessary to produce even more. We must prove that output, order, and discipline can improve. If not, in a few months, it could be the end of the nationalized mines." [105] Confronted with a spate of spontaneous strikes in April 1947, the CGT editorialists tempered their well-worn criticisms of the strikers: "Can we justifiably condemn the strikes? No, even though we think the strikes are inopportune, we understand why the miners are striking."[106] Nevertheless, the union continued to oppose strikes throughout the month of May. In June they called a special union meeting, drew up a set of demands, and launched a brief warning strike. Union communiqués called for a minimum wage that would change weekly in line with changes in prices, adding, "The miners have already won the battle of production. Now they want their just claims resolved." The miners' union began an orderly retreat from the battle of production.

5.

Coal Politics and the Cold War

rance's battle for coal ran up against important international issues in the late 1940s. From the French perspective, both the coal crisis and the deepening cold war became intertwined with questions of international relations, domestic politics, and economic recovery.

Few French leaders originally envisioned a rigidly bipolar postwar world. De Gaulle and his foreign minister Georges Bidault saw France playing an independent role standing "between East and West."[1] The not-so-hidden agenda behind the French position was to win a peace settlement that would protect France by keeping Germany weak. Thus, France's economic imperative for coal converged conveniently with a desire to prevent Germany from resuming its economic and military power in Europe. This approach became even more important as it became clear that France's other prewar suppliers, Belgium, Britain, and Poland, would not be capable of delivering the coal needed to supplement increased domestic production. But the French search for an independent role in foreign affairs and for "hidden reparations" in German coal collided with conflicting American objectives. Already, American and British policymakers had begun to reorganize the distribution of critical resources such as coal. Their actions were undertaken primarily to enhance the realization of longer-term goals of rebuilding Europe (including Germany) along Western capitalist lines and creating a Western alliance against the Soviet Union. Months before the term *cold war* had come into being, French inability to win coal reparations from Germany underscored the larger failure of its "German policy." In 1947 de Gaulle's independent "between East and West" strategy was abandoned as France joined the Americans in a struggle between two hostile world blocs.

Coal and the cold war also affected national politics in France. Throughout 1946 and well into 1947 the tripartite government continued to hold together. But the formal coalition masked a bitter struggle between Socialists and Communists for power in the nationalized industry and influence within organized labor. Tripartism came to an end in May 1947 when Paul Ramadier, the Socialist prime minister, ejected Communist ministers from the government for opposing its unpopular wage policies. But nearly five months before Ramadier's dramatic action, Robert Lacoste had taken decisive action to reduce Communist influence in the coal mines. And a bitter fight between pro-Communist and pro-Socialist factions for control of the CGT further poisoned relations between the two parties. Although the cold war did not create these problems, it did provide a new frame of reference for old conflicts that boiled over in a series of strikes in November 1947.

Coal and the cold war were also linked to economic problems in 1947. Inflation wreaked havoc on the French economy. The coal-mining industry, locked in the initial stages of an ambitious program of expansion, saw its fiscal stability destroyed by spiraling prices. Worse, raising the price of coal increased the inflationary trend throughout the economy as the coal-consuming industries passed along the added costs to their customers. With the economy sliding downhill, American assistance offered the only hope for France. But American policymakers, already deeply engaged in the fight against communism, were reluctant to provide economic assistance to countries where Communists held positions of leadership. In 1947 it suddenly seemed to make good economic sense to exclude Communists from the cabinet and to purge their members from important positions in the mines. When the Communists were removed, coal imports from America increased significantly. Additional increases occurred in anticipation of strikes by the mine workers in 1947 and 1948. Clearly, coal and the cold war played important parts in French economic planning. The Monnet Plan was based on an expansive coal program and on the assumption that extensive economic assistance was forthcoming from the United States in what became the Marshall Plan for European Economic Recovery.

IN SEARCH OF "HIDDEN REPARATIONS"

In July 1945, when the Big Three met at Potsdam, they found little agreement regarding coal reparations. Behind the scenes, however, American

TABLE 9.   French Coal Imports: Britain, Poland, and the Ruhr
(In thousands of tons)

1938 (ave.)	529	131	331
Jan. 1946	121	—	193
Apr. 1946	67	—	70
Jul. 1946	88	89	94
Oct. 1946	13	77	24
Jan. 1947	1	51	18

Source: INSEE, *Mouvement économique en France de 1938 à 1948,* 219.

policy on German coal began to take shape. President Truman ordered the U.S. Army in Germany to assume broad financial and supply responsibilities for distributing coal. Indicating the need to provide critical reparations for rebuilding the Allied nations, the president issued a directive implying that every extra ton of coal mined in Germany should go to France. Yet coal deliveries lagged far behind expected levels, prompting French protests and broadening support in France for more active steps to acquire coal from Germany (see table 9).

Jean Monnet, working out of France's Washington embassy in July 1945, requested larger U.S. coal exports in hopes of temporarily improving the coal situation. Monnet called for monthly shipments of 600,000 tons to France to cover the Allied army's coal consumption in France.[2] But American officials expressed reservations regarding the priorities set by French leaders. Some feared that France harbored hopes of regaining its former status as a major power, perhaps leading the tripartite government to swerve from American plans for European reconstruction. In preparation for Truman's meeting with de Gaulle, one American official complained that the French government was directing too much coal into channels for producing military equipment to supply a growing French army. Americans would not want to contribute to the relief and reconstruction of Europe, he warned, if France did not abandon the "uneconomic use of strategic raw materials" and use its resources to "get back to the road to economic stability."[3]

France seized control of the Saar coal mines in August 1945 and demanded American agreement that they be considered French property. At the Council of Foreign Ministers meeting in London in September 1945, French leaders invoked the "lessons of Versailles" by issuing stiff demands on Germany, including the separation of the Rhineland and the Ruhr from Germany. These actions caught the American officials moving in opposite directions. A dispute emerged between General Clay, head of the occupation forces in Germany, and the State Department, which sought French cooperation around a much broader set of issues. Ambassador Jefferson Caffrey, requesting emergency coal shipments to France in January 1946, emphasized the "importance of maintaining and if possible increasing coal exports to France because of political as well as economic reasons."[4] Meanwhile, American officials in Germany tangled with French delegates who wanted more German coal. Clay reported to the State Department that Germany could not possibly meet previous agreements on coal deliveries to France. Further, he questioned the value of German coal exports to France.

The debate over exports of German coal to France revealed the dilemma involved in trying to square European reconstruction needs with the requirements for German economic recovery. Put simply, although deliveries of German coal could assist in the recovery of other European countries, exporting it to France weakened efforts to rebuild Germany. In addition, America's position as an occupying power combined with the dollar's supremacy in international currency meant, as Clay noted, that the "United States [was] placed in a position of subsidizing shipments of coal from Germany to France."[5] France also drew fire from occupational authorities in Germany for using its veto power too frequently and for refusing to agree to American proposals for Allied control agencies in the absence of a more comprehensive agreement on German coal exports.

De Gaulle's successor, Félix Gouin, built his policy on German reparations (in coal and other materials) and American economic aid to modernize backward industrial equipment in France. Bidault continued as foreign minister and pushed the same program. In April 1946, Marcel Paul, the Communist minister of Industrial Production, traveled to Poland and secured an agreement for that country to resume its coal shipments, which had provided about 10 percent of the coal France imported in 1938. Deliveries of Polish coal began to arrive the following month, and in July, nearly 90,000 tons were exported to France. Among prewar coal suppliers (excluding the disputed Saar region), Poland's share of coal deliveries to France increased from 36 percent in June 1946 to 65 percent at the end of the year. But Polish deliveries failed to meet the agreed target of 100,000 tons of coal per month.[6]

French leaders next brought their case for coal to Washington. In the course of financial negotiations in March 1946, Léon Blum went into detail regarding French coal needs. Jean Monnet followed Blum with a battery of statistics, graphs, and projections that linked the need for coal with forecasts for economic growth. In April, economist John Kenneth

Galbraith, in a study for the State Department, argued on the basis of "agreed Allied policy" that the main source of coal for France should be Germany and that production of German coal should be maximized in order to help European recovery and to generate German foreign exchange. Disagreeing with estimates by American occupation forces in Germany, Galbraith wrote, "Even allowing for possible under-estimate in German requirements and possible over-optimism with respect to the rate of revival of German coal production, it is clear that a large German coal export will be available, probably sufficient to cover the whole of French needs under their proposed plan."[7]

"Month after month the haggling over coal went on," wrote Alexander Werth.[8] But James Byrnes's speech in Stuttgart in September 1946 stunned French officials with its call for rebuilding a united Germany without making any changes in the control of the Ruhr or the Rhineland. The speech by the American secretary of state was described in French circles as "the straw that broke the back of the de Gaulle–Bidault policy of the last two years." It indicated a new "pro-German" policy by America. In November 1946, British officials informed the French that coal exports would have to be scaled back even further. The announcement by the Americans and British that the two German zones under their control would be merged to create "Bizonia" implied that no special arrangements for sending German coal to France would be forthcoming.

In January 1947, Léon Blum, struggling to halt inflation with a dramatic price cut, sent a secret message to Britain's Ernest Bevin. Blum expressed a desire to visit London, primarily to discuss France's desperate coal needs, but also, as the U.S. State Department noted, "to talk of the possible negotiations of Franco-British alliance." British coal imports, which accounted for the largest deliveries of any country to France in 1938, had stopped altogether in the last months of 1946. But the British had no coal to offer Blum. And to make matters worse, the Foreign Office indicated to Blum, "in any decisions concerning coal supplies from the Ruhr, American agreement would be necessary in view of the economic merger of the British and American zones of occupation."[9] In perfect symmetry, the American occupation leaders in Germany declined to engage in discussions with the French regarding the recruitment of German workers for the French mines in 1947, arguing that "the problem of manpower in the (British and American) zones is a joint problem which, under our agreement with the British, should only be discussed jointly with the U.S. and Britain."[10] Ambassador Caffrey was sent to France with a note asking that the German war prisoners be returned within ten months.[11]

A frustrated Vincent Auriol, elected as the first president of the new

Fourth Republic, met with Caffrey and Secretary of State Byrnes in March 1947, accompanied by his acting foreign minister, Pierre Henri Teitgen. The French coal problem, if it continued, would "lead to uneasiness and uncertainty with grave political consequences," said Auriol. "The coal problem is the vital political question for France," said Teitgen. "The entire French reconstruction is in the balance. The future of France depends on present negotiations regarding Germany. The question is not a purely French problem but exists for all Europe. Germany should not be reconstructed before France and the other countries it ravaged. A strong France is indispensible to Europe and the world." Auriol concluded by utilizing the Versailles analogy: "A Germany stronger than ever sprang up from the Treaty of Versailles. Such a possibility should never be given to Germany again." [12] But any remaining hopes Auriol had for resuscitating France's German policy at the Four Power Conference at Moscow evaporated in the wake of the Truman Doctrine. The president's speech, delivered the day before the opening of the conference, upstaged the important meeting that brought together Marshall, Molotov, Bevin, and Bidault and was focused on issues involving Germany and Austria. Important agreements could not be reached. The Americans and British were already implementing their policies toward Germany. They were unwilling to support French proposals to "internationalize" the Ruhr but were willing to support French claims of the Saar region if it included reductions of coal shipments from Germany. This was the best that Bidault could get from Molotov who, unhappy with Truman's speech to the U.S. Congress in which the president resolved to provide American aid to any country threatened by communism, was even unwilling to give the Americans the satisfaction of Soviet agreement with them on the French Saar claims.

Caffrey, stationed in Paris, remained sympathetic to French demands for "hidden reparations" in German coal. But American policymakers considered the French energy crisis in a much broader, global context. Under American urging, the Allied Coal Allocation office, once the war ended, was transformed into the European Coal Organization. Then George Marshall, in preparation for what would be called the Marshall Plan, instructed George F. Kennan to form a policy-planning study on economic recovery in Europe. Again, the coal dilemma was at the heart of the matter. Should German coal be used to help Germany achieve self-sufficiency, thus reducing the cost of the occupation? Or should German coal be exported to France in order to contribute to rebuilding liberated Europe? Kennan responded by launching a "coal for Europe" program. Its purpose was to increase coal production in the Ruhr for European consumption. Kennan recommended that the program convey the impression, by means of wide publicity, that the campaign was led, not by the American government, but by a concerned American public.[13]

In the summer of 1947, to the horror of Clay and Americans in Germany, the British, working with local Social Democrats in the German zone, made plans to nationalize the German coal mines. Hurriedly, the State Department invited Britain to a coal conference in Washington. The conference began in August 1947 and lasted nearly a month. It resulted in the formulation of a tough American position against nationalization. Pressured by their American allies, the British agreed to drop the plan to nationalize German coal.[14] In Washington the episode sparked a chorus of voices in favor of attaching conditions against nationalization to American economic aid to all European countries. Writing from France, a labor historian, Val Lorwin, prepared a detailed background piece for the State Department explaining why such a policy would not be effective or appropriate for France.[15]

For energy-starved France, the only remaining option was to import more American coal. The flow of American coal to France increased rapidly in the troubled years of 1947 and 1948.[16] In the twelve months before May 1947, monthly shipments of American coal to France averaged 435,000 tons. But between May 1947 and March 1948, U.S. coal deliveries increased to an average of 1,161,000 tons per month. The pattern of monthly coal imports could be interpreted to show that deliveries tended to increase in anticipation of strikes by French miners. In the summer of 1948, on the eve of the October coal strike, coal stocks reached six million tons, the highest level since before the war.[17]

The German question, which was supposed to be the big issue in matters of economic reconstruction, was quickly becoming displaced by the issue of American economic aid. Truman's speech was interpreted in France to mean that the only way a country could receive economic aid was to be threatened by the Communists. That conclusion had an immediate impact on French politics. "The Communists are rendering us a great service," wrote Pierre Mendès-France. "Because we have a 'Communist danger' the Americans are making a tremendous effort to help us. We must keep up this indispensable Communist scare."[18] Raymond Aron, in a number of influential articles in *Combat*, reasoned that France might as well join with the Americans against the Russians and the French Communists. "For reconstruction, we are largely dependent upon the Americans," wrote Aron. "Without American credits even the present mediocre standard of living of the French people would be impossible." François Goguel wrote in *L'Esprit*, "All information from America agrees that a tidal wave of anti-Communism is today sweeping the country. The USA is undoubtedly determined to eliminate Communist influence not only in Central Europe and the Balkans, but in western Europe as well."[19]

ECONOMIC AID AND THE COMMUNISTS

American officials were disturbed by the presence of Communists in the cabinet, the nationalized industries, and the army and police. While they generally avoided official pronouncements to this effect, American policy-makers and congressional leaders made certain that French representatives clearly understood their concern with the idea of treating the Communists as a legitimate party of the government. Many influential Americans viewed the French Communists as agents of Soviet power in France. They were probably not aware of the degree of popular support for the PCF. In the view of many American leaders, the Communist presence was a dangerous aberration that could be checked by vigorous action. Election results in 1945 and 1946, however, convinced American officials who were monitoring the situation in France that ridding France of communism would require more than the oft-prescribed "surgical operation." Less conservative Americans viewed the success of communism in France as a protest against the inept economic system that had governed France before the liberation. Their emphasis was on improving the economic situation that allowed the Communists to "exploit" working-class discontent.

The coal crisis forced U.S. policymakers to learn more about the state of the French coal-mining industry, resulting in meetings between American representatives and leaders of the industry, including CGT officials. As Caffrey noted to Byrnes in June 1945, "It is generally agreed that an increased volume of coal production in France is essential to the maintenance of industrial activity even at present reduced levels, and that it is of critical importance in connection with the avoidance of social disturbances during the coming winter." Duguet, Communist leader of the miners' union (later named president of the Charbonnages de France), pledged the CGT's commitment to increased production but warned that social and economic policies would have to be altered in order to win the confidence of the miners. Richard Eldridge, labor attaché in the American embassy in Paris, participated in a coal conference in the Loire coal basin in June 1945 that brought together leading state, mine, and labor officials to establish plans to increase production based fundamentally upon improving labor conditions in the mines.[20]

The Communists' promotion of the battle of production surprised and perplexed some American officials because it failed to conform to their notions of communism. Rather than mobilize workers for the barricades, the Communists exhorted them to "produce, above all, produce!" What disturbed American policymakers was that the Communist policy appeared to give legitimacy to the notion that no French government could govern without the Communists. Irving Brown, an American anti-Communist union organizer working in France, expressed dismay with the way the Communists succeeded in wrapping themselves in the clothing of the French Resistance and the new "economic renaissance." H. Freeman Matthews, head of the State Department's Office of European Affairs, wrote: "The Communist tactical objective has been to demonstrate that France cannot be governed today without Communist participation."[21] French representatives, in their dealings with American officials, learned to exploit this American concern. A 1946 report of a meeting between a State Department representative and M. Bernard, who sought increased coal imports from America, noted that "the French official emphasized the importance of industrial improvement in stemming the tide of communism and pointed to the need for political stability of France."[22] In his memoirs, Jean Monnet described how Léon Blum, during his voyage to the United States to obtain coal imports and emergency financial aid, used a political argument to counter Americans who sought to withhold aid to France because of its leftist tendencies in 1946. "If we were unable to pay for the imports that are vital to our economy," Blum told the Americans, "you must realize that France would be placed, through material poverty and a sense of having been abandoned, in a situation from which one could not expect any reasonable way out." Monnet wrote that the men who governed the United States understood what Blum meant.[23]

While Communists used their influence in the labor movement as a sort of economic blackmail to retain their positions in the government, French officials were playing on American anti-Communist fears in order to obtain economic assistance. Many French leaders knew that once the Communists were out of the cabinet, the government's problems on the home front could increase at the same time the American incentive to send aid was diminishing. Thus, two weeks before Communist cabinet members were removed from their positions, an official of the Bank of France said, "We are not yet ready to face the CGT. Furthermore, it would be a mistake to break with the Communists on an economic issue."[24] A frustrated James Byrnes complained in October 1946 that, in dealing with coal matters, "we can't talk to anyone below Bidault's level since most of them are Communists."[25] Robert Lacoste, however, had not waited for the Americans to increase their pressure on the French to push aside the Communists. He performed his own "surgical operation" in the nationalized coal mines.

THE RETURN OF LACOSTE

In December 1946 Robert Lacoste resumed his former position as minister of Industrial Production. He wasted little time in making changes. Lacoste viewed himself as the main architect of nationalization, although the definitive law was introduced and enacted during the tenure of Marcel Paul. Speaking in the mining town of Harnes in September 1946, Lacoste commented that high production and good relations in the mines signaled the Socialists' success in nationalizing the industry and providing for more worker participation. But Lacoste had harsh words for the Communists. "If the nationalizations are to succeed, they cannot be governed by a political party," said Lacoste. "If a party is allowed to gain dozens of permanent officials and controls considerable amounts of goods, then the success of the nationalization will come to an end."[26]

One of the first things Lacoste did was to alter once more the composition of production committees by reducing the number of representatives selected by the mine workers to one. This left management responsible for naming the remaining three representatives.[27] The effect of this action was to greatly reduce the ability of mine workers to use their veto power over production plans as a means of offsetting management controls.

Then Lacoste turned to the task of making changes in the boardrooms. Lacoste issued a set of decrees in January 1947 that reduced the role of the CGT within management and spun a new web of state controls around coal policies. He changed the requirements for membership on the board of directors of the Charbonnages de France by requiring the state to select representatives with at least five years of administrative experience in government agencies. In addition, Lacoste enumerated a list of actions that could not be taken by the Charbonnages de France or the regional Houillères du Bassin without government approval. Another decree allowed the minister of Industrial Production to dissolve the boards of directors at the national or regional level if those agencies were considered to be failing in their responsibilities. Additional decrees compelled the Charbonnages and Houillères to submit their financial reports for evaluation by a group of state controllers.[28] The CGT protested Lacoste's actions, but to no avail. Addressing the Federation of Miners' convention in February 1947, Duguet contended that the five-year requirement was a bureaucratic way to remove CGT leader Léon Delfosse from an administrative post.[29]

The new decrees reduced the number of CGT representatives in the Charbonnages de France from twelve to six. Of the six representatives who were dismissed, five were Communists. In March and April Lacoste appointed the boards of directors in the mining basins of Provence, Lorraine, Cévennes, and Auvergne. He made certain that the union held only a few posts.[30] In June supplementary decrees specified that "each member of the administrative council must not belong to any of the groups he is not representing." This allowed for the removal of all Marcel Paul's apppointees who represented consumers or the state but also belonged to the CGT. Lacoste also shortened the term of office for board members from six years to three years and specified that one-third of the body would be renewed every year. This meant that several Paul appointees would complete their terms of office in 1948.

While removing CGT representatives from the councils, Lacoste reinstalled many of the old mining chiefs. Indeed, eleven administrators who had served on the Coal Mines Committees during the 1930s and the Coal Mines Organization Committee under the Vichy regime were appointed by Lacoste to board positions in the nationalized mines.[31] His actions angered the mine workers. But they were well received by the business leaders and state officials who in 1947 joined the chorus of protests against the financial operations in the nationalized mines.

THE FINANCIAL CRISIS

A financial crisis wracked the coal mines in 1947. It destroyed any possibility for fiscal solvency and forced industry leaders to plead for special government subsidies, thus drawing attention to alleged abuses committed by certain administrators. Critics charged management with incompetence and accused the Communists of politicizing the decision-making process. Union leaders cited problems facing the industry and pointed to the miners' efforts in the battle of production, but the debate sparked by the financial crisis unfolded in a highly charged political atmosphere where criticisms of certain policies meshed easily with rising cold war tensions.

Close scrutiny reveals that the financial crisis of 1947 was neither the result of errors committed by individual administrators nor a product of Communist subversion. The industry found itself in a situation that made fiscal solvency impossible. On one hand, labor costs and the cost of supplies increased steadily in a period of hyperinflation (see table 10). Considered from a different angle, the percentage of labor costs to the value of coal increased from 1938 to 1947 (see table 11). But while the cost of producing coal increased sharply, government policy attempted to hold down the sale price of coal as an anti-inflationary weapon and to boost profit margins for industrial consumers of coal.[32] The twin objectives of luring workers into the mines and investing funds to rebuild the industry

TABLE 10. Labor Costs as a Percentage of Production Costs

	1936	1947	1948	1952
Wages and Benefits	52.0	73.9	71.0	63.4

Source: Jocelyn Moniez, *L'Industrie charbonnière française depuis 1946* (Lille, 1959), 259, and Charbonnages de France, *Rapport de gestion, 1947, 1948, and 1952* (Paris, 1952).

TABLE 11. Labor Costs as a Percentage of the Value of Coal

1938	49	1949	43
1944	81	1950	46
1945	93	1951	44
1946	64	1952	40
1947	67	1953	39
1948	51	1954	36

Source: A. Chabert, *Les Salaires dans l'industrie française: Les charbonnages* (Paris, 1957), 163.

TABLE 12. Cost of Producing Coal v. Sale Price, 1947
(Francs per ton)

	Mar.	June	Sept.	Dec.	Average
Sale Price	1,389	1,364	1,346	1,746	1,461
Cost of Production	1,556	1,715	2,008	2,468	1,937
Balance	−167	−351	−662	−722	−476

Source: Charbonnages de France, *Rapport de gestion, 1948* (Paris, 1949).

proved incompatible with efforts to trim expenses to restrain coal prices. The financial problem facing the coal industry existed mainly because it cost more to produce coal than the government allowed the industry to charge for it.

The "Blum experiment," a 5 percent price cut in January 1947 (followed by another 5 percent price reduction in March), aggravated the problem. By March 1947 the cost of producing coal far exceeded its sale price (see table 12). The Charbonnages de France reported that the price cuts "destroyed the financial equilibrium" of the mines. In November the government raised coal prices in a step toward financial stability, but by the middle of 1948, the cost of producing coal once again outstripped the allowed selling price.[33]

Since the 1930s the mining companies had operated with deficits and had been kept above water by state subsidies. But in the political climate of 1947, the issue sparked a fierce debate. Some critics of the financial operations traced the problem back to a 25 percent wage increase granted to the workers in 1946. At that time the CGT, yielding to pressures within its ranks, reversed its position against wage increases and, anticipating disagreement from the government, made an overture to the national employers' association, the CNPF, for a wage settlement. While the wage hike was justified by the fall in workers' real wages, the Communists and the CNPF wanted the agreement for different reasons. The Communists wanted to show that they had not forgotten the material needs of the workers, especially in view of upcoming elections. For the employers, the agreement was intended to serve as a demonstration of good faith and as a justification for breaking the ceilings on industrial prices.[34]

CGT members of the board of directors of the Charbonnages de France, with President Duguet in the lead, pushed for the wage increase. By a majority of one, the board agreed.[35] Four months later, however, the government appointed a committee to investigate the wage decision of July 1946 and to determine a new sale price for coal. The investigating committee was headed by Étienne Audibert, an engineer who joined the Charbonnages de France in July 1947 and later became its president.[36] It was the first of many studies of the managerial and financial operations in the mines. In January 1947, Blum, Lacoste, and André Philip cosigned a decree that set up a commission to act as a watchdog over the operations in the mines.[37] A law of March 21 provided for parliamentary control and established subcommittees to review the operations of the nationalized and mixed enterprises.[38] Another investigating commission, led by the engineer Wahl, was created by government decree in November 1947.[39] Besides governmental inquests, two other studies of the industry figured in the debate. The first was a report by a Belgian Senate commission on the nationalization of the French mines. While pointing to some advantages, the Belgian report recommended leaving Belgian mines in the hands of the old owners.[40] The second study, Marcel Ventenat's *Les Expériences des nationalisations: Premier bilan*, which appeared in June 1947, was a scathing attack on the nationalizations.

None of the governmental studies were made public. The Belgian report and the Ventenat book, however, were utilized by opponents of nationalization. These reports contained little in the way of specific information. The Belgians drew their conclusions after spending a week in the mining basin talking with administrators. Ventenat, a civil engineer, introduced no new information. He simply compiled selections from parliamentary speeches and meshed them with statements from former owners and engineers. In an angry and one-sided polemic, Ventenat attacked high labor costs, argued against overstaffing, and claimed that the Miners' Statute had been extended to too many workers. He also contended, in what soon became a well-worn cliché, that the Communists had built a bastion of power in the mines in order to launch an insurrection in France.[41] Despite the lack of new information, these reports made an impact inside legislative circles, where many of the assertions raised by critics were assumed to be true.

Lacoste considered the offensive around the financial issue serious enough to warrant a vigorous defense of the nationalization. On May 30, Lacoste joined with Duguet in a press conference that sought to "shed light on a number of facts and problems that have been distorted by hasty and partial inquests." Duguet pointed out that prices of materials and supplies had increased much more rapidly than the price of coal. Lacoste stressed the necessity for modernization in order to increase productivity. "I would warn people against having any illusions," said Lacoste. "The mines cannot be modernized from one day to the next. This effort will require several years and very large imports of special material. And this effort should be supported by the entire country."[42]

One week later, when the Charbonnages de France asked for a subsidy to cover its deficit, an acrimonious debate erupted in the National Assembly. A deputy of the MRP attacked the notion that "the state will pay for everything." He criticized the overlapping of managerial functions and warned of the danger of allowing a key industry to fall into the hands of a political party.[43] René Mayer, speaking for the Radical Socialists, quoted sections from the Belgian report and criticized the "mixing of partisan politics into the life of the enterprises" and a growing "crisis of authority" in the mines. Lacoste again defended the industry. He argued that the high cost of labor was characteristic of coal mining throughout Europe. Individual output, compared to that of 1938, stood at 80 percent in France, 75 percent in Belgium, and 62 percent in Holland. Taking issue with those who claimed that cutting the cost of producing coal should be management's main goal, Lacoste said that France needed a continuation of the battle of production and asked the legislature to have confidence in the miners and their unions. He also pointed to the measures already being taken to correct many of the alleged abuses, including increased state control over financial aspects of the nationalized industries.[44]

Even as he spoke, however, Lacoste knew that the wave of postwar nationalizing had ebbed. By February 1947, *Nord-Industriel* came down squarely against nationalization, claiming it had generated big deficits. *Foreign Affairs* published an article by French economist Charles Rist, who argued that it had burdened the state with serious problems and should be abandoned.[45] Conservative political forces were reasserting themselves in France while the coalition between Socialists and Communists was dissolving rapidly.

Regarding coal policy, the two Left parties had shifted their goals in opposite directions in the two years since the liberation. At that time, the Communists favored centralized state directives from the minister of Mines and the director general while the Socialists argued for decentralization, worker participation, and tripartite boards of directors. But the Communists soon adopted most of the elements of the Socialist plan for nationalizing, especially after the Communists' influence in management began to wane. Meanwhile the Socialists moved to tighten the state's control. In 1947 Maurice Thorez introduced a bill to reform the nationalized industries that called for tripartite councils of workers, consumers, and the state and provided that these councils, rather than state-appointed general directors, would have the basic responsibility for the industry. But the Socialists no longer favored such an arrangement. Lacoste's new formula placed authority in the hands of a strong president and general directors who were named by the government. He also made sure that the state maintained strict financial controls over the nationalized industries.[46] Just as Lecoeur had used state power to enhance working-class representation in the mines, Lacoste utilized his ministerial authority to remove the Communists from leading positions in the mines. His actions were not lost on the mining engineers, many of whom were having second thoughts about their membership in the CGT-affiliated Syndicat National des Ingénieurs des Mines (SNIM).

THE DECLINE OF COMMUNIST INFLUENCE
WITHIN MANAGEMENT

Marcel Paul had named SNIM as the "most representative" union of cadres in 1946, but the organization fell into decline the following year.[47] *Voix du Nord* and *Nord-Industriel* both claimed that the SNIM's rival, the CGC-affiliated Syndicat des Ingénieurs des Houillères du Nord–Pas-de-Calais (SIHN), had displaced SNIM as the largest organization of engineers. The SIHN, formed ten years earlier in Lens, sought to represent the material concerns of engineers while also guarding the authority inherent in their profession. Thus efforts by SNIM to convince SIHN to merge with it went nowhere. For many of these engineers, membership in an organization dominated by the same workers they gave orders to made little sense.[48] In one of the early elections undertaken by mining engineers—to select administrators for the retirement funds in Pas-de-Calais in June 1947—the SIHN received 740 votes and the SNIM received 273.[49]

One did not need to look far for an explanation of the cadres' growing dissatisfaction with SNIM and the Communists. Engineers who had enrolled in SNIM had done so for a variety of reasons. Some gravitated toward the CGT because that union was the largest and most powerful in France. The CGT's Resistance legacy attracted others. It is likely that some engineers joined SNIM in order to deflect the threat of purges or to enhance their prospects for rapid advancement in the mines.[50] During the conflicts surrounding the naming of representatives to the administrative councils, the Socialists had charged that some of the Communist-backed engineers, including Georges, Dumez, Thomas, and others, had joined the Communist party in order to cover dubious Resistance records. Armanet, the SNIM president who was appointed general director of the northern mines, was sometimes accused of being a Communist by his critics. But Armanet was apparently a Socialist or at least he was close to the old confédéré wing of the CGT.[51]

The decline of Communist influence among the mining engineers was revealed in the failure of a Communist-backed reform plan for the northern mines. In February 1947, amid the hoopla surrounding the announcement of the Monnet Plan, Lecoeur, now serving solely as president of the miners' union, proposed a new "technical plan" for the coal mines. A management team would coordinate exploitation of all basin mines and reorganize the methods of payment in order to reduce conflicts between workers and management. The technical team would work shoulder to shoulder with the director of Personnel, Léon Delfosse.[52] The plan aimed to alter the policy of autonomy, which allowed each group of mines a high degree of flexibility in determining production plans. The various mine directors and top engineers considered autonomy necessary because of variations in the strengths of coal seams, different degrees of mechanization, and other factors that made no two mining sites identical. Autonomy meant that head engineers wielded a great deal of authority in the mine for which they were responsible. In turn, the engineers expected a certain degree of independence from central management. The directors and head engineers opposed the technical plan because it would reduce their authority and independence. But according to the CGT Federation of Miners, "autonomy amounts to irresponsibility, risks causing a serious crisis of authority at all levels, and produces an anarchic situation in the mines."[53]

The Communists hoped to win support for the technical plan from SNIM, but the results at the organization's second national convention showed that the Communists had become a minority force inside the union. Not only did SNIM delegates reject the plan, which they considered too centralized, but they also passed a resolution that affirmed the group's independence from political parties.[54] Moreover, of the eight officers elected at the SNIM convention, at least five represented the non-Communist tendency within the CGT. In the mines of Nord, the cadres opposed the plan and viewed it as an attempt to further subjugate them to the federation under the guise of greater efficiency.[55]

After the plan was rejected by SNIM, the leaders of the federation tried to convince the administrative council of the northern mines to adopt it, but to no avail.[56] The technical plan was opposed by Armanet, himself a CGT leader and the general director of the mines. Tabled for a month, the plan was finally defeated in April by a vote of ten to seven. The debate inside the council revealed the erosion of Communist influence among non-Communist unionists. SNIM representatives Armanet and Trégieur voted against the plan, prompting the Federation of Miners to criticize Armanet for the first time publicly and to demand Trégieur's removal as a labor representative.[57]

The Communists next attempted to rally the cadres to the technical plan by organizing a meeting under the auspices of the National Union of Engineers, Technicians, and Cadres (UNITEC). The Communists had built this organization as a Resistance grouping during the war, but it had remained virtually dormant for more than two years. Two engineers, Georges and Dumez, proposed the creation of "mixed production committees extending up to the summit in the hierarchy of the mines."[58] But the meeting was a failure because so few engineers attended. A week before the meeting, Armanet had recommended that management personnel not attend the UNITEC meeting.

The failure of the technical plan was a measurement of the decreasing ability of the Communists to shape policies in the mines. In 1946 Paul and Lecoeur wielded the authority of the state to promote higher production by replacing old-line managers with worker representatives. Out of office in 1947, and deprived of their ability to use the state's power, the Communists next attempted to direct policy through the regional administrative council. But they never held a majority in that body. Under these circumstances, Jean Armanet occupied a pivotal role because he worked closely with the head engineers of each mine. But Armanet gradually fell out with the Communists, and they found it necessary to strike out against the head engineers and Armanet himself. Two years earlier, CGT leaders had called off the purge commissions and welcomed the engineers with open arms into the CGT's SNIM. In 1947, stung by the failure of the technical plan, they unearthed the old theme of "insufficient purges."

The Communists may have had another reason to back the technical plan. In the spring of 1947 the "crisis of authority," conflicts between miners and managers, began to reemerge. Disputes over the setting of piece rates fueled much of the tension. A report to the administrative council of the mines indicated that the miners could not understand the complicated system of determining task rates. They viewed the system as arbitrary and capricious. In cases where the rate was set too high, the miners often tended to work up to the rate but hesitated to produce more coal for fear that the rate would be reevaluated and scaled downward. Where the rate was set too low, many tended to work as little as possible, knowing that they would gain the minimum wage and hoping that the task would be revised upward.[59] The Miners' Statute was supposed to prevent these problems, but the language of the statute could not cover every situation, leaving a certain amount of ambiguity in the rules governing the setting of piece rates. Engineers set the rates and informed the workers. If the workers had a problem, they could report it to the union steward, who could bring it to management's attention. Parity commissions set up to resolve disputes existed at the local, regional, and national levels.[60] Employee representatives made up one-half of the members of the parity commissions, but representative of the engineers and foremen sat on the employee side (rather than on the side of management). This meant that a situation could arise where the person whose ruling the worker was disputing was represented on the workers' side of the parity commission. If workers avoided the parity commissions on wage rate disputes, however, that increased their intentions of trying to win their point of view at the point of production. This created sharp conflicts in the mines, making management's job more difficult and contributing to rising absenteeism among management personnel.[61]

The technical plan could also be seen as a last-ditch effort to restore the miners' confidence in nationalization and the battle of production. The March issue of *Mineurs* supported the plan by arguing for more participation by the workers. The pit committees (no longer referred to as production committees) were now viewed as key organisms. The miners were urged to take the initiative to organize large meetings in the mines and to induce management to come. As the writer in *Mineurs* expressed it, "You should call a meeting in the mine, which should be enlarged to include management and technicians, the head foreman, and other foremen. This will, of course, involve many people, but after all, doesn't everyone have a role to play in reaching our objectives?"[62] The pit committees would assume a new role in relation to the engineer, "watching over him, clearing away all impediments, and guaranteeing the best organization of labor."

But mining engineers had little interest in attending large meetings initiated by the miners to discuss the best ways to produce coal in "their" mines. The technical plan sought to rejuvenate the pit committees, but it was too late. Two years earlier the union had agreed to turn the pit committees into production committees and to reduce their size to include only one or two mine workers. In January 1947, Lacoste had further reduced the role of workers in the production committees. There is little indication that mine workers rallied to the technical plan in the spring of 1947.

When the mine workers struck in June and July 1947, the engineers continued to work. Rejected by the leadership of SNIM, the Communist elements regrouped in UNITEC. Socialist members, including several of SNIM's former leaders, joined forces with the anti-Communist faction called Force Ouvrière (FO). Others joined SIHN. The CGT's experiment with SNIM had succeeded initially because of the willingness of many cadres to break with much of their professional and ideological training and join a union for the first time. Also, the Communists had shelved traditional criticisms of management personnel in exchange for labor-management collaboration in the battle of production. But SNIM was doomed when collaboration between workers and management broke down and the cold war began to split the world into two warring camps. The organization collapsed when the engineers found themselves hopelessly divided along pro-Communist and anti-Communist lines. Given the social background of the engineers and their position as managers in the mines, it was perhaps not surprising that they refused to follow the CGT after 1947. But the Communists also faced a challenge from within the ranks of the mine workers' union.

OPPOSITION WITHIN THE CGT: FORCE OUVRIÈRE

Opposition to the Communists developed slowly within the CGT Federation of Miners. A sense of hesitancy on the part of the oppositional forces stemmed from several factors. First, many key oppositionists were Socialists, and their strategy was often conditioned by Socialist policies at the national level. In Nord, the Socialist party was led by Auguste Laurent. It tended to closely follow the national stance of the party. In Pas-de-Calais, however, the influence of coal mining was more important than in the economically diversified Nord. Given the depth of Communist implantation in the mining areas, many Pas-de-Calais Socialists favored closer unity of action with the Communists. Indeed, Pas-de-Calais became a center of leftist socialism as its leader, Guy Mollet, sought to retain the party's Marxist ideology and turn it more resolutely toward industrial workers. At the same time, the towns of Lens and Liévin were old Socialist strongholds and a non-Communist confédéré tradition was also centered there. In Nord the Socialist leadership followed the party's national office in opposing unity of action with the Communists.[63]

The growth of Communist strength in the region made it harder for the Socialist party and its oppositionists in the CGT to formulate a clear-cut strategy. Part of the opposition favored unity of action with the PCF unionists, while another group sought to distance themselves from the Communists. The opposition faced a dilemma. Should it remain a loyal but not totally silent minority within the union in hopes of gradually increasing its influence among the workers and displacing the Communist leadership? Or should it organize itself into a faction and openly challenge the Communists for control of the union—even if it meant leaving the CGT if they lost? Non-Communist labor leaders who had retained their posts within the apparatus of the CGT Federation of Miners—Sinot, Morel, Lampin, and others—favored the unity approach. The most vocal proponents of a sharp break with the Communists were often former union delegates who had lost their positions in December 1944. These individuals fought a lonely and difficult battle in 1945 and 1946, spreading their ideas in *L'Espoir*, the Socialist weekly of Lens, and in the weekly journal of their political persuasion, *Force ouvrière*.

The unity approach seemed preferable to many Socialist militants, but the opposition's attempts to regain power by working within the existing union structures bore few positive results. Those who had lost their posts in 1944 were unsuccessful in seeking reinstatement at the next convention in 1946.[64] The opposition fared no better at the national level in April 1946, leading *Nord-Matin* to criticize the "totalitarian unanimity in the CGT" and to support the notion of building a movement for "independent unionism."[65] The summer and fall of 1946 brought little consolation to the Socialist unionists in Pas-de-Calais. In June *L'Espoir* warned party members that the Communists were approaching rank-and-file Socialists in attempts to form groups called "Friends of the French Workers Party." One month later, the Pas-de-Calais Socialists felt the sting of defection in their ranks when a section of the Young Socialists, which had fallen under the sway of Trotskyist activists, decided to leave the Socialist party. Election results in November 1946 offered no comfort. During the campaign, party leaders voiced some of the sharpest criticisms of the Communists that had been heard since the war. Yet the number of votes garnered by the Socialists dropped precipitously, leading *L'Espoir* and *Nord-Matin* to consider the elections "a grave setback."[66]

Inside the CGT, union oppositionists found it difficult to operate through normal union channels, which were often dominated by the Communists. In February 1946, *Force ouvrière* claimed that reports of the regional CGT executive board were never printed up and sent out to the unions. In April 1946, the union leadership proposed a plan to change the current system from one in which unions were organized at the regional level to one in which they were organized by groups of mines. When implemented, the decentralized system had the effect of strengthening the Communist hold on the union. Meanwhile the opposition blamed Communist control of the union newspaper, *La Tribune des mineurs*, for the fact that speeches of Socialist leaders were routinely ignored.[67]

Unable to make its influence felt within the union apparatus, the opposition created a faction within the union, making its criticisms more widely known and openly challenging the Communist leadership. It was the rank-and-file militants, as opposed to the non-Communist union officials, who took the first step toward becoming an organized opposition when a handful founded a group, Friends of Force Ouvrière, in September 1946.[68] For the first time since the liberation, the oppositionists began to raise publicly their differences with the Communists. E. Mériaux, the FO organizer in the north, explained that while the opposition was willing to admit to the seriousness of the coal shortage, they opposed the Communists' using the same tactics of the old companies to promote production, such as the Bedaux system, individual pay, and stakhanovism in the mines. "Today all the miners see that the old methods are being put into effect," wrote Meriaux. "But while we know that the majority of the workers oppose these methods, it is very difficult to know what to do about it without being called 'saboteurs of the French recovery.'"[69]

Although Friends of FO was formed in September 1946, actual FO groups did not surface until February and March 1947, and then in Lens and Liévin, old Socialist strongholds.[70] Gradually, the oppositionists organized groupings across the mining basin. A small FO group was formed in Douai. Various delegates and union stewards openly came out as FO activists in Courrières, Vermelles, and Ledoux. FO organizer Mériaux visited the mining towns, urging miners who had left the CGT to retake their union cards only after joining FO.[71] By the end of March 1947, FO members preparing for upcoming union elections added the secret vote to their list of demands. They sharpened their criticisms of Communist shop stewards and threatened to run on independent slates if they could not win the union's official endorsement.

The FO militants drew encouragement from the rapidly changing political situation. The dropping of Marcel Paul and Auguste Lecoeur and the actions taken by Lacoste to limit the influence of the Communists fed their enthusiasm. The all-Socialist temporary government and the Blum price cut in January 1947 seemed to indicate a new Socialist activism, leading a zealous writer in *l'Espoir* to describe the new government as "a workers' government of the extreme Left."[72] For FO unionists in the CGT Federation of Miners, the Communist reversal in the union of mining engineers seemed a portent of things to come. Ironically, the oppositionists began to push for continued high output at the same time the Communists were making a slow retreat from the battle of production. In December 1946, FO activists had considered the Communist exhortations to work hard an insult: "Safety issues and not production should be in the front rank of the miners' demands." But in January 1947 an FO member wrote: "The old slogan 'produce' launched by our union and by Lecoeur, Paul, and Croizat now begins to make sense."[73]

Non-Communist leaders of the Federation of Miners, seeking to avoid confrontation with the Communists, urged caution. Spinetta, writing in *Force ouvrière* in January on the subject of nationalization, urged the mine workers to "avoid a partisan spirit." A *Force ouvrière* report on the CGT Federation of Miners' convention noted the conciliatory attitude on the part of the Communists. The report expressed a sense of hope and caution:

> A completely different atmosphere pervaded the meeting, in contrast to those of the past two years. Duguet criticized the various factions but added that there would always be different currents within the union movement. He urged the miners not to taunt the minority and to give them representation equal to that of their strength. We feel the struggle that we have led for the past six months has not been in vain and that something has changed. We will soon see how this policy will be interpreted in the unions. Will we see a bit more understanding on the part of the majority?[74]

But speeches at a convention were one thing. The relationship between the two factions was much less amicable in the coal mines where FO began to organize. The FO oppositionists decided to try to place their comrades on the slates put forward by the union for the elections for delegate positions. In Loos-en-Gohelle the FO group boasted that a Communist delegate who had supported individual payment was forced to change his view in order to retain his post in the upcoming election. At a union meeting on March 30, FO activists peppered a Communist union steward with questions he could not answer and boasted that he would soon lose his post. The elections for safety delegate posts at the FO strongholds in Lens resulted in arguments over voting procedures and the final election tallies. In new elections held a month later in March, FO claimed the union had endorsed 13 of its 19 candidates.[75]

Ironically, the apparent victors in the April elections for representatives to the social security offices were neither the Communists nor the FO oppositionists. Instead the CFTC received roughly 30 percent of the vote, a remarkable feat considering that the group involved less than 10 percent of the mine workers. It seems likely that many workers voted for the CFTC to protest the internal struggle that was dividing their union. Sinot, writing in *Force ouvrière* in May criticized the "division in the union and sectarianism of some union leaders."[76] A few weeks later, Sinot (who was not a Communist) attributed the CFTC success to the fact that some CGT members "who don't understand the situation and act like fools" either voted for the CFTC or abstained. He criticized some members of the opposition—"those who, because they are in the minority, talk about 'parity' and 'separate slates.' There should not be rigid tendencies and factions in the union but rather different views that lead to the same goal."[77] At a meeting of the top leaders of the CGT Federation of Miners in June, Sinot introduced a "unity resolution" aimed at preventing separate lists for upcoming union delegate elections. Although the majority rejected his resolution, they agreed to a compromise that, in Sinot's opinion, was "less precise, but close to the same thing."[78] Hoping to avoid splits at the local level, the leadership instructed the miners to "establish single lists which satisfy all the workers regardless of political, philosophical, or religious convictions."

But instructions from the front office could not alleviate division within the union. In most areas, the two groups were unable to produce a single slate of candidates, so the two factions ran head-to-head. FO made some progress in Lens. A candidate who ran on the "independent unionism" slate narrowly defeated a delegate endorsed by the CGT leadership. An FO candidate for a full-time steward post placed second. Another candidate in Lens lost by only five votes. At Valenciennes and Mauberg, independent unionism slates opposed the official CGT candidates. In the other mining groups only one single list was obtained. In Nord, union meetings frequently degenerated into shouting matches, with the opposition demanding secret ballots and the Communists upholding the old tradition of raised hands. In May 1947, the FO group in Nord demanded "parity at all echelons" and threatened to run on separate slates. By the end of June 1947, FO in the northern mines decided to campaign on a separate slate, explaining: "Under these conditions, the only thing we could do was to run separate FO slates. We are not to blame for this, and besides, the union movement will benefit from a bit more clarity." In some cases, when leaders of the CGT asked FO members to run on the union-endorsed slate, they declined, refusing to become "hostages of the Communists."[79]

In the election for union delegate positions held on 8 July 1947, the CGT-endorsed slate won 73 percent of the vote, the CFTC captured 16 percent, and the "independent unionists" received 11 percent. Communist leaders heightened their criticism of the opposition. Soon the gap that had separated unionists who favored trying to work with the Communists and those oppositionists who had openly broken with them began to narrow. Thus when the leadership of the CGT union passed a resolution condemning the "splitters," three non-Communist leaders dissented: Maillet of Lens, Dubruq of Bruay, and Lampin.[80]

While both wings in the CGT national office sought to hold the Federation of Miners together, the rapidly evolving political situation and the growing restiveness of the miners pulled in opposite directions and toward a split. The strikes that erupted during the last week in June 1947 were largely spontaneous actions, partly caused by a shortage of decent bread. Neither the Communists nor the opposition promoted these strikes. The Communists said the strikes were inopportune but added that it was understandable that the miners would want to strike. The Socialists warned the miners to beware of Communist-led strike movements that would sabotage the reconstruction effort. Sinot claimed that the strikes were caused because an agreement that had been forged between both wings of the union and Robert Lacoste had been scuttled by the cabinet.[81] Despite efforts to end the strike by the union, a week after the order to return to work had been sounded, many miners continued to stay out of the mines.

Sporadic work stoppages erupted in August and September of 1947. The miners displayed a willingness to strike with or without the union's endorsement. Communist union activists, always uncomfortable with the strike ban, decided to roll with the growing trend. The oppositionists, former champions of the right to strike, sometimes succumbed to the restive mood of the workers, but they did so cautiously, fearing that soon they would be forced to come down squarely against Communist-backed strikes.

The heightened tension between FO and the Communists put an end to the tenuous coalition between the two labor factions. Yet the oppositionists hesitated to leave the CGT, labor's "old house," for fear of cutting themselves off from the mass of union members. Meanwhile, Communist union leaders were left wondering if they would be able to retain the loyalty of rank-and-file workers. Lacking further support from the state and facing a loss of influence in management, union leaders concluded that traditional forms of worker militancy, including strikes, would be needed if the union wanted to preserve the important gains that had been won in the first two years following the liberation.

THE STRIKE OF NOVEMBER 1947

On Friday, 14 November 1947, Léon Delfosse was dismissed as vice president of the Houillères du Nord–Pas-de-Calais. His firing triggered a walkout in the mines that was accompanied by strikes by metalworkers in Paris and Marseille. For the first time since the liberation, the CGT leaders gave their blessing to national strike action.

Virtually all discussions of postwar France refer to "les grandes grèves" of 1947 and 1948 as important events.[82] However, most accounts are very brief and rely on a small number of sources. In 1950 Georges Lefranc, a former staff member in the CGT national office in the 1930s, provided an early description of the 1947 strikes, but his contribution was really a discussion about why the Force Ouvrière oppositionists, with whom Lefranc sympathized, broke away from the CGT. Other early writings on the 1947 strikes viewed them primarily as products of the cold war. Likewise, newspaper reporters for Paris-based dailies as well as government leaders and politicians conveyed the impression that the strikes were subsidiary sideshows to the dramatic international events of 1947. A few writers suggested an economic factor behind the strikes, but this aspect was downplayed. Very few reporters or early researchers interviewed union leaders or rank-and-file strikers to find out why they walked off the job. The dramatic speeches in parliament made it into the written record, but the voices of the miners were usually absent from discussions of the "big strikes."

Despite some minor variations, the rough consensus among non-Communist writers is that the walkouts were political actions orchestrated by the Communist party, if not by the Kremlin itself. The most common explanations of PCF goals included one or more of the following: forcing the Communist ministers back into the cabinet, bringing down the government, derailing the Marshall Plan in France, preparing for a seizure of power. The strike was regarded as a failure because the workers' demands were not met and because the controversy surrounding the strike caused a serious split in the CGT.

American and French officials claimed that the Communists were planning an insurrection. But no real evidence was ever produced to substantiate such charges, although they were widely believed to be true by much of the public. Doubtless non-Communist leaders had the most to gain by cultivating the rumor that a Communist takeover was being prepared. But they also must have been aware that no evidence showed such a plot was imminent. The Communist interpretation has its own short-comings. Most of their leaders argued that the strikes were mainly economic, defensive actions, as if the PCF had no real political objectives. In fact, the political motives of the PCF were never fully revealed, and thus the connection between the strike and the party's goals could only be guessed at. Further, most of the standard discussions of the strikes are marked by an inability to conceptualize the role of the CGT, not simply as an arm of the Communist party, but as the main organization representing the economic interests of the workers.

The 1947 strikes are best understood by examining their evolution at the local level, disentangling the workers' motives from the political objectives of the PCF, and locating the strikes within a larger historical context. Within this framework, a different picture emerges. Initiated from below rather than from above, the strikes drew upon a broad-based desire to "do something" to make the economy respond to the drastic fall in real wages. Attempts to "politicize" the strikes from above (for example, by criticizing the Marshall Plan in the union newspaper) did not seem to motivate workers. But the strikes were political by necessity since decisions on wages and working conditions required governmental approval. By striking, the miners sought to change the government's policy. Halting work was a political action even if union leaders were reluctant to label the strike as political. Only if we consider the strikes in their historical context can we understand that workers were attempting to defend the advances that had been made. The miners were deeply concerned that nationalization, the Miners' Statute, union control over the social security funds, the cooperatives, the canteens, and other worker advances were in jeopardy and could be withdrawn unless workers stood up for their rights.[83] With the exception of sporadic wildcat strikes or brief "warning" strikes, the unions had refrained from leading a national strike for more than three years. The image of workers being unwittingly marched into class war by Stalin made good press copy, but it failed to reflect the reality that, for many workers, the union's willingness to take action seemed long overdue.

From the workers' perspective, the government was blocking the way to progress on the economic front and breaking promises that had been made. The dismissal of union representatives from key positions in the nationalized industries continued. In March 1947, Léon Delfosse and other CGT representatives were removed from the administrative council of Électricité de France–Gaz de France, where they had served as representatives of consumers. Although leftist groups generated strikes at Renault and other workplaces across the country in April and May that were strong enough to push the CGT into taking leadership of various

TABLE 13. Worker-Days Lost to Strikes, 1947
(In thousands)

Jan.	67	Apr.	96	July	283	Oct.	313
Feb.	63	May	508	Aug.	24	Nov.	7,546
Mar.	27	June	6,104	Sept.	361	Dec.	6,967

Source: INSEE, *Mouvement économique en France de 1938 à 1948*, 314.

strikes, the union's objective always was to end them. During those same turbulent months, the miners' union kept the lid on strikes in the northern mining basin. In June a special meeting of the miners' union called for a renewed struggle to upgrade the mining profession and raise wages. When negotiations died, a brief warning strike brought out nearly 150,000 mine workers (out of a total of about 190,000) in the northern basin. Other brief strikes occurred in June across the country in a spontaneous and uncoordinated fashion. The number of worker-days lost to strikes grew from 27 in March to 6,104 in June (see table 13). Between May 15 and July 11 *L'Humanité* continued to talk about the "battle of production" and highlighted Maurice Thorez's famous quote regarding the Popular Front strikes: "We must know how to end a strike." The CGT backed wage settlements in railroads, electricity, banks, and department stores. When public employees made their wage demands, PCF leader Jacques Duclos suggested that they accept the government's offer.[84]

The leader of the electrical workers' union, Marcel Paul, called for mediation to settle wage issues. In July, the CGT began talks with the employers' organization, the Conseil Nationale du Patronat Français (CNPF), aimed at settling wage issues for private sector workers. In August both parties reached agreement on an 11 percent wage hike, but this did not extend to the large public sector and was, in any case, quickly lost to rising inflation.[85] In October metro workers in Paris launched a work stoppage without the support of the CGT. The government decided to negotiate with the so-called autonomous unions (most important, FO), and a settlement provided for a limited-term bonus to help wages catch up with inflation. CGT leaders then called for the catch-up to be extended to other workers until national wage negotiations could begin in December. In the mines, railroads, electricity and gas, and other state-owned industries, wage settlements required approval by the Ministry of Industrial Production, with the Ministry of Finance holding a veto power.[86] Thus, no wage agreement, even a temporary action, could take place without the government's support. But the government, which now referred to itself as the "Third Force" government (located between the twin evils of Communism and resurgent Gaullism), showed a greatly diminished interest in negotiating with the CGT. Instead, government officials began bypassing the CGT and holding meetings with splinter groups. These problems in labor relations were not widely noted in the media. The attention of the public and the government was fixed mostly on the big international events that were unfolding as the cold war deepened, the Truman Doctrine and the Marshall Plan were adopted, and the Cominform was created.

But in the mines, the big news in October was the promulgation of a rule that allowed management to suspend pay formulas established by the Miners' Statute to workers who had committed an error or made a mistake. The miners protested and accused management of wanting to return to the old days.[87] Then a conflict over the raising of the sale price of coal resulted in the resignation of Victor Duguet as president of the Charbonnages de France. On November 6, Jules Moch, the Socialist minister of National Economy, announced a new coal price. The government allowed the sale price to rise by 60 percent from 1,350 francs to 2,160 francs but also repealed its decision in September to provide the industry with a subsidy. Moch indicated that the industry would be required to use such price increases to finance much of the cost of rebuilding the industry. Moch described his action as purely a simple measure of circumstance, but to the miners it indicated a return to the old and outmoded principles of economic liberalism. Duguet and other union leaders argued that raising the price of coal stoked the fires of inflation. Further, the government's action underscored an important shift in government policy: the cost of rebuilding the coal industry would no longer be born by the entire nation, but rather by those who bought coal or worked in the industry.[88] An angry Duguet called a special meeting of the administrative council of the Charbonnages de France on November 11. But he was unable to obtain a majority to protest Moch's action. The following day Duguet resigned, charging Lacoste with purging CGT members from representative posts in the nationalized industries. Proving that Duguet was right, Lacoste fired Delfosse a few days later and the strike erupted. "By firing Delfosse," said *Franc-Tireur*, "the government has set a match to a powder keg."[89]

Were the strikes political? Socialist leaders certainly believed they were. *Le Populaire* warned workers to "beware of a political strike." *Nord-Matin* echoed the same theme: "The Communists want to involve the northern miners in a political strike." Jean Lechantre wrote that "in the eyes of the Stalinists, the CGT is merely a political instrument."[90] Camille Delabre wrote bitterly, "When they were in the government, the Communists used to say that the strike was the arm of the fascists. Today the situation is changed. Any excuse is sufficient to launch the working class in a strike movement which will lead the country to ruin." Georges Procurer urged the miners to "denounce those who unleash strikes in order to satisfy their own dirty political ambitions." Abel Poulain called the strike "an attack against the nation."[91] No one knew how long the strikes would continue, but many government insiders and commentators were quick to suggest that the groundwork was being laid for a Communist takeover. The French press was described by Alexander Werth as being in "a state of incoherent emotional excitement." France seemed to be suspended dangerously while the world was splitting into two hostile camps. President Auriol's intelligence operatives described the coal strike in the north as "total" and warned of potentially ominous job actions in other mining areas.[92]

Labor representatives claimed the strike was basically economic. In the mines, union leaders called together the workers to formulate their demands, which can be summarized as follows:

- Raise the minimum wage.
- Institute immediate "catch-up" bonuses.
- Institute cost-of-living increase based on most recent three months.
- Rehire Delfosse as Charbonnages de France administrator.
- Compensate for silicosis at same rate as for job-related accidents.
- Compensate half the cost of domestic coal and travel to work.
- Set up the Comités des Entreprises.
- Adjust the piecework system to accommodate overtime and bonuses.

In addition to these demands, which were raised by the national miners' union, the CGT in Nord–Pas-de-Calais added these demands:

- Provide use of the mines facilities for union meetings.
- Distribute kindling wood in bunches of 20 at 20 centimeters' length.
- Speed up the implementation of the housing plan.
- Provide weekly meetings with union leaders at the group level.[93]

Of these twelve demands, six were clearly economic in nature. Two involved health and housing. The government had already approved legislation for the Comités des Entreprises; they simply needed to be implemented. Using the building of the mines for union meetings was not a surprising request considering that many miners did not live in the same area where they worked. Asking for weekly meetings with management at the group might have been a constructive suggestion. The closest the miners came to making a political demand was the call to rehire Delfosse, the workers' representative in management.

Nevertheless, it was not possible to build a wall between economic demands and political motives. "Since 1947 the CGT has launched strikes which were both professional and of a political character," wrote Goetz-Girey. "The two terms are not contradictory. The strike is launched generally to help promote wage demands or in order to improve working conditions, but it is placed in a context such that it has as its goal the exerting of pressure upon a government or public opinion."[94] The strikes were political because the only way to raise wages was to force a change in governmental policy. Attempts to negotiate had failed, and by the end of November the generalized strike wave had swept through key industries and services such as metals, automobile manufacturing, the railroads, the docks, and the Paris metro. Even if the demands were not specifically political, they were raised in an atmosphere that was highly charged in political terms. *Combat*, an influential daily newspaper of the moderate Left, saw the strikes as "very much like an attempt to strangle the economic life of the country."[95]

Auriol and other governmental leaders received a steady stream of information about Communist plans, supposedly leaked from high-ranking informants in the PCF. A report on November 20 claimed that the Communists, on orders from the Cominform, sought to discourage the United States from giving aid to France. The Communists intended to continue the coal strike and to shut down the metals industry. They would use shock troops to take over the communications, railroads, highways, radio, the postal service, and other services.[96]

Yet close observers of these events knew that there was more to the strike than signals from the Kremlin. "International Communist strategy does not of itself create strike potentialities," wrote Val Lorwin. "The strikes were made possible by the increasing discontent of the workers during the summer and fall of 1947. This discontent was not something the Communists called into being. When they went into the opposition, they simply released a powerful brake."[97] Without the economic crisis, it is doubtful that any number of directives from Moscow or anywhere else would have brought the miners off the job. But the workers' purchasing power was going in the wrong direction even though three years had passed since the liberation (see table 14). Lacking a cost-of-living provision, and unable to negotiate the wage issue, the miners' only recourse

TABLE 14. Buying Power of French Mine Workers, 1938–1948
(Underground and surface, 1938 = 100)

1938	100	1944	77
1939	98	1945	106
1940	80	1946	97
1941	74	1947	85
1942	77	1948	85
1943	70		

Source: INSEE, *Mouvement économique en France de 1938 à 1948*, 278, 317.

was to convince the government to forge a new wage agreement. As the strike spread, Lacoste argued inside the cabinet for a global settlement on wages. If this was not done, he stated, "the workers will offer great resistance to the government and it will be difficult to prevent strikes." Citing the "sentiment of workers' solidarity and blind obedience to the union," Lacoste warned: "If we don't do something starting today, we will have a generalized strike that will be impossible to break by force and will touch off a civil war."[98]

THE SPLIT IN THE CGT

Very few miners worked during the first week of the strike. At the FO stronghold at Liévin, 200 miners showed up for work, while 360 stayed away from the mines. A few miners worked in the Courrières mines and at Oignies. In the surface installations, most of the workers were off the job. In the 18 mines of the Douai group, the strike was total, with 22,500 workers off the job. Only in Valenciennes could the local authorities report a light return to work. Out of 7,600 miners, including POWs, 1,100 workers reported to the mines. One-third of the surface workers came to work.[99]

Hoping to end the action, the FO group in the CGT Federation of Miners drew up a resolution opposing the strike for the national committee meeting of the union on November 19 and 20. They also published a statement against the strike in the weekly edition of *Force ouvrière*. Several leaders of the CGT federation in Nord and Pas-de-Calais signed the statement, but the resolution was easily defeated by the majority of delegates. The strike was already spreading to the coal mines across France, and workers in other occupations were walking off the job. Rebuffed at the national meeting, the FO group from Pas-de-Calais called upon the workers to avoid "the developing agitation in the mines. We urge the workers, conscious of the need for union power and unity, to refrain from any agitation that compromises the national production and national independence." Veteran FO leader Maillet gloomily predicted: "If the CGT favors a total strike, it will signal the end of worker unity in the mining basin." [100]

FO activists tried to stem the tide from below, but with only limited results. Understanding that many miners who had little interest in striking nevertheless hesitated to express these views openly in large meetings, FO called for secret ballots. The group also criticized the Communists for launching strikes by "artificial" means, as when they locked up the lamproom, preventing workers from going underground, or when union stewards called the workers off the job. [101] The Communists usually opposed secret ballots, although such votes took place in some areas. Decisions to strike were made by raised hands at emergency meetings called by local union leaders or on instructions from union stewards that were passed along, pit by pit. This decentralized method made it nearly impossible for the opposition to derail the strike action. FO activists who were leaders in the CGT federation were bypassed in day-to-day matters once the strike began. But their leadership positions prevented them from breaking with the union and joining their comrades who opposed the strikes. Top FO leaders like Sinot and Lampin complained of being held hostage inside the CGT apparatus. Indeed, the Communist majority had no interest in expelling the FO activists. Three days before the end of the strike, *La Tribune des mineurs* published a communiqué, written earlier and signed by several FO leaders, that condemned strikebreaking. Recognizing the Communist tactic, Claude Bourdet wrote: "The FO is already organized, but the Communists in the CGT do not want to expel them and then be blamed for being splitters." [102]

FO and CFTC leaders made some brave attempts to rally the miners to return to work, but the results were disappointing. In pit number one of Liévin, the FO led a group of miners to the picket line and demanded a vote. At 10:00 A.M. the picket captains agreed; 317 voted to strike and 194 voted to return to work. But FO argued that 300 workers were still on the job when the vote was taken. The next day, FO led a crowd of 200 miners to work. They swept past the picket lines and descended into the mines. However, after one day, the miners stopped working, some claiming that they feared reprisals from strikers. [103]

During the second week, the union vowed to continue the strike and the government threatened to use police forces to guarantee the "right to work" in the mines. Seeking to stimulate support, the Federation of Miners organized a series of large demonstrations in the mining towns. But the unity that had marked the first week began to break down. FO took the lead in demanding a legitimate strike vote with secret ballots. "The situation is always the same," said one FO member. "Either the leaders draw up a list of demands and the miners vote with raised hands, or the union leaders simply call the strike themselves." [104]

Participation in picketing dropped off, but few miners returned to the job. One writer noted, "The situation is worse in Nord and Pas-de-Calais, where the workers will no longer cross picket lines. After working a day, they changed their minds and won't return. They say they don't want to work because they don't want to provoke an incident." [105] Crossing picket lines made most miners uncomfortable. Reports of reprisals involved name-calling, broken windows, and arguments between strikers and nonstrikers. Most miners avoided the work site and the picket line. They simply stayed home. Toward the end of the second week, picket lines were staffed mostly by Communist militants, often accompanied by their wives.

After waiting for nearly two weeks, the government finally proposed a bonus of 1,500 francs. However, striking miners would not be eligible. This obvious attempt to split strikers from nonstrikers proved a failure. CGT leaders pointed out that in its rush to punish the Communists, the government was attacking all miners who had struck. Far from splitting the workers from the Communists, the government's action seemed to leave the miners no choice but to continue the strike. Also, the government's meager economic concessions made it impossible for the reformist FO elements to pose as the real defenders of the workers' interests. Instead, they were left in the awkward position of defending the small minority of workers who had been willing to cross picket lines.

With negotiations stalled, Jules Moch ordered police and troops from the Compagnies Républicaines de Securité (CRS) to intervene on the picket lines to guarantee the "right to work." Strike leaders commandeered the large trucks that were parked in the Houillères truck yards and used them to mobilize "flying squads" of strikers to sites where the picket lines were under attack from the forces of order. In some cases, the strikers set up roadblocks and checkpoints in the roads of the mining basin. Sirens, which had been used during the war to warn of air attacks and later to announce strikes during the liberation, were utilized to rally strikers to picket sites that were no longer secure.

During the third week of strike, the mining region became a battleground. In Liévin nearly 400 miners, led by FO leaders, came to work but were driven away by rock-throwing picketers. At the central workshops at Oignies, nonstrikers physically dispersed the picketers and reoccupied the works. But in pit number five nonstrikers were injured when they attempted to dislodge strikers from their entrance to the mine. At

Bussy-Grenay, between Lens and Béthune, a few hundred miners went to work in two pits. But when they ascended, they were surrounded by a thousand strikers who had been waiting at the pithead. Shots were allegedly fired and some people were arrested in scuffles. A group of 50 CRS troops tried to restore order, but they were repulsed. Tear gas was used in an effort to disperse the crowd. But truckloads of reinforcements kept arriving. Within an hour nearly 3,000 strikers were on the scene. At Dénain, 2,500 demonstrators forced the CRS to withdraw and then reoccupied the pits. In the mines of Anzin, a few thousand troops, backed up by sixteen machine guns, dispersed the picket lines and occupied the Agache pit. In Bully, two CRS troops were kidnapped by the strikers. In these attempts to retake the mines held by police, Henri Martel and two other CGT militants were badly beaten by the police. When the mayor of Sans-en-Gohelle tried to lead 200 miners back to work, he was roughed up by the strikers. Police arrived but were surrounded by a crowd. The fight was a standoff.[106]

Maurice Thorez returned to the mining basin on December 4, Saint Barbé day, a traditional miners' holiday. The visit by the Communist leader contrasted dramatically with his previous excursion to the mining region. In 1945 Thorez the government official had shocked the mine workers with his undiluted call for production at a meeting at Waziers. Now he came to deliver what some unionists called the "anti-Waziers" speech. Thorez spoke to a crowd numbering nearly 20,000. Despite the cold weather, the rally was held outside and was preceded by a long march through the narrow streets of the mining towns. Thorez had spoken in a controlled atmosphere in the hall at Waziers, but now he addressed the crowd from a low stage, closely ringed by dozens of union officials and striking militants. Thorez saved his most bitter attacks for the Socialists. Léon Blum and Guy Mollet were raked across the coals. Auguste Laurent, the Socialist leader who edited *Nord-Matin*, was described as a "scab" for opposing the strike. Thorez attacked the Socialists en bloc: "Socialists of the Right and Socialists of the Left are all against unity and are all together in their long-standing hatred of the Soviet Union." Thorez's speech was remarkable for its reckless, almost adventurous, tone: "The choice is either combat or death; the death of the workers' movement, and the death of France as a free and independent nation." Roger Pannequin, a militant CGT member, was shocked by the speech. He viewed it as a declaration of war against the Socialists, an unrealistic and sectarian political strategy.[107]

In the fourth week, what had begun as a work stoppage turned into a series of military maneuvers. After a train was derailed on the Paris-Lille route on December 3, killing seventeen, the Communists were widely accused of sabotage. The CGT condemned the action and the Communists blamed right-wing provocateurs. An inquiry by Roger Pannequin concluded that the train had probably been derailed by the government or by railroad officials. Lecoeur, however, believed that local militants, acting without the permission of the leadership, had taken the action because they thought that CRS troops were aboard. Several reports testified that many strikers were armed with guns and clubs. One report stated that, at one point, the strikers and troops set up opposing lines and faced each other in a sort of modus vivendi. A communiqué issued by the Federation of Miners stated that "striking miners in the Moselle basin were marched into the mines with guns at their backs."[108]

Although CGT militants found their numbers dwindling on the picket lines, the government's unwillingness to negotiate and their use of troops did little to endear the government to the miners. FO leaders maintained that 80 percent of the miners opposed the strike, but Claude Outil of *Combat* asked, "If 80 percent of the workers want to return to work, then why are 90 percent of the miners still off the job? The only ones who firmly oppose the strike are the small core of FO members."[109]

As FO stood on the brink of leaving the CGT, local FO activists from Nord and Pas-de-Calais pushed the national FO leaders like Jouhaux toward an open split. Some of these local activists had been "purged" from the union leadership in 1944. Some had run head-to-head contests against "official" CGT candidates in various union elections. Forced to confront the Communist majority nearly every day for years as part of their work and political activity, these local FO militants were acutely aware of the need to avoid ambiguity in breaking with the Communists. Jouhaux and other top FO leaders were reluctant to leave labor's "old house." But local FO activists, after having led a back-to-work movement and facing physical confrontations with strikers, were in no mood to go back into a Communist-dominated union. At the November meeting of the national leadership of FO, the northern delegates pushed for a stronger statement against the Communists. At the December meeting, they demanded that all FO members who held leadership posts in the CGT resign immediately.[110] After a vote by the FO caucus, five members of the executive board of the CGT left the organization. They were followed by FO leaders from the various affiliates of the CGT. For the third time in its history, France's major labor federation had broken into two parts.

After its initial proposal had been rejected, the government waited another week before offering another proposal. Strikers would receive 800 francs if they returned to work by December 10. The CGT had decided to end the strike on December 9. However, on that same day Jules

Moch, recently appointed to the Ministry of Interior, ordered the military forces to occupy the entire northern basin, an act that seemed to be motivated less by necessity than by a desire for intimidation. The action prolonged the strike in an unorganized form. An estimated 20 percent of the miners refused to return to work because of the troop occupation, despite union instructions. Indeed, in the face of the military action, some strikers dismissed as fabrication press and radio reports that claimed the strike had ended. As late as December 14 *Combat* reported that only 25 percent of the miners in the Douai mines were on the job, and that picket lines were still up at some mines. Management attributed these problems to "bad transmission of union directives to the rank and file." The situation would soon normalize, they felt, once the troops had been withdrawn.[111]

STALEMATE OR DEFEAT?

The strike of 1947 was a setback for French workers, but in the mining region the result seemed more like a stalemate. The CGT had demonstrated its ability to strike, while the government showed its determination to resist strikes. The union did not win its economic demands or its demand that Delfosse be reinstated as a vice president in the northern mines. Workers did not receive pay for strike days, and many were imprisoned by the authorities for strike-related offenses.

Despite repression against strike activists, union leaders claimed that they had become strengthened by the young activists who had gained new experience in the nuts and bolts of class struggle. Pannequin noted that the CGT's return to militancy brought back the activists who had been disenchanted with the old "battle of production" line. Many Socialist miners had participated in the first week of the strike. The miners' union remained intact after the departure of FO leaders and their following. "After the strike," recalled Jean Wrobleski, "most of the miners, even the Polish workers, remained with the CGT and did not leave the union."[112] Delfosse retained his last administrative post as a member of the administrative council of the Houillères du Nord–Pas-de-Calais. Attempts by the government to pass a highly restrictive antistrike bill were shelved once the crisis abated. And the government implemented the 1,500-franc indemnity that had been promised, along with a 22 percent increase in family allocations. The CGT withdrew its forces to fight another day.

Despite wild claims that the Communists had launched the strikes as the first stage in an insurrection, the evidence suggests that the PCF sought to harness the untapped militancy and public frustration with the economy into a powerful movement capable of changing the government's policies—or, even better, the government itself. Perhaps the most telling proof that the PCF was not planning an insurrection was the fact that it never called for a massive show of strength in Paris.

While dismissing the notion that an insurrection was in the offing, however, some have estimated that the PCF leaders fomented the strikes in an effort to regain their governmental positions. But the Communists must have known that such an outcome was unlikely unless the government coalition fell apart. Communist leaders did estimate, however, that the strikes could make it so uncomfortable for the Socialists that they would be forced to leave the government and, it was hoped, regroup with the PCF in a new version of the Popular Front.

This electoral side of the PCF political strategy, however, was accompanied by two other important aspects: the party's public image and the international situation. As Annie Kriegel and Ronald Tiersky have shown, the PCF had the flexibility to project various public images that aimed to interpret or connect the line of the party with popular concerns. By backing the strikes, the PCF returned to its old role as "tribune of the people" and aimed at consolidating its following around a militant program of action. If such action rallied the Socialist rank and file and made the Socialist leaders uneasy with the government's wage policies, all the better. The international dimension was also important in 1947. Despite the interest PCF leaders had in promoting the "French road to socialism," they would defend the Socialist fatherland to the last. Made aware of the concerns expressed at the founding meeting of the Cominform, PCF leaders were not in the least bothered by the idea that strikes could jeopardize American economic assistance.

It is important, however, to disentangle the political strategies of the Communists from the CGT's objectives, which were never identical to those of the PCF. While the CGT favored new wage policies and a government of the Left, its affiliated organizations concerned themselves primarily with material grievances, workplace issues, and union rights. Union leaders were directed to consult all workers, even nonunion workers, to gain their input in the shaping of strike demands. Bypassing the FO oppositionists in creating the National Strike Committee proved that the CGT majority was committed to waging a well-organized strike, even if a minority of union leaders were opposed. But it did not prove that the CGT had any intention of backing an insurrection. Also, in November, the PCF suggested an emergency CGT meeting to consider a call for a general strike, but CGT leaders scheduled the meeting for December 19 and by that time the strike had ended.

If the strike did not result in a crushing defeat for the CGT, however, it is difficult not to view it as a defeat for the PCF. The chances that the Communists would be invited back into the government were reduced to nothing. The possibilities for a Communist-led "government of democratic unity" seemed even more remote. Rather than move the Socialists from the Third Force into a Popular Front configuration, the strike and the split in the CGT had driven a powerful wedge between the two parties. The PCF retreated to the old sectarian "united front from below" strategy in dealings with the Socialists, who now moved much closer to the Americans. As the strikes were winding down, John Foster Dulles, a U.S. representative to the Four Power talks on Germany that were being held in London, came to France to meet with government officials and de Gaulle. At a press conference in Paris, Dulles underscored the importance of rebuilding Germany and commented favorably on the government's tough stand against the strikes. "What was happening in France was far more important than what was happening in London," said Dulles.[113] His statement recalled once again the connection between French coal policies and the cold war. The struggle to win German coal reparations had become a fight against communism. The old social and political bloc that had resisted the Nazis and liberated France was now divided into two warring camps. Within a year, they would once again choose sides in a final confrontation in the mining region.

6.

The Miners' Strike of 1948

n 1948 the coal miners put down their tools once more in one of the most controversial strikes in French history. A number of factors combined to transform what might have been an ordinary work stoppage into a massive and deadly confrontation between the CGT miners' union and the government.

The economic situation continued to deteriorate as inflation sapped workers' real wages—and no end seemed to be in sight. The stagnating economy created a broad base of support for labor action. In the month of September (even before the miners had taken their strike vote) nearly half a million workers participated in work stoppages affecting 6,000 firms. In addition, the government's attitude toward efforts by organized labor to improve the situation made it seem that a strike was the only way to get the government's attention. So serious was the situation that the reformist non-Communists of FO and CFTC were compelled to break off talks with the government and join the CGT in a two-day warning strike in September.

Inside the mines, the "crisis of authority" reemerged. When disputes occurred, union leaders no longer compelled workers to resolve the problem while keeping up production. Among miners, the notion that the gains of the past were endangered was widespread. In September a number of new administrative rules issued by Lacoste convinced many union delegates and labor activists that the government would eliminate them from their positions unless a successful strike took place. The cold war atmosphere, which gave labor conflicts a sense of inevitability, convinced Socialist leaders and other non-Communist political officials of the need to wage a high-profile war against the strikers and their union. Meanwhile the Communists followed a sectarian, adventurous strategy by leading the CGT into a major strike without knowing how to end it.

Everything added up to a formula for industrial strife. When the strike began in October 1948, the unions were united and almost no coal was mined. When the strike ended, 56 days later, the CGT and FO unionists were at war with each other, nearly 3,000 union activists were jailed, and a majority of miners had gone back to work. Both the government and the CGT looked for a showdown, but for different reasons. Government leaders wanted American policymakers to recognize the reality of the Communist threat and their willingness to "get tough" with communism. The Communists utilized industrial action to consolidate their position among French workers and to reassert their old role as the peoples' tribune. The party's electoral strategy now called for a "government of democratic union," but its leaders surely understood that it would not arrive soon. Party leaders also hoped that industrial action would help to keep France out of the cold war's Western orbit.

As in the 1947 work stoppage, the CGT's strike goals and the workers' motives for striking were not identical to the political objectives pursued by the Communists. From the union's perspective, each of the big strikes was necessitated by the dismal economic climate. But there were important differences in the way the miners' union mobilized its members. In 1947 the miners had sought to defend nationalization of the mines. But in 1948 the emphasis shifted to defending union rights and the workers' standard of living. Also, in 1947 the mine workers had walked out in solidarity with other workers in a generalized strike wave. But in 1948, after a week or two of widespread labor action, the miners found themselves alone, facing military forces, on the picket lines. Another difference concerned strategy. In 1947 the CGT leaders realized that it was time to call off the strike when workers started voting with their feet to return to work. Top PCF leaders concurred, and the strike was ended. In 1948, however, the miners' union displayed a lack of leadership by failing to provide an orderly retreat from an untenable situation.

STRIKE IMPETUS: COMINFORM OR CRISIS OF AUTHORITY?

Top government leaders claimed that the stimulus for the strike came not from the northern coal fields but from Moscow. Minister of Interior Jules Moch believed that Zhdanov himself had given the orders to strike in June, three months before the strike began.[1] Moch immediately consulted with Léon Blum and outlined a vigorous set of countermeasures: "1) requisition by the army of all the vehicles of the nationalized enterprises in order to prevent their use by the strikers for transporting commandos and distributing food as had happened last November; 2) encircling, from a distance, the mining basins in order to occupy them in case of suspension of security; 3) reaching an agreement with FO and the other unions if possible." Moch's scenario prefigured the events of the strike. His comprehensive plan to contain and defeat a miners' strike was formulated months before the miners cast their ballots in a strike vote. Moch brought together a large force of military leaders, police, and local security forces with his strategy to thwart a strike. Large amounts of coal were stockpiled.[2]

But while Moch envisioned a strike emanating from Moscow, another source was found in the inner workings of the mines, where the crisis of authority escalated between labor and management. The minister of Industrial Production, Robert Lacoste, sought to lower production costs and to restore authority in the mines, but the ouster of CGT representatives after the 1947 strike shifted the debate from within management to the workplace. In the coal mines, underground workers openly argued with foremen and engineers. For CGT activists, the days of labor-management cooperation were history. The union merely released the floodgates on a growing stream of discontent. Union officials looked the other way as workers turned grievances into limited job actions or chronically failed to show up for work.

"In 1946," explained a writer in *L'Espoir*, "a union official or a delegate would threaten a worker who slackened in his work effort or who interrupted the work day in a conflict with a foreman. Today, the same steward might actively take up the grievance and call a meeting of as many workers as possible. He can even invite the foreman, knowing full well that the foreman will not come. And he can take an 'I can do nothing attitude' when some of the workers decide to leave work early or to stay home from work tomorrow."[3]

A strike in March demonstrated how disputes originating at the point of production could spark a spontaneous strike movement. On March 12, eighteen workers at the Escarpelle pits in the Douai mines walked off the job, protesting a wage cut that had followed a recent drop in production. The strike spread quickly. The next day in Liévin, miners struck to demand that elected stewards who had been suspended for striking in November 1947 be rehired. In Bruay 3,000 miners demanded that the head of safety in the mine be elected, not appointed.[4] Within two days an estimated 40,000 miners were off the job in the northern mines.

The March strikes showed that the CGT, although weakened by the stalemate in December 1947, continued to maintain influence with the miners. In the elections for delegate posts in February 1948, the CGT captured a strong majority.[5] The strikes also forced the smaller unions to follow the CGT or appear as strikebreakers. The Socialists attempted to convince miners to stay on the job. *Nord-Matin* complained that the Communists were "exploiting all methods in order to draw around them many strikers."[6] Lampin wrote in *Force ouvrière* that the agitation failed to correspond to the workers' real demands.[7] His comrade, Sinot, warned: "For two weeks (the Communists) have unleashed a gymnastic of partial and limited strikes. These are the prelude to larger movements currently in preparation."[8]

The CGT, however, limited the strike to the mines, and it ended after only a few days. The miners' union, hoping to deflect charges that they were striking in a deliberate effort to increase inflation, demanded either a wage hike or a price cut.[9] The union also voiced the need to recall delegates who had been dismissed by management. "The delegates have a responsibility to defend the workers," said Delfosse, "but the workers must also defend the delegates."[10]

Explosions in the mines claimed the lives of sixteen workers at Courrières in April and seven more young miners at Liévin in September. The Federation of Miners demanded enlarged powers for the safety delegates.[11] In September, the headlines of *Liberté* rang with the angry words of the father of one of the young miners killed at Liévin: "In order to save money, they have killed my kid." The union argued that the disasters could have been prevented. Two days before the explosion at Liévin a steward had reported a dangerous accumulation of coal dust and had called for safety measures to be taken. In speeches delivered at funeral services, Lecoeur and Martel urged the miners to fight to increase the role of the stewards.[12] After the Courrières disaster, Lecoeur assailed the management personnel, describing them as "assassins who sacrifice safety for productivity."[13] *La Tribune des mineurs* accused management of following the commands of Lacoste in order to produce coal at the lowest possible price.[14]

The resignation of a former ally and director of the northern mines, Jean Armanet, underscored the reality that the CGT had lost most of its friends in management. Despite the differences between CGT and the government, Armanet had successfully mediated during the strikes in March 1948. But *La Tribune* charged that Armanet had abandoned the miners. "The miners can no longer rely upon any administrators because they have all become weakened and corrupted. They no longer represent the same interests as the mine workers."[15]

While the CGT sought to strengthen the role of elected stewards as a means of protecting the miners, critics of the industry sought to do precisely the opposite. An investigation of the mines launched by the government in November 1947, under the direction of an engineer named Wahl from the Department of Bridges and Roads, was completed in April 1948. The Wahl report was never made public. The Federation of Miners requested to see the report, but the request was denied.[16] However, *Creusot des cadres*, the monthly newspaper of the CGC, published excerpts from the Wahl report. It contended that low productivity resulted from a "crisis of authority" at all levels of management, which prevented engineers, supervisors, and foremen from enforcing discipline. This crisis was aggravated by the politicization of the nationalization, and the report recommended that composition of the administrative councils be further modified to allow "independent personalities, chosen by their competence" to manage the mines. Chronic absenteeism had to be curbed, the work force needed to be reduced, and a better means of linking wages to productivity was required.[17] According to *Nord-Industriel*, the Wahl report proposed altering the composition of the administrative council because of the "preponderance of wage earners on that body" and because the Miners' Statute prevented management from acting against unjustified absenteeism.[18]

The resignation of M. Guillaume, president of the Charbonnages de France, in April 1948 lent weight to the criticism advanced in the Wahl report. In his letter of resignation, Guillaume maintained that the Charbonnages de France was a "rubber-stamp" body within which "political forces played a dominant role." The regional bodies had too much power, and high production costs and low productivity in the mines could not be solved without "restoring the power of the management."[19]

In the months preceding the miners' strike, *Nord-Industriel* published a number of articles on the coal industry. Henri Billemont called for trimming the heavy "social expenditures" that forced labor costs upward. *Nord-Industriel* also chided the government for yielding to the pressures of the *grèves tournants* when the miners won a small bonus in August. In September, *Nord-Industriel* published an article entitled "Disorganization in Our Coal Mines," which pointed to absenteeism and "social agitation" as the critical problems. "The workers think they are still on vacation. Many workers are coming to work one-half hour late or else come up from the mine earlier than they are supposed to. And this seems to be an organized activity." For Billemont, the Communists, backed by their Soviet bosses, were behind the social agitation in the mines. Like Jules Moch, Billemont expected big strikes in the fall. In early September, he confidently predicted a "general strike in October."[20] "The cadres are unanimous in saying that the real crisis is the crisis of authority," claimed *La Vie française*, a Paris-based business weekly. "Since the war, the authority of the cadres has been greatly abused. The simplest disagreement can cause a big argument that wastes hours of production time."[21]

TABLE 15. Absenteeism in the Mines of Nord–Pas-de-Calais,
June–September 1948
(In percentages)

June 21–27	16.27	Aug. 10–16	17.71
June 28–July 4	16.90	Aug. 17–22	14.71
July 5–11	14.95	Aug. 23–Sept. 4	17.05
July 12–18	14.74	Sept. 6–12	18.12
July 19–24	14.27	Sept. 13–19	20.33
July 25–Aug. 1	14.52	Sept. 20–26	18.65
Aug. 2–9	14.64		

Source: *Nord-Industriel* (Lille, 1948).

Absenteeism became more widespread. Rumors circulated to the effect that miners were avoiding work to go fishing. Miners argued, half humorously, that it made more sense to miss work and catch fish than to spend half a day's wages to pay for a fish. In fact, the percentage of workers absent from work in the mines remained relatively low throughout most of the summer. Only in September did it begin to rise, as the weekly statistics from *Nord-Industriel* demonstrated (see table 15). The miners' federation linked absenteeism to the increase in work-related accidents.[22]

Absenteeism reflected a larger "social malaise" noted by French observers in the summer of 1948. Going fishing, arguing with a foreman, or exaggerating an injury or illness in order to stay home from work were various ways in which this mood was manifested. Monthly statistics showed that in 1948 large numbers of underground workers, estimated by Didier Philippe at nearly 80,000, began leaving the mines. Management recruited 60,000 underground workers from France and other countries in 1948.[23] The sometimes stable profession was becoming a revolving-door job, and the high mobility of workers left its mark on the mining towns. The housing shortage remained in effect and many workers continued to live in rude barracks or doubled up with fellow miners in houses owned by the mines. A writer in *L'Espoir* decried the fact that Lens, previously well-kept and attractive, had deteriorated to the point that "former visitors and old residents who return to Lens would simply not believe the change."[24]

Striking was another way workers reacted to the malaise. During the summer of 1948 nearly ten million workers participated in what were called the "grèves tournants": limited, often localized strikes. By September the economic situation had become so difficult for workers that the CFTC and FO, always reluctant to take strike action and deeply afraid of a Communist-inspired general strike, reluctantly called a two-hour work stoppage at the end of the month.

THE LACOSTE DECREES

Seeking to curb absenteeism and end the crisis of authority, Robert Lacoste issued directives that touched off a wave of discontent and served as the catalyst for the miners' strikes of 1948. The "Lacoste decrees," issued in September 1948, provoked little interest in the national press. But in the mining basin, according to André Théret, they "were the object of scrupulous examination by the workers."[25] The decrees sought to strengthen management's authority, reduce absenteeism, and eliminate 10 percent of the positions in the offices and surface installations of the mines.

Henri Martel summarized the union's criticisms. "Management," said Martel, "can decide against permanently hiring a miner for political reasons or because of his union activities."[26] One decree allowed the immediate firing without appeal of all miners with six unjustified absences in six months or twelve in six consecutive months. This affected all miners, but it hit especially hard at those who had struck in November or March. Also, the decrees altered the procedure for settling disputes and taking disciplinary action. The Miners' Statute provided for five stages of disciplinary measures: a warning, a fine, suspension, demotion in rank, and termination. Only the first two measures were immediately applicable, and suspension could be undertaken only after agreement had been reached in a parity commission. But the Lacoste decrees allowed a suspension to take effect immediately and without going before the commission.[27]

Lacoste also sought to reduce by 10 percent the office staff and surface workers of the mines. Because most of FO's members were employed in the surface works, the struggling new union had serious misgivings about the layoffs. Sinot, the FO leader, raised the threat of unemployment in the mines.[28] Earlier, the CGT had agreed on the need to compress the work force in surface installations, but they now opposed Lacoste's methods. The parity commissions were again circumvented, and the power to review layoffs was placed solely in the hands of the general director.[29]

An additional feature of the Lacoste decrees fanned the anger of many miners: control and management of the accident and relief funds passed from a quasi-autonomous and representative body of mine workers into the hands of central management of the mines, a change that Martel claimed "returned the miners to the arbitrary ways of old."[30] A writer in *Travaux de l'action populaire*, a Catholic labor monthly, commented that this aspect of the decrees, while perhaps justified by abuses, nonetheless indicated "an insufficient understanding of the social atmosphere and the state of mind of the miners and of the attachment they hold for these relief funds for which they fought so stubbornly in the past."[31]

Although neither management nor the union publicly admitted it, many believed that most of those who were to be sacked would be union militants, particularly since the parity commissions could now be bypassed. Lacoste contributed to this sentiment when he stated in a radio speech that "those who truly love their work are surrounded by too many parasites and other people who think of other things besides extracting coal." "We can see why these people are upset by the lay-offs of the Lacoste decrees," wrote a hostile editorialist in *Voix du Nord*. "This time it is a different purge that they are worried about."[32] Sulpice Dewez, leader of a group of "independent unionists" in the mining region, was even more specific. "People talk a lot about the Cominform and about the economic situation, but not about the real reason behind the strike. The fact is that the Lacoste layoffs will hit particularly hard at those 'Communist creatures' that Lecoeur and Duguet have put in the unproductive apparatus of the mines."[33] Because the union stewards saw the decrees as an attempt to remove them, they were willing to go to great lengths to keep the strike going in 1948.

Yet the real or imagined witch-hunt against union militants should not obscure the fact that the Lacoste decrees aimed at resolving the crisis by reducing the union's power in relation to management. "There is no doubt that the Miners' Statute, with the use of the parity commissions of discipline and conciliation, have curiously weakened the authority of management in the mines," wrote an observer in *Travaux de l'action populaire*. "The worker representatives in these commissions have usually been able either to prevent all penalties or at least reduce the severity of the penalty." But the engineers themselves also contributed to the "shirking of authority" because "the fear of finding themselves in a situation of *contestation* and of having to defend the decisions they made in front of the workers has led the engineers in many cases to abstain from disciplining a miner. Lacking proper educational training in public discussion, they often find themselves intimidated by the mine worker leaders, whose ways of thinking and feeling are foreign to engineers." Yet, this observer pointed out, the parity commissions were necessary and constituted a step forward: "The dismissals of mine workers have been abused in the past."[34]

THE CGT PREPARES: "UNITÉ D'ACTION"

In July, Benoit Frachon proposed a new CGT strategy called "unité d'action." He urged all CGT unions to unite with other unions in joint action. The CGT strategy resembled the old PCF tactic of the "united front from below." While encouraging FO and CFTC members to join the movement for higher wages, the CGT also continued to criticize the top leaders of FO and CFTC, hoping to split the rank and file from the leadership.

The new CGT strategy received its first test in the coal mines. In July a resolution from all three unions in the mining basin of Aveyron called for an increase in the minimum wage. The CGT attempted to duplicate that effort in other basins as well. In August the CGT aligned their wage demands more closely to those of the CFTC and FO. The federation then publicized the fact that all three unions had essentially the same wage demands and called upon the non-CGT workers to join a larger, united movement.[35] In September the CGT urged all workers to become involved and advocated more democracy in the unions. Frachon stated that "we have remained behind the movement of the masses" and he called for the CGT newspaper, *Le Peuple*, to be "opened up" to the workers.[36]

FO and the CFTC wanted nothing to do with the CGT appeal for unity. But both small unions had fared poorly in the elections for stewards in February 1948. FO had captured only 20 percent of the votes to the CGT's 75 percent. The CFTC received the remaining few votes. Moreover, the two smaller unions found it nearly impossible to defend the government's wage policies among the workers. FO and the CFTC had formed a lobbying coalition in March 1948 to engage the government in wage talks that produced nothing. During the March strikes, FO had assured workers that important governmental action was forthcoming. Throughout the spring and summer, *L'Ouvrier des mines*, FO's weekly in the northern coal basin, elaborated on their organization's efforts to win wage increases for the workers. FO leaders urged the government to act quickly. By July 25, however, a disappointed Lampin entitled his article on recent negotiations "Patience Has Its Limits."[37]

Initially, the FO-CFTC coalition separated itself from the CGT by refusing to support wage hikes in favor of cuts in prices. Eventually, however, the coalition presented wage demands. The minority unions consistently warned the miners of the dangers of working with the CGT. As a writer in *L'Ouvrier des mines* saw it, "We should consider the Communists as lepers and have no contact with them."[38] The CFTC observed that the CGT was "playing a double game" and warned the miners to avoid falling into a dangerous trap.[39]

By the end of September, however, the CFTC and FO suspended talks with the government and organized a two-hour work stoppage. Although the CGT was not invited, the federation was more than happy to join this limited strike movement. CGT militants mobilized as many workers

TABLE 16.   Strike Vote by Group in Nord–Pas-de-Calais, September 1948

Mining Group	Number of Workers Enrolled	Number of Voters	Voters "for" Striking	Percent-age of Voters "for" Striking	Voters "against" Striking
Auchel	19,135	14,753	12,986	93	1,767
Bruay	18,990	13,753	11,543	86	2,210
Béthune	26,664	16,674	14,088	82	2,586
Lens	20,514	13,807	11,137	79	2,670
Liévin	10,833	7,222	6,353	86	869
Hénin-Liétard	32,457	23,665	20,481	83	3,184
Oignies	7,457	4,455	3,907	91	548
Douai	25,133	17,189	15,804	94	1,385
Valenciennes	23,207	14,974	12,812	87	2,162
All mining groups in France	317,506	244,322	218,616	89	25,086 *

* Does not include abstentions and nullified votes.

Sources: Françoise Salion, "Les Socialistes et les grèves du Nord et du Pas-de-Calais, 1947–1948" (Lille, 1971), 81, and Georges Lefranc, *Les Expériences syndicales en France de 1939 à 1950* (Paris, 1950), 216.

as possible and staged large rallies at Bully-Montigny, Hénin-Liétard, and Bruay. The CGT proclaimed the action a great success and proof of the value of "unité d'action." [40] The Lacoste decrees had appeared a week earlier and the federation used the Friday afternoon work stoppage as an excellent launching pad for a strike vote scheduled for the following Monday.

The Socialists, however, were less certain of the value of the work stoppage. *Nord-Matin* decided against reporting on the demonstration. FO termed the action a success but urged the workers to be patient. [41] *Syndicalisme*, the CFTC weekly, voiced a similar message of caution. In 1947 the CGT had been accused of using undemocratic procedures in calling the strike. In 1948, however, the union guaranteed wider distribution of the strike demands and used printed ballots rather than voting by the raised-hands procedure. The results of the strike vote were subject to some debate, but essentially the vote revealed broad support for the strike (see table 16).

The CGT claimed a smashing victory by pointing to the fact that 89 percent of those voting had favored a strike. FO, after a last-minute meeting, decided to counsel workers to abstain. Later, Sinot of FO charged that "only 56 percent of the miners voted to strike; 44 percent abstained at the call of FO."[42] However, Sinot's figures included all the absent workers (about 17 percent), those who voted against a strike, 12,000 prisoners of war (who could not vote), miners who had not yet returned from their vacations, and those who simply chose not to show up for the vote. Depending upon how one preferred to interpret the results of the strike vote, between 55 percent and 90 percent of the miners—a strong majority—chose to strike in October 1948.

MOCH'S MOBILIZATION

With Jules Moch at the helm, the government undertook elaborate measures to defeat the miners' strike. Four days before the strike began, the trucks and cars of the mines were brought to Lille and Arras for routine inspection. Moch put them under armed guard.[43] In one fell swoop, the minister of the Interior deprived strikers of their means of transporting teams of miners in flying squads to bolster picket lines across the basin. The trucks had also been used during the 1947 strike to collect and distribute food to the strikers and their families. "This would be Moch's first victory," wrote Angelli and Gillet. "The trucks were sorely needed by the miners."[44] Moch had already crafted an elaborate system of communications, setting up special radios and telephones between the prefects and the "problem areas" and linking together the mining management from the different mining regions. In case these lines might be discovered and cut by the strikers, radio transformers were installed in areas that were considered to be safe.[45] In the Nord, the management of the mines decided to evacuate the horses from the mines—5,000 in all—apparently responding to rumors that the CGT intended to starve the horses in a desperate effort to blackmail the government. This rather bizarre precaution indicated to the miners that the strike would be very long.[46] Two days before the strike began, *Liberté* reported that several companies of Algerian soldiers had arrived in the mining town of Cambria. A trainload of an estimated 500 soldiers from Germany moved westward by truck from Lille to Arras and Douai.[47]

On the first day of the strike, Auguste Leceour addressed the miners with a message of optimism. "I have directed some good strikes in this mining basin," he said, "but I have never known a strike with such perfect organization and remarkable unity."[48] The CFTC supported the strike for 48 hours, and FO, while not publicly associating itself with the strike, nevertheless told its members to avoid trying to return to work.[49] Reporters noted that the picket lines, though dominated by the CGT, also included CFTC and FO members.[50] Georges Lefranc, no partisan of the 1948 strike, stated that "the enthusiasism was general" during the first week.[51] In Paris, Jefferson Caffrey, the American ambassador to France, wrote to the American secretary of state: "There is real evidence that the trend which resulted in the split between Communist and non-Communist trade unions (the capital event of postwar France) has come to a stop and may be reversed by a trend toward unity, in which the superior organization of the Communists would prevail."[52] A Socialist labor leader wrote that "the work stoppage was total on the first day of the strike because no one is opposed to a warning strike."[53] Spinetta, an FO leader, wrote that "many miners did not participate in the referendum organized by the CGT, but all will go along with the strike." He added that the "despair of the miners" contributed greatly to the success of the strike: "Daily life has become impossible and the government's promises have not been kept."[54]

Unanimity, however, did not mean that the miners had gleefully gone into the strike, as an FO writer noted: "The first day of a strike has never seemed so gloomy."[55] Michel Hincker, reporting for *Combat*, wrote, "I have seen many strikes before, but this one stands out. The atmosphere is cold, almost painful. In these brick villages, now free from the smoke and the dust, the people continue to lead a normal life . . . this normal life, which has satisfied ministerial envoys, is deceiving. All the personnel, except for a few in Valenciennes, have stopped work. . . . A general strike is beginning and dozens of thousands of miners and their wives are embarking upon a difficult adventure." Hincker asked the miners where they thought the strike would lead. "Most strikers shrug their shoulders," he wrote, "Their faces are grave and cautious."[56]

Attempting to engage rank-and-file members of FO and the CFTC in joint strike action, *Liberté* and *La Tribune des mineurs* published the names of local Socialists who opposed the Lacoste decrees.[57] Meanwhile, the minority unions feverishly urged the government to reach a settlement. Lacoste convoked meetings with the three unions on October 5. The minister of Industrial Production offered a modest across-the-board bonus, a 15 percent pay raise based on seniority, and a special allocation to surface workers with 30 years of experience. Although the CFTC and FO had initially supported much higher wage demands, their representatives claimed to be satisfied with the government's offer. FO termed the government's offer "an uncontestable improvement" and called for a referendum on the results. The CFTC concurred and called off its 48-hour strike.[58]

Representatives from the CGT, however, were not impressed with the government's wage offer. They organized eight mass meetings in the mining basin to report on the negotiations.[59] Predictably, these meetings resulted in a further mandate to continue the strike. To the CGT, vital issues such as the Lacoste decrees, the power of the stewards, and the cost-of-living increase had not been addressed. But the government had given its final offer. On the evening of October 6, Lacoste took to the radio airwaves. He declared that the CGT demands were unacceptable and that "all necessary measures" would be taken to end the strike.[60] *Combat* predicted that Lacoste's speech would not be well received in the coal fields. *Franc-Tireur* warned the government: "Negotiate with miners; don't provoke them!"[61]

DÉTENTE AND ESCALATION

The strike held firm during the first week. The Federation of Miners issued a communiqué that welcomed "the massive return of workers to the CGT" and saluted the "rank-and-file FO and CFTC members who stayed off the job." Talks were informally suspended, but there were some signs of a détente during the second week, raising hopes that a settlement could be found. *Nord-Éclair* and *Combat* noted "astonishing calm" in the mining basins.[62] A dispute over security in the cokeries was settled between October 8 and October 11 by meetings between the CGT, the government, and local authorities.[63] Jean Charvin, a reporter for *La Gauche* wrote: "In the cokeries the CGT leaders have managed to guarantee their security despite a partisan rank and file who wanted a total strike."[64] Auriol, influenced by information from Jules Moch's alleged informant in the PCF's politburo, saw signs of détente on the strike front. "Among the Communists," wrote Auriol, "many fear being swept away by the movement, and they do not hide this feeling from the union leaders. Many have torn up their union cards because they feel their comrades are being maneuvered. Others continue to strike, but they do not want confrontations and riots."[65] Indications of accord also came from the east. In Lorraine, where iron miners had been striking for several weeks, the CGT and the government reached an agreement on October 12 that offered some concessions and gave rise to hopes that a similar settlement could be found in the coal mines.[66]

Yet by midweek, it became clear that the strike situation would probably get worse before it improved. Anticipating a long and "hungry" strike, the federation organized caravans of thousands of miners' children, who traveled outside the basin to spend time with the families of other workers.[67] Louis Delaby, the CFTC leader, recognized that the food shortages would be grave, and he urged that contributions be sent to the CFTC headquarters.[68]

More ominously, the disputes over the "right to work" and the security of the cokeries and the pumping systems grew in intensity. In the eastern part of the basin, at Anzin and Ledoux, FO and Gaullist militants began leading larger numbers of miners back to work, inevitably prompting minor disturbances and vandalism and some fights. *Liberté* routinely attacked "provocateurs" and vandalism, but Lecoeur and Martel spoke to the stewards and stated that the enemies of the strikers should not be able to appear publicly in the streets.

The security problem was even more complex and serious. *Combat* noted on October 11 that "in one-half of the pits of Nord and Pas-de-Calais, the strikers refuse to allow management to do all the work they feel is necessary. This is the first time this has happened."[69] The FO engineers' union charged that strike committees prevented them from carrying out necessary tasks regarding security in the mines. Clauwaert, editor of *Nord-Éclair*, wrote that the strikers had pressured the elevator operators to cease work, thus compelling the security crews to descend by ladders.[70]

The CGT maintained that the strike committees would guarantee security in the mines. As early as October 5, however, the union threatened to call off security crews in the Lorraine mines because the police had occupied the mines even before the pickets were set up. Duguet issued a statement that "the maintenance of police at the entrances to the mines could heighten the problem of security crews all over France."[71] The message was clear: the CGT considered the withdrawal of security crews as a possible response to military occupation. But the government viewed the "liberation" of the mines as a necessary element in defeating the strike. The dispute had reached an impasse and stood on the verge of escalation.

FO leaders pressed for a new strike vote. But who would organize such a referendum? The CGT blasted the FO proposal as "an appeal to treason."[72] FO next called upon the government and the Charbonnages de France to organize a new referendum, but to no avail. A communiqué revealed their disappointment: "The public powers and the managers of the Charbonnages de France are afraid to organize a referendum."[73] Auriol pressed Lacoste for a new referendum, but the minister of Industrial Production commented that the mine directors feared it would produce an overwhelming abstention vote.[74] One week later the CFTC urged arbitration as a means of settlement, but the idea was turned aside by the government. In the old days, when the mining companies ruled, a strike could cause the government to intervene as a "neutral" party in the public interest. But in 1948, the government had become owner, leaving no neutral body for the miners to appeal to.

While these efforts to negotiate a settlement were dying, military forces under the direction of Jules Moch tightened the ring around the northern basin and began to dislodge strikers from the mines of the Moselle region. A skirmish in front of the mines resulted in the death of a Polish miner in Merlebach. In response, the Federation of Miners warned that failure to retract the police and military forces would produce a limited withdrawal of security crews for a 24-hour period beginning on Monday, October 18. This bold threat by the CGT unleashed a rapid chain of events as the strike raced from a stalemate to a test of strength. Moch immediately convened a "war council" meeting of cabinet members, civil and military authorities, and regional officials. By early Saturday morning, the group issued a warning to the miners that "measures will be taken with full force."[75]

In the Centre Midi and in St. Étienne some pits could be flooded if maintenance was withheld for one or two days. Moch's special antistrike team, IGAME (Inspecteur général de l'administration en mission extraordinaire), gathered in Lyons the following day and mapped out a set of military maneuvers to defeat the strike. Documents collected by Angelli and Gillet reveal that the IGAME group sat down with mining engineers to study aerial photos taken by reconnaissance airplanes to help military forces discover the best points of attack. The following day a convoy of several kilometers in length—police, CRS, the horse-riding *gardes mobiles*, and government soldiers—paraded through the mining basin in order to demoralize the strikers. Next, the roads leading to the mines were sealed off, and each pit was isolated.[76] The forces of order moved pit by pit through the basin in St. Étienne and the Loire, removing barricades erected by the strikers, arresting those who resisted, and occupying the mines. *Combat* reported that fifty persons were wounded in clashes between strikers and police in the Loire basin.[77]

At the local level, however, union leaders and local authorities made some attempts to prevent a bloody confrontation. In St. Étienne, for example, the miners' representatives and the prefect met all night on October 18. The miners explained, "We love our mines, but we do not want the police here," and they promised to guarantee security once the police were withdrawn. But in the morning the CRS moved in quickly, using tear gas to disperse the strikers.[78] A communiqué issued by the Federation of Miners also suggests that in some areas union leaders had postponed the decision to halt security until a later date. But the CGT national office denied that any agreements had been reached. "The union has issued several warnings; not only have they not been heeded, but the police violence has multiplied."[79] Even so, *Nord-Éclair* wrote that the security crews in the north had taken the necessary measures on the morning shift and that six of the seven cokeries functioned according to an earlier agreement reached between local union leaders and management.[80] But in the afternoon of October 18, Léon Delfosse gave the order to suspend security in Nord and Pas-de-Calais;[81] Jules Moch tightened the military belt around the northern basin; and the strike escalated once more.

STRIKE OR WAR?

On Tuesday, October 19, the strikers at the Verquin mines began to organize a meeting at the entrance to the mines but were dispersed by the police and CRS. However, a reporter from *Voix du Nord* stated, "In the afternoon, the strikers returned, arriving eight hundred strong, organized into a procession with red flags at the head. Two engineers and a chief foreman were roughed up after attempting to remove some barricades. . . . Beside these strikers were women and children, many of whom were armed with large clubs."[82] A battle erupted between several hundred strikers and 25 CRS forces. *Voix du Nord* added that seven CRS cars came within a kilometer of the battle but refrained from taking any action. The CRS troops withdrew.

At Noeux-les-mines, 500 strikers penetrated the mine and threw out all the engineers and supervisors. They also damaged the home of a chief foreman.[83] A police official, inspector Bourdon, was seized by the strikers and forced to march through the *corons* without his trousers, a penalty that had been meted out to German troops captured by Resistance forces during the liberation. "During the Occupation," *Liberté* wrote of Bourdon, "he arrested and tortured patriots and sent several to Germany, where they died."[84] In Béthune, 4,000 men and women marched to the police station and demanded the release of seven strikers who had been thrown into jail. The crowd grew to between 7,000 and 8,000. A police official, a Socialist named Pé, received a delegation of miners and agreed to release the arrested miners but not to drop the charges.[85]

These violent counterattacks by the strikers often caught the forces of order off guard. In the Gard region in southern France, 30 CRS were captured and held by the strikers, who seized their weapons, jeeps, and other materials. In response, Lacoste delivered an address on the radio on October 20 in which he warned that the government would not be intimidated by these threats and added, "Our stocks of coal will allow us to wait."[86] Martel answered Lacoste by claiming that the miners could hold out, if necessary, "for two months on a single potato per day." Duguet told a rally of miners: "We will fight like lions to protect our right to strike." *Combat* called the strike a standoff.[87]

Responding to the strikers' counteroffensive, the Council of Ministers met in a special session on October 22. Jules Moch told the council that the situation had deteriorated. Auriol wrote: "In the Loire, the Gard, and St. Étienne, the forces of order have been attacked by large numbers of striking miners and have suffered some serious losses. Two hundred and fifty CRS and gendarmes have been wounded. . . . In Nord and Pas-de-Calais, the tension increases. The security is no longer assured except in a sporadic manner. The pits are barricaded. The police station at Béthune has been under seige."[88] Moch claimed to have seen a letter written to the editors of all Communist newspapers that declared the aim of the strike was to bring down the government. He added that certain Communists saw the strike as a prelude to the installation of a people's democracy. Moch said that more troops were soon arriving, from North Africa and Germany, to guard against an insurrection. He concluded that the time had come to begin arresting strikers for sabotage.

Jules Moch's testimony seems to have greatly shaped the discussion and eventual outcome of this emergency meeting. Lacoste raised the question of negotiations with the CGT, but Queuille answered that the government could not undertake discussions with any organization that interrupted the security of the mines. The policy of "no negotiations" remained in effect while the cabinet agreed on several "state-of-seige" measures:

1. The "class of 1948" reserve group was ordered to report for duty.

2. CRS could shoot after a warning had been issued.

3. Prefects could prohibit public and private meetings.

4. Foreigners participating in demonstrations could be expelled.

5. Prefects could censor and seize any newspapers that supported the actions of demonstrators.

Bolstered by the government's decision to expand his powers, Moch quickly launched the offensive in the northern mining region. The minister of the Interior explained: "I had hesitated to launch our general offensive . . . [but] the determining factor had been the impatience of the miners to be 'rescued.' A young FO member wrote me: 'Don't you know that here we speak of an "occupation" by the Communists, as the Germans occupied our region four years ago and that we hope to be delivered from them? What are you waiting for?'" The operation began on October 24 as military forces, moving in at night, occupied the eastern end of the basin in a line from Valenciennes to the Belgian border. This area was chosen not by chance but because the CGT was relatively weaker there, partly because many workers were Belgians who commuted to work in France and also because FO was more firmly implanted in the mines of Valenciennes and Ledoux.[89] An embryonic but active Gaullist movement in the mines existed there as well: *Voix du Nord* noted on October 23 that "the RPF miners have decided to sign up with FO and the CFTC and to devote themselves body and soul to putting an end to the CGT strike."[90]

In the morning, the miners awoke to see the mine entrances and streets occupied by military forces. "The miners," *Combat* wrote, "were surprised by the large numbers of troops and by their sudden arrival."[91] Once the eastern end of the basin had been occupied on October 28, the troops cleared the center of the region, which, in Moch's words, "formed a single liberated zone eighty-five kilometers long."[92] On October 30, troops moved into Pas-de-Calais and took the mines around Bruay-en-Artois. Then, after resting the troops for two days, Moch moved to take the 42 pits in the CGT strongholds of Béthune, Lens, Liévin, and Courrières. The strikers could not maintain picket lines against military forces. In Carvin and other mines the strikers erected barricades, but most strikers abandoned the pickets. On November 1 *Combat* estimated that one-half of the pits in Nord and Pas-de-Calais had been deserted.

However, the authorities faced the task of getting the miners back to work. Some strikers began receiving requisition orders to return; failure to appear carried a penalty of one month to a year in prison and a fine.[93] By the third week of the strike, most miners had spent their remaining wages. Credit became more difficult to obtain. The Federation of Miners printed and distributed special food coupons to be presented to local shopkeepers instead of cash. The CGT promised to back up these notes, but some shopkeepers refused to accept them. Under these conditions, FO and the CFTC began leading groups of miners in a return to work, setting in motion skirmishes and fistfights in front of the mines, the intervention of CRS troops, and usually the withdrawal of the picketers. "In all the official proclamations," wrote *Combat*, "the 'right to work' has replaced 'security problems' as the main problem."[94]

An atmosphere of war pervaded the mining basin. If some miners saw the military forces as "liberators," more, it seems, were repulsed by the helmeted and armed soldiers, the jeeps, tanks, and trucks that patrolled the streets and the main roads. Many of the troops brought in from Germany spoke in a dialect that evoked memories of the Nazi occupation. Equally as foreign were the North African troops or the groups of "displaced persons" from eastern Europe who were sent to work in the "liberated" mines.[95] *Croix du Nord* described the "trenches and foxholes built around the mine entrances" and the large barricades built by the strikers at pit number two at Lens.[96] Two miners were arrested in Béthune on charges of "distributing revolutionary literature to the soldiers."[97] *Nord-Éclair*, on October 27, listed some of the strikers arrested: at Somain, seven strikers were jailed for a noisy demonstration against supervisors and engineers; a CGT mine steward was arrested for "obstructing the right to work"; another striker, incarcerated for carrying a club, was sentenced to five days in prison; he was joined there by two Italian workers. In Thivencelles, nine Poles who were picketing were arrested, tried, and sentenced on the same day. *Nord-Éclair* commented: "Their prison terms (two months) should be followed by expulsion, which will allow them to taste the benefits of 'people's democracy,' which fundamentally, it seems, are closest to their hearts."[98]

The government considered itself at war with the striking miners. While Moch commanded the forces that occupied the northern mines, the cabinet discussed a report from a "high-level military authority" who advocated even tougher methods. "Soviet Russia is making war preparations, not on the Elbe but rather in the mines of Nord and Pas-de-Calais. Is this a strike or a war?"[99] Roger Pannequin reflected that "the communiqués of the non-Communist press were written as if they were emerging from the headquarters of an army in the midst of a campaign. The tanks, armor, and soldiers used against the miners stimulated these would-be strategists."[100] Dominique Desanti, a left-wing journalist who spent eight weeks in the north covering the strike, claims that the "desperate actions" of the miners can be understood only within an atmosphere of war. She correctly noted that the fear that war could erupt at any moment was a sentiment that emanated from Moscow as well as from Paris and Washington.[101]

While the government had decided on a military solution, the Communists operated within a mental framework dominated by war psychosis. During the miners' strike, Thorez's oft-quoted proclamation that "France will never make war on the Soviet Union" became a ritualistic phrase for all Communist party speakers. But Thorez had forgotten his great quotation from the Popular Front strikes. Too much emphasis on "proletarian internationalism," as they defined it, led the Communists to lose sight of the limits of how far the rank-and-file miners were prepared to go in order to reach the strike demands. As the strike came to be seen as a hopeless affair, many union leaders pressed inside party channels for some type of orderly retreat. When the CFTC and FO began to lead workers back to the mines, some local CGT leaders made overtures for negotiations at the local level. But the national office of the CGT felt that such discussion worked against a national settlement, and it informed the various groups that "discussions on the local or regional plane are not only useless but are prejudicial to the movement and the cause of the miners. The solution to our demand and the security problems can be found only at the national level, in Paris, where the government must assume its responsibilities and reopen talks that they have deliberately broken with the Federation of Miners."[102] Such a posture by top CGT leaders lent credence to charges that the striking miners aimed to topple the government. On the other hand, the federation did have the responsibility to win a national agreement, and it could have been that local settlements would work against such a possibility.

Undoubtedly, some miners hoped to bring down the government or to fan the flames of violence, including a certain number of ex-Communist party members, and former Resistance fighters and anarchists who plunged into action alongside the Communists. Moch claimed that internal documents of the Communist party used the slogan "No enemies on the Left." A legal scholar named Durand, who followed the entire range of Left and trade-union periodicals during the strike, noted that many non-Communist leftists played active roles in the strike. But the warlike atmosphere also fostered a situation wherein groups of particularly militant strikers went beyond the instructions of their union leaders in attacking scabs or participating in acts of terror and vandalism. "A lack of perspective combined with the well-tested practice of violence, had strongly led the Communist miners, individually and collectively, beyond reasonable limits," recalled Pierre Villon, a Communist leader. "In an atmosphere marked by the cold war and the preparations for war against the Soviet Union, the notion that they risked becoming clandestine, as well as the Cominform's analysis, led them to see each battle as the last."[103]

As the troops drew the circle tightly around the sector of Bruay, Béthune, and Auchel, *Nord-Éclair* noted that "the CGT stewards who for the past few days have preached revolt are not so visible around the entrances to the mines." François Mitterrand, the Socialist minister of Information, emerged from a Council of Ministers meeting on October 28 and stated, "The government wants to demonstrate that the working class will not follow Communist agitators."[104] Too often, Mitterrand noted, the less important agitators were jailed while the top union leaders who gave the orders were allowed to go free.

However, the military solution left difficult questions unanswered. Claude Bourdet criticized the Communists for their sectarianism, but he also criticized the government. In an article entitled "Death Trap," Bourdet wrote: "The government is headed toward one of the most deceptive victories. Aided by the nation's indignation and viewing the occasion for revenge against the PCF, a revenge that forgets four years of economic setbacks, the government has lost its cool head and is now being swept away by a current that risks taking it very far: authority to shoot, expulsion of foreign workers, mobilization of reservists, censure of the press, in short, a real state of seige. From there it will lead toward imprisonment of CGT leaders and the prohibition of the Communist party." Such a situation, Bourdet wrote, also made it difficult for FO to succeed: "The workers have reached the limits and we must respond to them and negotiate. It is a poor strategy to try to divide the mass of workers from their leaders. Rather than dreaming of imprisoning the leaders, we must discuss these matters with them." [105]

In one of the last CGT strongholds, Liévin, the strikers battled CRS troops for several hours using grenades and molotov cocktails. But they were soon beaten back, seven were injured, and many were arrested. The same scenario took place in Béthune, Avion, and other mines. [106] The strike could not hold, but the government's victory was fragile. As a writer for *Combat* expressed it on November 3: "The despair of the miners does not stem solely from their military inferiority. The strike, hardened and disciplined for a month, today begins to crumble, consumed by extreme poverty in the miners' households. And not one of their demands have been met. The government has had its say because of the weight of its arms and slowly the miners will begin to return to work. But the real conflict has not been resolved. In the final analysis, the government's success will be fragile." [107]

Food shortages pressed the miners to return to work. In November the CGT mobilized its entire national apparatus in efforts to collect food supplies and money for the strikers, raising between 200 and 500 million francs. [108] In Nord and Pas-de-Calais 50 tons of potatoes and a similar amount of other foodstuffs were collected and distributed to the striking miners. [109] Generous donations came from miners' unions in Belgium, the Netherlands, Italy, Scotland, and the countries of eastern Europe. [110] But donations could not hope to feed so many miners, as the Federation of Miners disappointedly indicated in a communiqué of October 25. [111]

Unable to continue the strike in the mining basin, the CGT turned to other unions and urged them to launch solidarity strikes. The result was a brief wave of strikes based mainly among workers who unloaded and transported coal—dockers and railroad workers. "In Dunkerque," according to *Voix du Nord*, "the dockers have not unloaded coal for several days. Eight hundred dockers are on strike. In Calais they were persuaded to work, but are very hostile to the unloading of coal." [112] The railroad workers passed a resolution on October 28 that would stop trains of coal from entering France. [113] But these strikes were partial and lasted only for a few days. North African and other troops were brought in to unload coal while local authorities requisitioned striking dockers. In the railroad workers' union, where FO was relatively strong, instructions to continue a 24-hour strike, issued by Communist and CGT union leaders, were only partially followed. The occupation of the mining basin also prompted sporadic strikes among metalworkers in Valenciennes and Anzin. But solidarity strikes could not win the miners' strike. Unlike the situation in 1947, the miners struck virtually alone in 1948. "During the 1948 strikes," recalled Roger Pannequin, "the miners were in the front lines of combat. They had been the force that had always held when the others had begun to cave in. But in 1948 they were isolated. Admired but isolated; aided but isolated." [114]

ISOLATION AND DEFEAT

Isolation bred defeat. "When will the strike end?" asked the miners, strikers and nonstrikers. Inside the political bureau of the PCF, CGT leaders posed the same question. The ensuing discussion revealed disagreement between some CGT leaders (Frachon? Lecoeur?) who believed that an orderly retreat was needed and other PCF leaders, including Duclos and Thorez, who wanted the strikes to continue. The debate lasted for more than two hours and concluded with a decision to continue the strike. Perhaps against their wishes, many CGT union leaders continued to press their members to stay off the job. By this time many union delegates and other activists had been arrested and were in jail. Others feared pursuit by the authorities. Communiqués from the Federation of Miners appeared less frequently.

On October 30, the CGT national office (not the Federation of Miners) issued a statement to all French miners describing the difficulties facing those who continued to strike and urged them to hold fast: "During the next two days you are going to be bombarded by speeches and invitations to quit striking. You are going to be submerged in lies. . . . Three deaths wait to be avenged; hundreds of your comrades now in prison wait for you to liberate them. With thousands of police and soldiers, with tanks and artillery against unarmed miners, they can take the pits. But they cannot force the miners to return to the mine and that is what counts. . . . Tuesday, as one man, you will be united and on strike." [115] But Tuesday came and went, and the situation became more difficult. Despite rumors of a possible reopening of talks, calls for binding arbitration, and aborted attempts to negotiate at the local level, no negotiations took place. Apparently convinced that the union seriously aimed to topple the government, the authorities simply resolved to deal the miners a dramatic defeat. And for the striking miners, impending defeat made isolation inevitable.

Relations between the two Left parties virtually ceased to exist during the strike. The Socialists used the occasion to heap abuse on the Communists and to take revenge against the PCF members for years of intimidation. Socialist leaders toured the basin speaking to anxious citizens about the strike; at the same time the local authorities prohibited several meetings organized by the Communists.

For their part, the Communist militants broke all precedents in their criticism of Socialist leaders. Describing the Section Française de l'Internationale Ouvrière (SFIO) as "moribund," the PCF urged all sincere Socialists to leave the SFIO and to join the newly formed United Socialist Party (PSU), an ephemeral grouping of Left Socialists and Communist sympathizers.[116] On November 5, Thorez outlined the type of coalition that could constitute a "government of democratic unity," and in an unprecedented act the general secretary of the PCF excluded the SFIO and substituted the fledgling PSU.[117] Such tactics, however, did not draw rank-and-file Socialists to the side of the Communists. As Pannequin noted, the strike movement in 1948, from the very beginning, was launched against the wishes of the Socialist miners.[118] Worse, as Pannequin understood, it tended to drive the Socialist workers back into the arms of their leaders. Falling back on old political habits, Communist leaders in the CGT began to refer to the Socialist leaders as "social-fascists."[119]

In subsequent years, Communists criticized the practices employed against Socialists during the 1948 strikes. Lecoeur, propelled into the top echelon of the PCF after the strikes, found himself demoted and then expelled in 1954. Charges against him included following a sectarian attitude toward the Socialists and failing to make correct distinctions between Socialist leaders and Socialist workers.[120] Later the PCF *Manuel* echoed these same criticisms of Communist relations with the Socialists and added that this attitude, combined with the prolongation of the strike, helped turn the miners' strike into a strike by a minority of workers.[121] In 1971 an internal document produced for the PCF by Roger Grimaud surveyed Socialist-Communist relations since 1944 and pointed to the dangerous and sectarian policies adopted by the Communists during the 1948 strike.[122]

The strike also brought into action some of the most rabid anti-Communists in the region. De Gaulle's Rassemblement du Peuple Français, which had made such a splash in the November 1947 elections, began to openly organize its cells in the mines during the strike. For the first time, Gaullist mine workers distributed tracts and sold their newspaper, *Le Rassemblement ouvrier*, in the mining basin. It chided the CFTC and FO for their "lack of combativity" and boasted of several "incidents" between its militants and those of the CGT. The Gaullist group participated in the FO-sponsored attempt to register nonstriking workers who wanted to return to work. The RPF group sought to make the Communists illegal and demanded that the authorities arrest Frachon, Lecoeur, and Duguet.[123]

"The strike gets longer and creates divisions among the miners," claimed the headlines of *Croix du Nord*.[124] Strikebreakers were roughed up by strikers, quarrels erupted between miners' wives in the grocery stores, and children sometimes fought in the streets or on the school grounds. In some cases the wives of striking miners threatened to take their children and leave. At one point, Dominique Desanti reported, some Algerian workers who had been commissioned to work in the mines, were attacked and badly beaten by strikers. "They didn't speak French or Ch'timi, so we had to make them understand," explained the striking miners.[125] Louis Lengrand, a veteran mine worker who had been newly promoted into the lower ranks of management as a supervisor, offered a poignant description of the intense feelings of alienation and guilt that he felt when he crossed the picket lines.[126] According to Lengrand, out of forty-four supervisors in his mining group, only five or six descended, and most of those who refused to work were subsequently demoted into the ranks of the workers. But those who worked faced public ostracism in the mining towns. In this desperate and divisive situation, the conflicts between strikers and nonstrikers increased. FO and CFTC militants lodged complaints with the authorities, charging strikers with physical assaults and damages to property (usually broken windows).[127] At the same time, the strikers recounted several examples of police brutality.[128] The deep cleavages that resulted from the conflicts remained for many years.

Jules Moch and Robert Lacoste had believed that the occupation of the mining basin would prompt a rapid return to work by most miners. However, despite food shortages, the back-to-work movement required nearly two weeks to fully develop. Statistics on participation in the strike, produced by Baseilhac of the administrative council of the northern mines, indicate that as late as November 12, roughly one-half of the underground miners were still off the job. Surface workers returned more quickly.[129] By the time the CGT leadership called off the strike on November 25, roughly three-fourths of the underground workers had returned to the job. A hard core of strikers remained out to the last: the union militants, the staff of the labor organizations, party cadres, and those who believed that management would never allow them to return to work.

Nearly 3,000 strikers were convicted of various offenses.[130] Moch reported that 1,041 strikers were arrested in Nord and Pas-de-Calais; Delfosse claimed the number was higher. In January 1949, 700 strikers remained in prison in Béthune, and 350 were incarcerated in jails in Douai and Valenciennes.[131] According to André Théret's account of the situation in the mines of Bruay, on the day of the return to work, 790 workers and office workers were prohibited from returning to their old jobs. In December, after nearly one month of waiting, these workers were finally given the terms for returning to their jobs. In some cases, they could be rehired by making a formal apology for their participation in the strike. In other cases, strikers were compelled to publicly renounce all union activities. The number of workers who were rehired totaled 526, leaving 264 without jobs. At Lens, more than a thousand miners were not allowed to return to their old jobs at the end of November, although some were rehired in January 1949.[132]

Workers who were terminated or suspended faced aggravated problems. After eight weeks of striking, without food and after having stretched personal credit beyond its limits, these workers found themselves deprived of the benefits they had formerly received: health care and medicine, supplementary food rations, water, and maternity care. Many miners and their families were evicted from housing units provided by the mines. Because they had not been laid off, they could not qualify for unemployment benefits. Forced to find alternative work, some miners had secured jobs in the auxiliary works of the mines, until management ruled that expulsion from a job in one part of the mines extended to all posts under the aegis of the nationalized mines. Consequently, many strikers were forced to leave the region or to find work in construction or steel mills.

Those militants who retained their jobs returned to a working situation marked by a new form of isolation. "When it was not possible to lay off all the 'agitators' without seriously reducing the level of production," recalled Pannequin, "the mines grouped all the Communist miners together in the same workplace, creating 'red workshops.' Miners concentrated together in this way were able to make a decent wage. But they no longer had contact with the non-Communist workers. This tactic was used by certain engineers, especially those who needed to prove their loyalty because they had previously shown weaknesses for the CGT or UNITEC."[133] In January 1949, J. M. Domenach described the repression against CGT militants. "The leaders or those alleged to be the leaders were systematically hounded by the police—trade union stewards, town councillors, former Resistance members. This vast system of repression and blackmail was directly aimed at the miners' trade union. Several 'ringleaders' were dismissed the day the strike ended: 'You'll be sent for when wanted.'"[134] With many of the union delegates incarcerated or missing, the mass of mine workers were left without many of their veteran leaders. Théret recounted that in Bruay a delegation of miners went to the mine director on the day after Christmas in an effort to find out when they could return to work. The delegation was led by a municipal councillor because all the union leaders were in jail.[135]

THE MINERS' STRIKE: MYTH AND REALITY

The defeat of the miners' strike in 1948 marked an end to nearly 20 years of intense social conflict in the northern mining basin. The government's victory symbolized the end of the threat of a Communist-inspired and labor-backed social revolution. As Herbert Luethy wrote: "In the autumn of 1948 northern France was first a besieged and then an occupied zone, and, so far as the rest of France was concerned, all this took place in a foreign, unknown land; it was as if there had been a rebellion in Madagascar. . . . The management of the nationalized industry announced at the end of the eighth week of the strike, that in view of the almost complete return to work, it regarded the strike as ended, and that workers who stayed out longer would be regarded as having been dismissed. This would in any case have been the end of the matter, even if the CGT had not ordered a return to work next day. It was the unconditional surrender of the northern French 'Soviet republic.'"[136] Another observer, David Schoenbrun, made similar comments: "I was at Lens, in the heart of the coal fields, and saw the [Senegalese] colonials charge the workers' barricades with drawn bayonets. Their strength was so formidable that resistance was hopeless. Moch broke the strikes and also broke the myth that had paralyzed political leaders for months: the belief that Thorez could seize power overnight by giving the signal for a working-class insurrection."[137]

In retrospect, it is remarkable how far "the myth" was taken for reality. As Alexander Werth suggested in 1948, "the French bourgeoisie had won a resounding victory over the working class, and the Communist bogey had greatly helped it in achieving this result."[138] Jacques Armel, an economist and writer for *Combat* made the same point when he wrote about the "defeat of the French working class":

> All this hullabaloo over changes of governments is neither here nor there; the truth is that what looks like a political crisis is in reality a profound social crisis. . . . The French bourgeoisie has been very skillful in dividing the French working class and in getting itself incorporated into the framework of international capitalism. In three years it has accomplished an astonishing revival.

Having made one concession after another, the French working class now has its back to the wall. Thanks to it, production has risen, and industrial and agricultural prices are rising. . . . Having always trusted the government's promises, which were never kept, it is now helplessly seeing itself suffocated by frozen wages, having already witnessed the most unfair distribution of the national income. In the name of a freedom, from which it derives no benefits, our working class is conscious of having won the battle of production and of having lost the battle of wages.[139]

But while some writers saw in the miners' defeat the end of the myth of a Communist-led workers' revolt, the PCF cultivated its own myth around the miners' strike. The Communists celebrated the miners' courage and class consciousness, partly to obscure the fact that the government had administered a very real defeat to one of the CGT's strongest federations and partly to restore the sagging confidence of Communist militants who saw their beloved party being pushed and pulled to the margins of political power. Dominique Desanti suggests that the creation of this peculiar "myth of the miners' strike" silenced would-be critics among Communist intellectuals by pitting class-conscious "workers" against vacillating "intellectuals." As the strike dragged on, Desanti suggested to Lecoeur that the strikers were reaching their limit and that the stores were cutting their credit. Lecoeur shrugged his shoulders. "The intellectuals are always afraid. If I were like that, I could never lead anyone." But the myth could not totally obscure the reality of defeat, and in 1949, wrote Desanti, party membership in the mining basin dropped, although party members did not speak of it publicly. "The miners, beaten, discouraged, went back to work and the CGT faced deep disaffection," wrote Desanti. "Unemployed, in debt; disagreements would last a long time in the *corons* of the mining communities. The miner ceased being a model."[140]

The reality of the strike was that each side had created its own myth. While publicly proclaiming the destruction of the French economy by striking miners, government leaders knew that sufficient amounts of coal had been stockpiled and that the Americans would provide special shipments to compensate for what was lost during the strike. Similarly, while Jules Moch spoke of Communist plots to destroy the republic, he failed to produce any real evidence to support these widely publicized charges. When it came to attacking the Communists, beating back workers' attempts to increase wages, or demonstrating that the government would not be bullied, the government's version of the myth was freely invoked. By contrast, the PCF-inspired myth was built on exaggerated accounts of the numbers of miners on strike and the "triomphaliste" claims in the

Communist and CGT press. The myth had a reality in the desperate but bold attempt by the coal miners to force a final change in the government's policy on wages and to rescind the Lacoste decrees. Yet the myth also blinded the PCF leaders to reality and prevented the CGT from making an accurate assessment of the situation. The union did not bring large numbers of strikers together to consider possible options once the strike became deadlocked. A desire to maintain the myth prevented top political leaders from listening to those CGT leaders and rank-and-file unionists who understood after the first three weeks off the job that the strike could not be won. While they continued the myth-building around the miners' strikes, the Communists failed to provide wise leadership for the labor movement. The miners and their union paid a heavy price.

7.

Economic Integration and the Retreat from Coal

The failure of the long and bitter miners' strike epitomized the defeat of the French working class.[1] It also marked the end of Left-initiated reform in social and economic policies. After state control was extended over the civilian airlines system in 1948, the nationalization effort came to a halt. Most features of the French welfare state were in place by 1949. The government lifted controls on prices in 1948. In 1950, the government allowed collective-bargaining wage agreements, but only after FO initiated a strike for the right to bargain on wages and was joined by the CGT and CFTC.

The start of the new decade also coincided with the beginning of what some regarded as the French "economic miracle." During the 1950s, the French economy grew at the rate of 4.5 percent, outpacing both West Germany (4.3 percent) and the United States (3.3 percent). Writers began to refer to "the new French revolution." For the first time since the 1870s the French birthrate increased to become among the highest in Europe. While this economic growth can be traced to many sources, three key components can be identified: economic integration, industrial modernization, and new economic policies.

The creation of the European Coal and Steel Community (ECSC) was the first important step toward European economic integration. Once again coal issues and the question of the future of Germany were linked. The ECSC was essentially built upon an agreement by France and West Germany to pool their coal mines and steel mills. This seemed to make war between the two historical antagonists unlikely, if not impossible. It also provided an important precedent for further efforts to integrate the economies of Europe, culminating in the creation of the Common Market. If the French and the Germans could agree on integrating their economies, why couldn't the rest of western Europe do the same?

Modernization of industry was another key component in French economic recovery. Marshall Plan assistance helped French firms to purchase new equipment and machinery. Also, many delegations of employers and employees participated in "productivity missions" that traveled to America to learn new ways of organizing production. In the coal mines, modernization meant the long-awaited arrival of electric conveyor belts and new coal-cutting equipment.

But integration and modernization alone could not produce the economic miracle. Rather, these two objectives were part of a new type of economic thinking that drove industrial policies in France after 1950. In his important study of French economic theory and practice in the twentieth century, Richard Kuisel defined the French neo-liberal policy as a new synthesis of economic management based on state direction, utilization of "corporatist" bodies, and relying on market forces wherever possible. The coal-mining industry exemplified those elements after 1950. Through its planning mechanisms, the state established targets for coal production and coordinated these efforts with other sectors of the economy. Leaders in the Charbonnages de France, together with state mining engineers, guided the industry's development. Private interests with important concerns regarding coal were also allowed to participate on some level in establishing coal policies. Market forces were brought to bear on the coal-mining industry after 1948 as the goal of increased production yielded to the necessity for higher productivity and lower energy prices. When the ECSC broke down protectionist barriers and expanded the coal market, the French industry was compelled to keep coal prices in Nord and Pas-de-Calais in line with those of German coal.

Coal production rose, the energy crisis abated, and the economy grew in the 1950s. Modernization made French industry more productive and competitive. But the miners saw some negative realities in the economic miracle. If much of the original impetus for the new synthesis in economic thinking had come from the Left and organized labor, it was state administrators, businessmen, and politicians who implemented the new policies. "The new synthesis of economic management and the market also marked the failure of more radical alternatives," wrote Richard Kuisel. "Neo-liberal institutions and policies were built over the broken dreams and bold designs of socialists, syndicalists, and doctrinaire corporatists."[2] The coal-mining industry retained some policies from the period of nationalization, notably the Miners' Statute, a housing program, and parity commissions, but in addition, market factors were brought to bear on decisions regarding production targets, labor costs, recruitment of miners, layoffs, and mine closures.

For the miners, modernization and the introduction of coal-cutting machines further reduced the autonomy of the hewers in the extraction process. Economic integration meant that miners' wages in France would be dragged down close to the lowest wage levels in the enlarged labor market. Workers lost representation in management and the union was weakened. Many miners were pessimistic about the future of their occupation. The image of the mine workers as labor's vanguard began to fade.

THE ECSC: THREE VIEWS

The true origins of the European Coal and Steel Community remain partly shrouded in mystery. The early drafts and papers used to prepare the "Schuman Plan" were burned the day before its announcement in May 1950.[3] Moreover, the coal and steel plan was crafted entirely behind the scenes, outside the purview of parliamentary or public scrutiny, by a small group of economic experts and well-connected politicians led by Jean Monnet.[4] Monnet feared that such a bold idea would be snuffed out by partisan debate arising from public fears of German economic revival. He also knew American support would be needed to put the project in place.

Monnet's vision was larger than coal and steel: he viewed the coal and steel pool as the first step toward a united Europe. After his idea died on the desk of Prime Minister Bidault, Monnet won the support of the foreign minister, Robert Schuman. Schuman, who had studied in Germany, spoke fluent German and came from the Lorraine region near the German border, and he agreed to back Monnet's project. Schuman was very interested in doing something original and important. The coal and steel plan was a novel approach to the old problem of Franco-German rivalry, but it also reached forward to the tantalizing idea of "Europe." Monnet's motives were more complex. He searched for a way to assuage French fears of a German revival while partially blocking the return of "Malthusian" industrial policies and "the old rut of limited, protected production."[5] François Caron observed that the founders of the ECSC (and the Common Market) were inspired by the desire "to make French producers restructure under pressure from foreign competition."[6] Derek Bok noted that the goal of the ECSC was to expand supply in order to lower prices, with the understanding that this could not be achieved immediately, but only incrementally.[7]

Another view of the ECSC emerged from across the Atlantic. From the first days of the liberation, the Americans had been concerned about what was regarded as the French tendency toward economic and industrial independence. "Communist policy on industry differs very little from de Gaulle's," wrote a State Department official after the general's departure in January 1946. "Each for his own reasons wants to organize French industry for freedom from too close dependence on non-French cooperation. Neither aims at self-sufficiency but both feel that close interdependence with the outside world would make France too vulnerable to political as well as economic pressure."[8]

American plans to rebuild Germany and integrate it into the Western alliance had been frustrated by French opposition and demands for coal reparations. But even after the agreement had been reached regarding the coal of the Saar region, the coal problem reemerged, this time in relation to Marshall Plan funding. Seeking to reduce French dependence upon coal imports, the French Commissariat du Plan of 1947 had assigned an important role for developing French coal: roughly 18 percent of Marshall Plan funds used for production in France went into the coal mines.[9] But in its first year, most of the Marshall Plan funds given to France were used to import coal and food from the United States. Marshall Plan aid to France in 1948 covered most of the cost of importing coal from America and the Ruhr.[10] In 1949, American coal exporters, faced with lagging demand at home, pressed for more foreign aid for coal and an end to quotas on coal exports. Marshall Plan countries took nearly half of the coal exported by the United States.[11] In Paris, the American Office of the Special Representative (OSR), later to become the Agency for International Development (AID), underscored American concern with the heavy emphasis French officials placed on developing their coal industry. The chief of the European coal section in 1949 highlighted a contradiction between American occupation policies in Germany and its attempt to underwrite economic recovery in France.[12] It made little sense to hold the price of German coal to a minimum for export to France while simultaneously pouring large amounts of American aid into the smaller French coal industry, particularly when the French refused to price their coal at the same level as German coal. Thus the Americans declared in August 1949 that European coal prices must always be held below that of American coal.[13] More detailed discussion of coal-pricing problems suggested an "uncertain future for French coal mining" and criticized the French investment program for coal as too high. The Americans urged France to divert funds from the nationalized industries to private enterprise.[14] The OSR called for a slowdown in French investments in oil, railroads, and coal, in anticipation of future coal deliveries from Germany.[15]

American policy-makers were quick to see the advantages of a Franco-German coal pool. Indeed, their role in the genesis of the project remained unclear (were the preparatory papers for the Schuman Plan destroyed to obscure the role of key Americans in crafting Monnet's plan?). Surveying the Marshall Plan at its halfway point, in April 1950, Richard Bissell, director of operations for the ECA, urged stronger efforts to integrate Europe by breaking trade barriers, creating a larger coal market, introducing competition, and eliminating less productive mining operations.[16] Marshall Plan head, Paul Hoffman, warned the Office of European Economic Cooperation (OEEC) in October 1949—a full six months before Monnet wrote up his ideas for consideration by Bidault—that European failure to establish economic integration could result in the termination of American aid. "The substance of such integration . . . would be the formation of a single large market within which quantitative restrictions, monetary barriers to the flow of payments and, eventually, all tariffs are permanently swept away."[17] Also in October 1949, McCloy, from the American embassy in Paris, suggested an international authority to govern the industrial policies in coordination with other inter-European agencies.[18] Six months later, Hoffman's friend Jean Monnet secured Schuman's support, discussed the plan with Secretary of State Dean Acheson, and then presented the Schuman Plan to the French Cabinet in May 1950. The plan put the entire coal and steel industries of France and Germany in the hands of a High Authority representing France, Germany, Italy, and the Benelux nations. Discussions with the British proved unsuccessful, partly because the French never expected to win their support and partly because the Labour party was not willing to push its recently nationalized coal and steel industries into wide competition. German industrialists backed the plan because it increased their influence in Europe, allowed for more rapid mergers and concentration within industries, and preempted nationalization of the German mines. The Schuman Plan greatly excited American officials, who saw it not only as a symbol of European unity, but also as a peg upon which they could hang German rearmament.[19]

For French miners, however, the plan offered little. Monnet, speaking at the signing of the ECSC treaty in April 1951, foresaw a general improvement in the standard of living for workers.[20] But in making his first presentation to the French Cabinet members a year earlier, Monnet had indicated that the plan's focus on productivity would involve closing a substantial number of French mines and laying off miners.[21] Étienne Hirsch, one of Monnet's colleagues, estimated that France would be forced by competition to eliminate 20 to 30 percent of its steel capacity.[22]

Union leaders complained that the plan's objective of equalizing wages and working conditions might not be beneficial to French miners. They pointed out that the poor wages and working conditions prevailing in Germany might be imported to France in the name of equality. The CGT predicted an upturn in unemployment and deterioration of living conditions for workers.[23] The Communists called the Schuman Plan "an economic Munich." They distributed pamphlets that contained drawings of workers being loaded into boxcars (marked "STO," the acronym for forced labor during the Occupation) for work in Germany. Leaders of the CGT miners' union predicted a further rollback of the reform in the mines.[24] Frachon traveled to Berlin for a meeting with German union leaders aimed at building international worker solidarity against a "third world war."[25]

Monnet indirectly confirmed the miners' notion that their wages and conditions were better than those of Germany. Seeking to clarify American questions in a meeting in May 1950, he stated that, from the French perspective, equalization of life and work in various national industries meant raising of standards and not leveling.[26]

Equally important, from the perspective of French miners, the Schuman Plan limited the ability of miners to use the strike to enhance their bargaining power because the government could simply increase coal production in Germany to cover the losses in French production. Protests by the CGT, however, proved ineffective. The policies governing the High Authority were hammered out by committees, with a consultative role for three non-Communist unionists from the CFTC and FO.[27] To their credit, the CFTC and FO representatives were able to win limited forms of assistance, including retraining and job placement services, for workers displaced by coal mine and steel mill closings.

Some French conservatives, fearing German economic domination, also opposed the plan.[28] Raymond Aron editorialized in *Figaro* in support of the French steel owners.[29] "The most determined opposition came from the iron and steel producers," wrote Jean-Pierre Rioux. "Backed by the CNPF [the main employers' organization] they hoped to organize their own lucrative cartels. It was the backing of the nationalized industries—the Charbonnages de France, then the SNCF [railroads] and the Régie Renault, all important consumers of steel—which allowed Schuman and the planners to surmount this opposition."[30] Thus the nationalized industries helped to lead the private sector into a competitive environment. In the final analysis, however, it may have been strong American support that pushed the plan to fruition, opening the way to a shift in coal policy from energy independence to economic integration.[31]

NATIONALIZATION RECONSIDERED

By 1954, the French coal industry had evolved considerably. The "economic feudality" of 1944 stood reformed and vindicated after several years of record production and climbing levels of productivity. With few exceptions, industrialists, business leaders, and heads of state economic agencies lessened their criticism of the coal-mining industry. In 1951, Lafond and Ricard, two top leaders of the Conseil Nationale du Patronat Français (CNPF), France's most important employers' organization, officially called a halt to polemics between their organization and the nationalized industries.[32] Writing in a new business journal concerned with energy, *Revue française de l'énergie*, Alfred Sauvy saluted the industry for its progress, noting that productivity in the French mines had surpassed interwar levels, while other countries with industries in private hands had not been able to do so.[33] While French coal mines had ranked among the lowest in productivity in Europe during the interwar years, in the early 1950s the miners' productivity outpaced that of their counterparts in the Low Countries, Belgium, and even Germany (see table 17). The Monnet Plan report for 1949 recorded the beginning of a big increase in productivity in that year.[34] Meanwhile a new state commission established as a watch-dog over the nationalized sector, the Commission de Vérification des Comptes des Entreprises Publiques (CVCEP), published four reports between 1949 and 1953. The commission found increased productivity as the industry's chief success.[35]

Two related factors lay at the heart of increased productivity: modernization and steady compression of the work force. New equipment such as conveyor belts, coal cutters, and new transport systems were intro-

TABLE 17. Productivity of Underground Coal Miners in Western Europe, 1938–1954
(In kilograms per worker per day)

	1938	1946	1954
France	1,229	926	1,515
Germany	1,916	1,191	1,492
Belgium	1,085	817	1,098
Low Countries	2,369	1,583	1,497
Britain	1,510	1,400	1,614

Source: Charbonnages de France, *Rapport de gestion, 1947–1955* (Paris, 1956).

TABLE 18. Modern Equipment Availability, 1938–1955

	1938	1946	1955
Conveyor Belts (km)	92	45	485
Locomotive Tractors	900	680	1,973
Rock Loaders	6	52	630
Electric Motors	0	250	7,852

Source: Charbonnages de France, *Rapport de gestion, 1955* (Paris, 1955).

TABLE 19. French Coal Miners, 1945–1954

	Underground	Surface		Underground	Surface
1945	195,219	98,112	1950	167,697	81,655
1946	211,189	107,821	1951	168,958	77,633
1947	216,195	103,885	1952	164,990	73,896
1948	190,786	92,341	1953	155,307	70,526
1949	186,416	88,612	1954	149,493	67,620

Source: Charbonnages de France, *Rapport de gestion, 1946–1955* (Paris, 1956).

duced between 1949 and 1952 (see table 18). Modernization plans for the mines, unveiled in February 1949, were drawn up by a commission headed by a key industry veteran, Lafitte-Laplace, in close consultation with American officials.[36] Marshall Plan aid, in the form of loans used for the purchase of American-made equipment, formed a central pillar of the modernization program.[37] Surface installations were rebuilt in order to consolidate activities to fewer sites. By 1949 twenty-two new surface projects were under construction in Nord and Pas-de-Calais.[38] The introduction of new equipment and modern surface operations allowed the industry to reduce the number of extraction sites. Less productive mines were closed when coal stocks accumulated. From 1946 to 1951, the number of mining sites in the northern coal basin fell from 109 to 98. By 1956 the number fell further to 73.[39]

The blue-collar work force in the mines was progressively trimmed. The number of coal miners had peaked in 1947 at 329,000. Ten years later their numbers had fallen by more than 100,000. The compression of the work force had begun with the Lacoste decrees in 1948 and continued into the 1950s (see table 19). The sharpest drop in the number of underground workers came on the heels of the miners' strike in the

TABLE 20. French Coal Mine Management Personnel, 1946–1952

	Supervisors/Technicians	Engineers/Managers
1946	13,502	1,906
1947	15,195	2,034
1948	15,806	2,015
1949	16,590	2,002
1950	16,336	2,052
1951	16,452	2,042
1952	16,540	2,062

Source: Charbonnages de France, *Rapport de gestion, 1947–1952* (Paris, 1953).

winter of 1948. The Monnet Plan for 1949 reported a 30,000 drop in the number of underground miners employed from July to December of 1948.[40] More than 23,000 of them (roughly 75 percent) left the mines of Nord and Pas-de-Calais.[41] Meanwhile the number of managers and technicians increased after 1947, a fact frequently noted by the miners' union (see table 20). Some of the increase in cadres was related to the development of the annex industries, which required more technicians than workers. A greater factor was the growth of mechanization, which required an increased supervisory staff and a larger role for technical services.

Under state direction, coal mining's financial balance sheet improved for the first time in decades, breaking a long cycle of deficits. Being in the black, however, had a different meaning for an industry located in the public sector. Nationalization changed the industry's mission from making profits to producing coal at the lowest possible price. Labor economists, especially CGT's André Barjonet and Jean Duret, were among the first to highlight the ways in which pricing policies in the nationalized sector assisted in the process of accumulation in the private sector.[42] Michel Toromanoff noted how the coal industry, with its controlled price schedule, provided an "indirect subsidization of the coal clients by lowering the industrial price of coal."[43] The cheap coal policy had been part of the first Monnet Plan in 1945. The hope was that the state could use its controls over pricing in ways that would limit inflation. This objective was obscured during the years of coal shortages, hyperinflation, and violent strikes. But by 1953, Maurice Byé, although not a proponent of nationalization, recognized that after 1948 the cost of coal had risen at a level significantly lower than that of industrial prices.[44] A similar finding was made by J. Grondien in an article in *Revue française de l'énergie* in 1950 (see table 21).[45] It is probably not possible to know to what extent

TABLE 21.   Coal Prices v. Industrial Prices, 1948–1954
                (1949 = 100)

	1948	1949	1950	1951	1952	1953	1954
Industrial products	84	100	105	165	192	187	176
Coal price	84	100	106	127	142	139	139

Source: INSEE, *Mouvement économique en France de 1944 à 1957* (Paris, 1958), 269.

the private sector and the chief consumers of coal—the railroads, electrical plants, the steel and chemical firms, and other large and small industries—benefited from state-directed pricing policies. The shift in emphasis from productionism to productivity, from coal at any price to coal at a lower price reflected the industry's new mission under public ownership.

Decision making in the coal mines steadily shifted from the regional level to the Charbonnages de France in Paris. The last two CGT representatives were removed from the Charbonnages de France after the 1948 strike. Only non-Communist unions were permitted representation. The CVCEP consistently urged that workers be allowed only a consultative role. In 1953 the term of FO leader Léon Jouhaux expired. That same year the government of René Mayer issued decrees that further reduced the number of administrative council members named by labor and consumer groups, resulting in a de facto end to a representational management model. "The nationalized industries," said Jouhaux, "have been transformed into staticized organisms." [46]

Success in the coal-mining industry, however, was built on the backs of the mine workers. While coal mining broke decisively with a long tradition of technological backwardness and low productivity, the situation for French coal miners deteriorated. Faced with a policy of rationalization and retrenchment, the heroes of the battle of production became the victims of modernization.

The strike defeat in 1948 greatly weakened the union and made it harder to defend workers' concerns. A group of mine workers who moved up to become foremen in the 1950s recalled that after the 1948 strike the top managers adopted a much tougher attitude toward workers and middle management. "It was a regime that was much harder, less liberal than before 1948," said Georges Pierrot. "The top management demanded greater production and they used more penalties," recalled Robert Volan. "It seemed like they wanted to retake what they had lost, and as the union was weaker after the strike, they knew it would be a long while before the miners could strike once more." "A worker who was not very polite to a supervisor would receive a fine," recalled Tadek Chudzinski. "If he had six days of absence from the job, he could be fired. You could really see the change. The boss had contol over everything."[47] Like many of his fellow workers, Chudzinski left the mines in 1949.

The introduction of coal-cutting machines, for example, allowed for a further expansion of longwalls mining and a loss of control by chief miners in the process of production. The old crew system was only a memory in most mines. Groups of hewers used machines to extract the coal and were paid on an individual basis according to output. They were closely supervised by a chief miner, whose job was to implement a production plan directed by the mining engineer.

A feeling of pessimism gripped the mine workers. Reprisals and dismissals of safety delegates and union stewards thinned the union of some of its most experienced leaders and rank-and-file activists. The government took control of the miners' cooperative in 1948 and scaled back its program of housing for the coal miners beginning in 1949.

Management stopped training apprentices in the early 1950s for a number of years. Organized labor found it very difficult to moderate management's power within the structures of the nationalized mines. The "glass house" had become a distant, impregnable tower. Once the coal shortage had been overcome, the emphasis on higher productivity increased the risk of layoffs. In 1949 the production targets established by the Monnet Plan were scaled back, and soon the miners were haunted by the specter of mine closings.[48] Addressing the miners at the CGT convention in Pas-de-Calais in 1950, Auguste Lecoeur asked: "How do we keep our region from becoming a desert?"[49]

As French energy consumption began to move away from coal and toward other sources, economic planners confronted the large cohort of coal miners, survivors of the battle of production, who felt they had won job security under the provisions of the Miners' Statute. Several sociologists studied the attitudes of coal miners in the 1950s, mostly in order to suggest what could be done to circumvent the problems caused by retrenchment and layoffs. Alain Touraine interviewed miners about their attitudes toward their work and the future of their occupation and then compared their responses to those of workers in the building trades. He found that miners generally had a negative perception of their métier and maintained a relatively pessimistic view of their future in coal mining. The miners' unionism, Touraine concluded, was less an instrument of defense or negotiation than an emotional and nearly unanimous expression of opposition to a global system of work.[50] Serge Moscovici found that the miners had mixed feelings about modernization. Most miners deplored the increased numbers of engineers and cadres in the mines. They tended to see management as bureaucratic and somewhat invisible compared to the period before 1950. Older miners, who constituted a growing majority in the 1950s, recalled that their situation had been better in the late 1940s when they enjoyed a somewhat privileged position in relation to other workers. Moscovici concluded that although the miners were not absolutely opposed to nationalization and technological change, their perspective on these issues had been profoundly shaped by the liberation experience, the split in the labor movement, and the strikes of 1947 and 1948.[51] As miners became older, concern with silicosis increased, and many miners complained that the new methods of extracting coal were more dangerous because they generated a much finer form of coal dust.[52] In 1949, 314 miners died from silicosis; in 1952 the number increased to 389; and the following year 487 miners died from silicosis.[53] One miner commented that he felt sad to send his son into the mines, but the family needed his son's paycheck since he was now too sick to work.[54]

While the CGT continued to be the dominant union among the miners, the labor movement remained divided along political and religious lines (see table 22). Union membership declined, and miners generally were unwilling to strike to win their demands. The Communists dropped the old habit of describing the miners as the vanguard of the proletariat. Pushed to the margins of political life and facing a decline in membership, the PCF searched for enemies within. In the early 1950s veteran leaders André Marty and Charles Tillon were accused of being police agents and were expelled. Arthur Ramette, Communist leader in Nord and Pas-de-Calais, was charged with financial mismanagement, demoted, and then expelled. Delfosse was dropped from the PCF Central Committee. Secondary union leaders like Roger Pannequin and André Théret were frozen out of key party and union posts.

TABLE 22. Miners' Delegates Elected by Unions, 1949 and 1952

Unions	Underground Workers		Surface Workers	
	1949	1952	1949	1952
CGT	148	127	66	57
FO	31	33	29	24
CFTC	13	18	18	16
Total	192	178	113	97

Source: Val Lorwin, *The French Labor Movement* (Cambridge, Mass., 1954), 180.

Auguste Lecoeur's turn came in 1954. Promoted to the position of secretary of organization in 1950, Lecoeur soon became the third most important Communist in France, behind Thorez and Duclos. He became a member of the PCF Secretariat, along with veteran leaders Thorez, Duclos, and Marty. Lecoeur took charge of the party's membership and recruitment efforts, a tough job in a period when sectarianism and cold war isolation limited the PCF's strategy. Lecoeur emphasized member-to-member outreach, including special house calls, in order to bring old members back to cell meetings and into party activities. He established a network of party stalwarts whose job it was to involve more party members in its activities. Lecoeur also attacked sectarian practices and argued for substituting the word *sections* for *cells* in order to make the PCF seem less insurrectionary and more inviting to newcomers. When Thorez went to Moscow for an extended medical treatment for cancer and Duclos was arrested (during the "pigeon affair"), Lecoeur served as the PCF's top leader. In the Chamber of Deputies he proved to be a forceful speaker for the PCF. Lecoeur came to be regarded as Thorez's heir apparent, although party insiders knew that the two men were not on friendly terms. Thorez complained that Lecoeur wanted to put him in his grave before he had died. Lecoeur also incurred the wrath of Thorez after he publicly criticized a drawing of Stalin by Pablo Picasso that Lecoeur found to be lacking in the principles of socialist realism. Lecoeur had also had sharp disagreements with Jeannette Veermersch, Thorez's wife, who played a big role in internal party affairs when Thorez was in the Soviet Union. Following the massive strike wave of 1953, which caught the PCF leaders by surprise, Lecoeur criticized the PCF for not providing leadership for the union movement. But he soon found himself under attack from Thorez. Lecoeur was charged both with sectarianism (for the tactics used during the 1948 strikes) and opportunism (for his proposal to change *cells* into *sections*). Unable to perform self-criticism that was sufficient to satisfy Thorez, Lecoeur went to Lens and composed a scathing attack on Maurice Thorez, Jeannette Veermersch, and Jacques Duclos. The publication of Lecoeur's *L'Autocritique attendu* assured the expulsion of the former Communist leader. The 44-year-old militant then passed through several political phases, including "national communism," democratic socialism, and, finally, Gaullism.[55]

Shorn of its leaders and tied to the narrow political strategy of the PCF, the CGT Federation of Miners faced the mine closings and other problems in a state of disarray. They criticized the other unions but worked to contain strikes in the mines, arguing that the miners were too demoralized to support a strike. They attacked management's productivity schemes but lacked any influence in management that could have altered those plans. A comparison of Victor Duguet's speeches at CGT conventions provides one indication of how the thinking of key labor leaders had evolved since the days of the battle of production. In 1946 Duguet lauded the miners for their front-line effort in the battle for coal. In 1948, during the miners' strike, the union leader praised the miners' courage in the face of armed troops. But in 1951 Duguet focused on the toll taken by accidents, silicosis, and mine closings. He painted a picture of misery and near hopelessness. Achilles Blondeau, a leader of the Federation of Miners in the north, described how the expansion of the piecework system combined with repression against union militants had reduced the ability of the miners to defend their interests.[56] The Communists began to take a dim view of nationalization after 1950, reverting to their earlier criticisms of state ownership and economic planning. "The state," exclaimed Lecoeur at the national convention of the CGT Federation of Miners in 1950, "is even more rapacious than the employers."[57]

THE RETREAT FROM COAL

France's investment in its struggling coal industry began to pay dividends in the 1950s. Increased mechanization and the centralization of surface installations helped to increase productivity. Small, marginal mines were closed. Production stabilized and the number of mine workers was reduced by 70,000 between 1949 and 1955.[58]

Coal policies responded both to the Second Modernization Plan and the European Coal and Steel Community.[59] The second plan underscored a basic commitment to a market economy. For French coal, this meant increasing productivity in order to keep prices low and make French industry more competitive. When the veneer of European unity was removed, the ultimate economic goal of the Schuman Plan was to acquire larger amounts of coal at cheaper prices by rationalizing western Europe's coal-mining industries.[60] The French coal industry, streamlined and retooled, pioneered French entry into European competition, and later the Common Market, by striving to keep coal from Nord and Pas-de-Calais competitive with Ruhr coal prices.[61]

The drive to hold down French coal prices proved successful in the 1950s and 1960s (see table 23). Coal prices remained steady from 1951 to 1955, rose slightly until 1959, and remained constant throughout the 1960s. Efforts to hold down the price of coal, however, inevitably confronted the old problem of high labor costs, which had accounted for 75 percent of the cost of producing a ton of coal in 1947. The drive for higher productivity, however, succeeded in reducing labor costs from

TABLE 23. Coal Prices, 1949–1969
(In new francs)

1949	27.71	1956	46.39	1963	63.52
1950	31.01	1957	51.24	1964	64.44
1951	37.12	1958	55.22	1965	64.44
1952	42.17	1959	62.22	1966	63.33
1953	42.35	1960	62.22	1967	63.33
1954	42.96	1961	62.22	1968	65.65
1955	42.98	1962	62.22	1969	67.06

Source: Bureau de Documentation Minière, *Annuaire statistique*, 1948 to 1969.

1950 to 1956 to around 60 percent.[62] In relation to the value of a ton of coal, there was a steady decline in labor costs from 1947 to 1954 (see table 11, page 00).

In the late 1950s, the industry's future was clouded by increased competition with oil. While energy consumption in France increased during the 1950s, coal's share of the national energy market declined from 78 percent in 1949 to 54 percent in 1960. The percentage of energy provided by French coal fell from 60 to 45 percent during the same period (see table 24). Most of the losses went to foreign oil, especially cheap crude oil that flooded the European market toward the end of the 1950s. This dramatic penetration by oil is partly explained by decisions of state officials and businessmen in France. The Finance Ministry, for example, favored the expanded use of oil because it required no state investment despite its relatively low price. When the third plan stressed the need to prepare France to enter international competition, the Ministry of Industry also tilted toward oil in order to escape the rigid labor costs in coal. French oil company leaders built a coalition of politicians that opposed placing excise taxes on heavy fuel oil. Despite protests that the switch to oil would jeopardize France's future economic security, the retreat from coal continued.[63] "The decline of coal," wrote Saumon and Puiseux, "appeared 'unavoidable' to all the experts as soon as they were certain that large petroleum reserves were available at a very low cost."[64]

In 1960, the minister of Industry, Jeannenny, announced a new plan for the coal-mining industry that scaled down production for the first time. "From now on," wrote Jeannenny to the Charbonnages de France, "coal production should not be determined by predictions of consumption, but rather by the cost of producing coal, taking account of the prices of foreign coal that could be imported as well as the price of competing forms of energy."[65] Jeannenny's plan triggered a new round of pit clos-

TABLE 24. Coal Production, Consumption, and Percentage of Primary Energy in France, 1949–1963

			(Millions/tons)		
	French Coal Output	Total Coal Consumption	Total Energy Consumption	Coal as Percentage of Total Energy Consumption	French Coal as Percentage of Total Energy Consumption
1949	53	69	88	78	60
1950	53	66	88	75	60
1951	55	71	99	72	56
1952	57	70	100	70	57
1953	55	66	97	68	57
1954	56	67	102	66	56
1955	57	71	109	65	52
1956	58	78	120	65	48
1957	60	80	121	66	49
1958	60	73	121	60	49
1959	60	70	121	59	49
1960	58	70	129	54	45
1961	55	71	134	53	41
1962	55	75	145	52	38
1963	51	75	158	47	32

Source: Bureau de Documentation Minière, *Annuaire statistique,* 1949 to 1966.

ings, protests, and further retrenchment. French mine workers attempted to halt the retreat from coal with strikes at Decazeville and finally with a general strike in March 1963. The miners won government assistance to limit the impact of retrenchment, but the strike did not result in a decisive fuel shortage in France. Unlike the 1940s, when the coal shortage forced the government to intervene and to accommodate some of the miners' demands, in a period of energy abundance, the miners lost their bargaining power and retreat from coal continued.

Seduced by cheap oil and eager to avoid high labor costs, French business and state managers accelerated the abandonment of coal. However, the formation of OPEC and the spectacular oil price increases in the early 1970s exposed France's economic vulnerability. In 1950, French energy production had supplied 70 percent of the nation's energy needs, reflecting a strategy of energy independence. But that percentage had fallen below 25 percent when the oil embargo forced France to confront a new "energy crisis" in 1973.

Conclusion

Acentury has passed since the first collective bargaining agreement in France was signed between coal companies and the miners' union in Arras (Pas-de-Calais) in 1891. To-day, however, nearly all of the coal mines of the region are closed. Much of the coal reserves have been exhausted, and the cost of continuing to mine the remaining coal seams is prohibitive. In the space of a generation, the coal mines that once occupied the foremost position in the economy have become relics of industrial archeology and frag-ments of the collective memory of retired mine workers. Nationalized industries have also fallen out of favor throughout Europe, and a trend toward privatization reaches into all corners of a global economy. Orga-nized labor in France and America enjoyed a great revival in the 1930s and 1940s, but both movements face seemingly intractable obstacles to-day. Given these changes, what value can be derived from a study of coal mining and mine workers in France?

First, there is value in setting the record straight regarding nationaliza-tion, the union's role in the battle of production, and the controversial strikes. The focus on coal also illuminates two critical developments in postwar French history: the Left's rise and decline and the ways in which state intervention laid the basis for economic expansion. Finally, the French experience with industrial policy offers valuable lessons for orga-nized labor.

Government's role in French coal mining increased steadily in the twentieth century. Because France imported and produced this strategic material, the government maintained a constant and compelling interest in coal output. Coal policies emerged through the interaction of coal operators who held government concessions to extract coal, state mining engineers who were trained to manage the industry, and mine workers as represented by their labor organizations and political allies. However, the precise mix of input from the various actors varied a great deal, usually in relation to shifts in the balance of power between workers and owners and changes in the political complexion of the government in power. During the war years of 1914–1918 the industry depended upon government action and subsidies to keep it afloat. Reflecting a desire for labor peace during wartime, the government instituted limited forms of worker participation in the production process. After the war, the government financed a rebuilding effort of the mines. But the coal operators abandoned wartime experiments with worker participation by eliminating union representation on production committees. Instead, the companies sought to cut labor costs by initiating new forms of rationalization of the labor process. During the depression years the state again intervened to stabilize the industry. The Popular Front elections and strikes in 1936 pushed the unions back into the equation, forcing the government to broker new labor policies, including the eight-hour day, vacations with pay, and a prohibition of the "scientific management" systems opposed by the coal miners. But the collapse of the Popular Front government in 1938 and the German victory in 1940 largely erased the union's victories.

German forces occupied the northern mining region from 1940 to 1944 and subjected the coal industry to the demands of the Nazi war machine. The industry's chronic problems—technological backwardness, recruitment difficulties, labor discontent—emerged in bolder relief and forced the government to intervene in almost every aspect of the production process. A group of "modernizers" within the French government initiated efforts to streamline administrative control, encourage investment in modern equipment, and set rational production targets. At the same time, several Resistance "think tanks" were busy developing plans to reform the economic system once the war ended. Mine workers faced declining living and working conditions during the occupation. Food was scarce, wages were low, and labor relations under the aegis of German military forces were marked by conflict and repression. Although the government had outlawed labor organizations, it permitted a handful of moderate union leaders to present the concerns of the workers to the authorities. Meanwhile, the CGT miners' union reorganized as a clandestine force, led primarily by the network of Communist activists who had formed pit committees in the mines. A work stoppage organized by northern coal miners in May 1941 was the first strike in France to protest the Nazi occupation and a portent of the popular forces that would be unleashed once the occupation forces had receded. War and occupation had created a new consensus for radical change and forged a popular movement that aimed at implementing those changes. By the time the liberation began, the issue was not whether or not the coal industry would be reformed, but rather how much control would be assumed by the state and what kind of a role would be offered to organized labor.

After the liberation, the government seized control of the coal mines and set up a provisional nationalization. A drastic coal shortage weakened the war effort and blocked the way to economic recovery. The new government struggled to satisfy the concerns of industrial consumers, the old companies, and mine workers. It was easy to promise the miners a new beginning but difficult to resolve the old problems that had required state intervention in the first place. The miners, defiant and "lean and hungry" after years of economic deprivation and political repression, walked off the job. They backed the politicians' calls for nationalization, but for them it meant dismissing a large portion of the management personnel, ending the food shortages, and putting workers in decision-making positions. As coal production dropped dangerously, the top official assigned to administer the region by General de Gaulle reported that a semirevolutionary situation was unfolding in a vacuum left by the collapse of traditional forms of authority. In this crisis situation, the CGT miners' union proved to be the only force capable of restoring order in the mines, but the task was achieved only with great difficulty. Union leaders who had organized strikes against the old coal bosses and the Germans now found themselves trying to convince angry wildcat strikers to return to the mines and extract more coal. They were helped when Maurice Thorez, top leader of the French Communist Party, returned to his native region to denounce strikes and promote the "battle for coal." Gradually the wildcat strikes ended and the union joined with the government in a common effort to promote higher production.

From 1945 to 1947 the CGT miners' union broke with long-standing union traditions by banning strikes, fostering cooperation with management, and leading an all-out effort to increase the production of coal. The union wove together a pattern of patriotism, solidarity, and voluntarism to stimulate the miners to work hard to overcome the coal shortage. But behind the slogans and rhetoric was a trade-off between labor and the government. Union leaders assumed the job of restoring order, preventing strikes, and settling disputes between miners and management. In exchange, the unions demanded complete nationalization, worker representation in management, and solid improvements in wages and benefits. The production drive championed the notion of labor-management cooperation, an idea that made sense at a moment when engineers, for the first time, had joined a union of mining engineers affiliated with the

CGT. Another important factor in generating cooperation between labor, management, and the state materialized in 1946 when Auguste Lecoeur, the leader of the miners' union in the northern basin, was named under-secretary to Marcel Paul, the Communist minister of Industrial Production. Lecoeur was given the responsibility of overseeing the progress of the nationalized coal mines, and he made every effort to extract more coal. Legislation that definitively nationalized the industry and provided for worker representation was enacted. Also approved was a Miners' Statute that codified a new list of workers' rights. During the battle of production, the old triangular relationship between operators, unions, and government was altered as the mining companies' role came to a close and the union's strategy was coordinated with the Ministry of Industrial Production and the district mining engineers. It marked the high point of cooperation between labor, management, and the state. Nevertheless, Lecoeur's efforts to replace veterans of the old mining companies with union activists proved only partly successful and generated a storm of controversy. The battle for coal produced positive results. In 1946 coal production surpassed prewar levels at the same time as the union's influence in coal policy peaked.

France's battle for coal had an impact on international issues as the cold war developed. French leaders sought to win "hidden reparations" in German coal, but American policy-makers had focused their attention on rebuilding Germany as a key player in an anti-Soviet alliance. The Americans were particularly concerned about Communist participation in the French government, a fear that French leaders learned to utilize when making requests for economic assistance. During a reshuffle of the cabinet in December 1946 the Communists retained their ministerial posts, except for Marcel Paul in the Ministry of Industrial Production. Lecoeur lost his government post and the new minister, Robert Lacoste, accelerated the gradual removal of Communist union officials from leading positions in the nationalized sector. A growing financial crisis offered critics of nationalization new incentives to reduce labor's power in the coal mines. Insolvency in coal mining in 1947 was rooted in factors that had little to do with the actions of any administrator—high labor costs, hyperinflation, and the government's attempt to slow inflation with price cuts. But that reality did not prevent parliamentary approval for a variety of measures that reduced labor's role in the mines. Meanwhile, the CGT encountered an opposition movement within the union of mining engineers and among the mine workers. Conflicts within the CGT reached a climax during the general strike of December 1947, which was triggered by the dismissal of a CGT leader as a vice president of the northern mines. Government officials saw the strike as the first step in a

Communist insurrection. The union's objectives were mainly economic in nature, but the strikes were also political. The union's goal in 1947, and in most major strikes in coal mining since the 1880s, was to force the government to alter its wage policies. But the government refused to yield and sent troops to occupy the northern mines. The strike ended in a stalemate. A group of union leaders denounced the Communists and left the CGT to form a new federation called Force Ouvrière. More unionists were dismissed from positions in the nationalized mines for strike activities, and the slogans of the battle of production were buried forever.

A longer and even more bitterly contested strike erupted in 1948. What began as an economic dispute turned into a deadly confrontation that continued for two long months. The cold war atmosphere gave the conflict a sense of inevitability as both the government and the CGT committed themselves to a fight to the finish. When Interior Minister Jules Moch ordered troops to occupy the mines, the union called out the mining security crews for a 24-hour warning strike. The government responded by arresting strike leaders and requisitioning mine workers. Attempts by the CGT to spread the strike to other sectors achieved only limited success, and, after two weeks, miners began to trickle back to work. Once the strike became a military battle, the union was bound to lose. CGT leaders failed to find a way to end the confrontation even after it was obvious that the strike would be successful. The 1947 strike had ended in stalemate, but the 1948 strike ended in defeat.

Labor's setback marked the end of the social and economic reforms of the postwar period. It also coincided with the beginning of two decades of economic growth in France. European economic integration began to be a reality with the creation of the European Coal and Steel Community in 1951. French coal policies, now designed by state officials in concert with mining engineers and industrial consumers of coal, shifted from energy independence to increasing French competitiveness within the European coal market. Modernization of equipment helped raise production while reducing the number of mine workers. This improved productivity and allowed the state to keep coal prices low. The CGT complained that merging the coal industries of western Europe could lower standards for French miners and lead to mine closings. But the labor movement, weakened by the 1948 strike and divided into political and religious factions, no longer possessed much influence within the decision-making process in the mines. The battle for coal had been won, but the coal miners who had fought in the front lines received only partial portions of the fruits of victory. As the industry declined in importance, the heroes of the battle for coal became the victims of retrenchment.

Notes

INTRODUCTION

1. For example, see Maurice Allais, *La Gestion des houillères nationalisées et la théorie économique* (Paris, 1953), and Monique Maillet-Chassagne, *Influence de la nationalisation sur la gestion des entreprises publiques* (Paris, 1956).

2. In 1984 the Brookings Institution held a conference in Washington, D.C., and invited French business leaders, elected officials, and civil servants to explain French industrial policy to interested Americans. The papers and some of the discussion were published by Brookings. Although these offered some good information about the current period, the role of labor organizations in industrial policy was virtually absent. Also, historical perspectives were mainly limited to the last two decades. See William J. Adams and Christian Stoffaes et al., eds., *French Industrial Policy* (Washington, D.C., 1986).

3. For example, see David Thomson, *Democracy in France Since 1970* (London, 1964), and Alfred Cobban, *A History of Modern France*, vol. 3, *1871–1962* (Middlesex, England, 1965).

4. By far the most important local work on the northern coal-mining region has been done by Étienne Dejonghe, professor of history at the University of Lille III. See Étienne Dejonghe and Daniel Laurent, *Libération du Nord et du Pas-de-Calais* (Paris, 1974), as well as several important articles cited elsewhere in this book. Other examples of local or regional history that bear on the coal mines are Michel Delwiche and Francis Groff, *Les Gueules noires* (Brussels, 1985), and Évelyne Desbois, Yves Jeanneau, and Bruno Mattei, eds., *La Foi des charbonniers: Les mineurs dans la bataille du charbon 1945–1947* (Paris, 1986). *Revue du Nord* has also published a number of articles that illuminate aspects of the history of the coal-mining industry in northern France.

5. For example, see Alfred J. Reiber, *Stalin and the French Communist Party* (New York, 1962).

6. Georges Lefranc, *Essais sur les problémes socialistes et syndicaux* (Paris, 1970), 109–10.

7. Marcel Ventenat, *L'Expérience des nationalisations: Premier bilan* (Paris, 1948); Jean Rivero, *Le Régime des nationalisations* (Paris, 1948); and Marcel Pellenc, *Le Bilan de six ans d'erreurs* (Paris, 1950).

8. David Pinckney, "The French Experiment with Nationalization, 1944–1950," in *Modern France*, ed. Edward Mead Earle (New York, 1964).

9. Mario Einaudi, Maurice Byé, and Ernesto Rossi, *Nationalization in France and Italy* (Ithaca, N.Y., 1955), 6, 28.

10. Warren C. Baum, *The French Economy and the State* (Princeton, N.J., 1958), 50.

11. John Ardagh, *The New French Revolution* (New York, 1968), 15. See also Herbert Luethy, *France Against Herself* (Meridian, N.Y., 1955), 55–56.

12. Ardagh, *New French*, 14–15.

13. François Caron, *An Economic History of Modern France* (New York, 1979), 223.

14. Jean-Jacques Carré, Paul Dubois, and Edmond Malinvaud, *French Economic Growth*, trans. J. P. Hatfield (Stanford, Calif., 1975).

15. John B. Sheahan, "Experience with Public Enterprise in France and Italy," in *Public Enterprise*, ed. William Shepherd (Lexington, Mass., 1976), 147, 161.

16. Andrew Schonfield, *Modern Capitalism: The Changing Balance of Public and Private Power* (London, 1970).

17. Stuart Holland, *The State as Entrepreneur* (London, 1972), 7.

18. Richard Kuisel, *Capitalism and the State in Modern France: Renovation and Economic Management in the Twentieth Century*, (Cambridge, England, 1981).

19. Claire Andrieu, Lucette Le Van, and Antoine Prost, eds., *Les Nationalisations de la libération: De l'utopie au compromis* (Paris, 1987).

20. State theorists include Ralph Miliband, Nicos Poulantzas, Erik Wright, James O'Connor, Claus Offe, Goran Therborn, and Fred Block. Many of the most important articles on state theory have appeared in *Politics and Society, New Left Review, Socialist Review*, and *Kapitalistate*. Fred Block makes an important point: "There are certain periods—during wartime, major depressions, and periods of postwar reconstruction—in which the decline of business confidence as a veto on government policies doesn't work. These are the periods in which dramatic increases in the state's role have occurred." Fred Block, "The Ruling Class Does Not Rule: Notes on the Marxist Theory of the State," *Socialist Revolution* 33 (1977): 24.

21. Darryl Holter, "Mineworkers and Nationalization in France: Insights into Concepts of State Theory," *Politics and Society* 11 (1982).

22. Claire Andrieu, "La France à la gauche de l'Europe," *Le Mouvement social* 134 (1986).

23. Commenting upon PCF leader Maurice Thorez's trip to the mining basin in an effort to end wildcat strikes in 1945, Fernando Claudin wrote: "To read Thorez' speeches at this period gives the impression that France was in the middle of building socialism and that the central task for the workers was to get under way an economy which they controlled." Fernando Claudin, *The Communist Movement: From Comintern to Cominform, pt. 2* (New York, 1975), 332–33.

24. Desbois, Jeanneau, and Mattei, eds., *La Foi des charbonniers.*

25. Rolande Trempé, *Les Trois Batailles du charbon, 1936–1947* (Paris, 1989).

26. Robert Goetz-Girey, *Le Mouvement des grèves en France, 1919–1962* (Paris, 1965), 38, 42.

27. Edward Shorter and Charles Tilly, *Strikes in France, 1830–1968* (London, 1974), 139.

28. Georges Lefranc, *Les Expériences syndicales en France de 1939 à 1950* (Paris, 1950), 151–60.

29. Adolf Sturmthal, *Left of Center: European Labor Since World War II* (Urbana, Ill., 1983), 70. See also Jean-Daniel Reynaud, *Les Syndicats en France* (Paris, 1975), 99–100.

30. Val Lorwin, *The French Labor Movement* (Cambridge, Mass., 1954), 108–10.

31. Val Lorwin, "Communist Strategy and Tactics in Western European Movements," *Industrial and Labor Relations Review* (April 1953): 384.

32. Reiber, *Stalin*, 179.

33. Political scientists and sociologists who observed politics in western Europe during the 1950s and 1960s were puzzled by the persistence of working-class electoral support for the PCF. The Communists were easily dislodged from positions in the apparatus of the state, but they remained firmly implanted in organized labor. Rather than dropping radical ideas and following middle-of-the-road political leaders, the French workers continued to back Communists in union elections and at the ballot box. Richard Hamilton tried to explain why French workers were still radical by focusing on the impact of occupational setting on political attitudes, based largely on public opinion surveys taken in the early 1950s. Hamilton found that the day-to-day work of Communist militants in the workshops was the single most important reason that half of the French workers voted Communist "with monotonous regularity" from 1945 to 1956. Richard F. Hamilton, *Affluence and the French Worker in the Fourth Republic* (Princeton, N.J., 1967), 21, 37.

34. Annie Kriegel, *Les Communistes français* (Paris, 1970). An interesting variant of Kriegel's "counter-society" thesis has been developed by Ronald Tiersky, who sees the PCF as building a counter-society in which the party offers alternating "faces" to the public as well as its members. See Ronald Tiersky, *French Communism, 1920–1972* (New York, 1974).

35. Georges Lavau, "The PCF, the State, and the Revolution: An Analysis of Party Policies, Communications, and Popular Culture," in *Communism in Italy and France,* ed. Donald L. M. Blackmer and Sidney Tarrow (Princeton, N.J., 1975), and Irwin Wall, *French Communism in the Era of Stalin: The Quest for Unity and Integration, 1945–1962* (Westport, Conn.: 1983).

36. Annie Lacroix-Riz, *La CGT de la libération à la scission, 1944–1947* (Paris, 1983).

37. Annie Lacroix-Riz, "Majorité et minorité de la CGT de la libération au XXVIe congrès confédéral, 1944–1946," *Revue historique* (October–December 1981): 477.

38. Donald Reid, *The Miners of Decazeville: A Genealogy of Deindustrialization* (Cambridge, Mass., 1985), 172.

39. George Ross, *Workers and Communists in France: From Popular Front to Eurocommunism* (Berkeley, Calif., 1982), 28.

40. The role of American policy toward western Europe is being reevaluated as documentation becomes available. Over the years, two conflicting views have held sway. One holds that the Truman Doctrine and the Marshall Plan saved western Europe from Soviet domination. Another contends that U.S. leaders used economic superiority to move France off an independent road and into an anti-Soviet alliance. Literature from the late 1940s through much of the 1970s falls into one of the two camps. Early literature on the Marshall Plan, for example, stressed American benevolence, but too often with a boosterish slant that lacked critical analysis. See H. B. Price, *The Marshall Plan and Its Meaning* (Ithaca, N.Y., 1955). More recent observers have questioned the value of American aid and the motives behind it. Gabriel and Joyce Kolko argued that America's deflationary strategy for western Europe succeeded in returning the old establishment to power but failed to improve the situation for the working classes. See Gabriel and Joyce Kolko, *The Limits of Power* (New York, 1972). Charles Maier drew from this research but focused instead upon the interplay between American leaders' desire for an economically integrated Europe and the efforts by European countries to advance their own national goals as much as possible. See Charles S. Maier, "Supranational Concepts and National Continuity in the Framework of the Marshall Plan," in *The Marshall Plan: A Retrospective*, ed. Stanley Hoffmann and Charles S. Maier (Boulder, Colo., 1984), 29–37.

41. An attempt to connect coal policy with the emerging cold war appears in Darryl Holter, "Politique charbonnière et guerre froide," *Le Mouvement social* 130 (1985).

42. See Yves-Marie Hilaire and Joelle Bourgeois, "Les Militants Ouvriers des années trente," in *De Blum à Daladier: Le Nord–Pas-de-Calais, 1936–1939*, ed. Marcel Gillet and Yves-Marie Hilaire (Lille, 1979), 205–24.

43. Darryl Holter, "Labour Leadership and Left Politics in Northern France, 1929–1949," *Studies in History and Politics* 5 (1986).

CHAPTER 1: FRENCH COAL MINING, LABOR, AND THE STATE

1. Michel Delwiche and Francis Groff, *Les Gueules noires* (Brussels, 1985), 10.

2. Ibid., 42.

3. Georges Tiffon, *Le Charbon* (Paris, 1983), 18.

4. Houilléres du Bassin du Nord et du Pas-de-Calais (HBNPC), *L'Histoire et l'avenir du bassin minier* (Douai, 1976), 3–4.

5. Donald Reid, *The Miners of Decazeville: A Genealogy of Deindustrialization* (Cambridge, Mass., 1985), 10–11; and Marcel Rouff, *Les Mines de charbon en France au XVIIIe siècle* (Paris, 1922), 76–77.

6. Marcel Gillet, "The Coal Age and the Rise of the Coalfields in the North and the Pas-de-Calais," in *Essays in European Economic History*, ed. F. Crouzet (London, 1969), 183.

7. Rouff, *Les Mines*, 589–90.

8. Reid, *The Miners*, 14–15; Warren C. Baum, *The French Economy and the State* (Princeton, N.J., 1958), 171; and Gillet, "Coal Age," 183.

9. René Gendarme, *La Région du Nord* (Paris, 1954), 49.

10. Charles Kindleberg, *Economic Growth in France and Great Britain* (Cambridge, Mass., 1964), 19.

11. Marcel Gillet, *Les Charbonnages du nord de la France au XIXe siècle* (Paris, 1973), 124.

12. R. Priouret, *Les Origines du patronat français* (Paris, 1963), and Gillet, *Les Charbonnages*, 129–30.

13. R. Cadel, *Dix Ans de nationalisation des charbonnages de France* (Brussels, 1956), 8.

14. Christopher H. Johnson, "The Revolution of 1930 in French Economic History," in *1830 in France*, ed. John M. Merriman (New York, 1975), 163–64.

15. Gillet, *Les Charbonnages*, 117–24.

16. Reid, *The Miners*, 15.

17. Ibid., 123–24.

18. Étienne Dejonghe, "L'Ingénieur exploitant dans les houillères du Nord–Pas-de-Calais et sa formation," in *L'Ingénieur dans la société française*, ed. André Thépot (Paris, 1985), 141.

19. Rolande Trempé, *Les Mineurs de Carmaux, 1848–1914*, vol. 1 (Paris, 1971), 43.

20. Ibid., 687.

21. B. R. Mitchell, *European Historical Statistics, 1750–1970* (London, 1978), 186.

22. François Caron, *An Economic History of Modern France* (New York, 1979), 159–60.

23. Marcel Gillet, *Le Bassin du Nord et du Pas-de-Calais de 1815 à 1914: Étude économique et sociale* (Douai, 1975), 54.

24. On the coal-mining métier, see Tiffon, *Le Charbon*, 36–42.

25. Donald Reid, "The Limits of Paternalism: Immigrant Coal Miners' Communities in France, 1919–1945," *European History Quarterly* 15 (1985): 99.

26. Philippe Ariès, *Histoire des populations françaises* (Paris, 1948), 97.

27. Ibid., 99.

28. Philippe Guignet, "L'Émeute des quatre sous, ou les voies de la protestation sociale à Anzin, mai 1833," *Revue du Nord* 219 (1973).

29. P. Guillaume, "Grèves et organisation ouvrière chez les mineurs de la Loire au milieu du XIXe siècle," *Le Mouvement social* 43 (1963).

30. Marc Simard, "La Situation économique de l'entreprise et rapports de production: Le cas de la compagnie des mines d'Anzin, 1860–1894," *Revue du Nord* 258 (1983).

31. Reid, *The Miners*, 126.

32. On the national Federation of Miners, see Diana Cooper-Richet, *La Fédération nationale des mineurs: Contribution à l'histoire du syndicalisme français avant 1914* (Paris, 1976).

33. Reid, *The Miners*, 140.

34. On Basly, see Joël Michel, "Syndicalisme minier et politique dans le Nord–Pas-de-Calais: Le cas Basly (1880–1914)," *Le Mouvement social* 87 (1974).

35. Trempé, *Les Mineurs*, 825–26.

36. See Jacques Julliard, "Jeune et vieux syndicat chez les mineurs du Pas-de-Calais," *Le Mouvement social* 47 (1964): 11, and Reid, *The Miners*, 144–45.

37. Rolande Trempé, "Le Réformisme des mineurs français," *Le Mouvement social* 65 (1968): 106–7.

38. Joel Michel, "L'Échec de la grève générale des mineurs européens avant 1914," *Revue d'histoire moderne et contemporaine* 29 (1982): 228–29.

39. Trempé, *Les Mineurs*, 826–29.

40. Georges Lefranc, *Essais sur les problèmes socialistes et syndicaux* (Paris, 1970), 109–10.

41. Robert Lafitte-Laplace, *L'Économie charbonnière de la France* (Paris, 1933), 10, 32–33, 168.

42. M. Olivier, *La Politique du charbon, 1914–1921* (Paris, 1922), 110.

43. Ibid., 111.

44. Tom Kemp, *The French Economy, 1919–1939* (London, 1972), 34.

45. Richard Kuisel, *Capitalism and the State in Modern France: Renovation and Economic Management in the Twentieth Century* (Cambridge, England, 1982), 71.

46. HBNPC, *L'Histoire et l'avenir*, 7.

47. For an overview of the reconstruction effort see M. Parent, "L'Effort de la réconstruction du bassin houillère," *Revue de l'industrie minérale*, May 1921. See also M. Georges, "Le Développement de la production en 1923—Nord et Pas-de-Calais," *Revue de l'industrie minérale*, 8 January 1929, and M. Sorré, *Les Ressources de l'outillage de la région du Nord* (Paris, 1933), 185.

48. Lafitte-Laplace, *L'Économie charbonnière*, 220.

49. Jean Romeuf, *Le Charbon* (Paris, 1949), 108–9.

50. Odette Hardy-Hemery, "Rationalisation du technique et rationalisation du travail à la compagnie des mines d'Anzin, 1927–1938," *Le Mouvement social* 72 (1970): 4.

51. Rolande Trempé, *Les Trois Batailles du charbon, 1936–1947* (Paris, 1989), 142.

52. On the Bedaux system see Hardy-Hemery, "Rationalisation," 17–22; G. Friedmann, *Problèmes humains de la machinisation industrielle* (Paris, 1946), 348–63; and H. Verdinne, "Le Problème de l'organisation scientifique du travail dans les mines," *Annales des mines de Belgique* 46 (1945–1946): 831–78.

53. Czeslaw Kaczmarek, *L'Émigration polonaise en France après la guerre* (Paris, 1928), 131, for 1922–1925; and Lafitte-LaPlace, *L'Industrie charbonnière*, 197–98, for 1919–1921 and 1926–1929, cited in the best study in English of Polish miners in northern France, Gary Cross, *Immigrant Workers in Industrial France: The Making of a New Laboring Class* (Philadelphia, Pa., 1983), 81–98 (84).

54. Georges, "Le Développement de la production en 1923 dans les mines du Nord et du Pas-de-Calais," *Revue de l'industrie minérale*, 8 January 1924.

55. Cross, *Immigrant Workers*, 85.

56. M. Georges, "Renseignements statistiques sur les mines du Pas-de-Calais en 1924," *Revue de l'industrie minérale*, 1 August 1924.

57. Cross, *Immigrant Workers*, 85.

58. Jean Chardonnet, *Le Charbon* (Paris, 1948), 167.

59. Pierre Parent, "L'Industrie houillère française," *Revue de l'industrie minérale*, 1 August 1939.

60. Productivity for underground workers rose from 966 kilograms per worker in 1929 to 1,136 kilograms per worker in 1938. Institut National de la Statistique et des Études Économiques (INSEE), *Mouvement économique en France de 1938 à 1948* (Paris, 1950), 218.

61. *Le Mineur unitaire*, 20 March 1935.

62. Hardy-Hemery, "Rationalisation," 33.

63. Parent, "L'Industrie houillère," 8.

64. Maurice Demouveau et al., "Les Relations entre le communisme et le socialisme dans le Nord et le Pas-de-Calais de 1919 à 1934," *Revue du Nord* 221 (1974): 213–45.

65. Samuel Cohn, "Schism and Loss: The Adverse Effect of the Division of the French Labor Movement on the Wages of French Coal Miners" (Unpublished paper, Madison, 1988), 3.

66. Raymond Hainsworth, "Les Grèves du front populaire de mai et juin 1936: Une nouvelle analyse fondée sur l'étude deces grèves dans le bassin houiller du Nord et du Pas-de-Calais," *Le Mouvement social* 96 (1976): 5–9.

67. *Réveil du Nord*, 30 March 1931. On labor in northern France during the 1930s, see Yves-Marie Hilaire and Joelle Bourgeois, "Les Militants Ouvriers des années trente," in *De Blum à Daladier: Le Nord–Pas-de-Calais, 1936–1939*, ed. Marcel Gillet and Yves-Marie Hilaire (Lille, 1979), 161–83.

68. Charbonnages de France, Carton 78, Dossier II.

69. Cross, *Immigrant Workers*, 191–92.

70. Edmond Gogolewski, "Les Polonais en France avant la seconde guerre mondiale," *Revue du Nord* 61 (1979): 660.

71. Yasmine Chudzinski and Jacques Renard, *Paroles et mémoires du bassin houiller du Nord–Pas-de-Calais* (Lille, 1981), 59, 79.

72. Ibid., 68.

73. Cross, *Immigrant Workers*, 196, 205.

74. Hainsworth, "Les Grèves," 10.

75. Joel Michel, "Mineurs, tullistes, métalurgistes: Le Nord dans le métropole, 1919–1939," *La Qualité de la vie dans la région Nord–Pas-de-Calais au 20ème siècle* (Paris, 1975), 69.

76. Yves Le Maner, "Les Communistes du Nord et du Pas-de-Calais de l'agonie du front populaire à la guerre," *Revue du Nord* 277 (1988): 364, and Hainsworth, "Les Gréves," 9.

77. Hainsworth, "Les Grèves," 8.

78. Chudzinski and Renard, *Paroles*, 61, 87.

79. Janine Ponty, "La Communauté polonaise de 1936 à 1939," in *De Blum*, ed. Gillet and Hilaire, 193, 197.

80. Reid, "The Limits," 108.

81. Trempé, *Les Trois Batailles*, 142.

82. Aimée Moutet, "La Rationalisation dans les mines du Nord à l'épreuve du front populaire: Étude d'après les sources imprimées," *Le Mouvement social* 135 (1986): 88–92.

83. In 1938 the rate of unionization in the mines of the Pas-de-Calais approached 100 percent. See Le Maner, "Les Communistes," 364.

84. Étienne Dejonghe, "Ingénieurs et société dans les houillères du Nord–Pas-de-Calais de la Belle Époque à nos jours," in *L'Ingénieur*, ed. Thépot, 177–78.

85. Dumoulin was a leader in the strongly anti-Communist group in the CGT. See Peter Arum, "Du syndicalisme révolutionnaire au réformisme: Georges Dumoulin," and Marie-France Rogliano, "L'Anticommunisme dans la CGT: 'Syndicats,'" *Le Mouvement social* 87 (1974): 35–62, 63–84.

86. Le Maner, "Les Communistes," 367.

87. Val Lorwin noted that most workers did not follow Communist calls to strike against Daladier's modifications of the 40-hour law. He expresses surprise that the miners' union, "disciplined, though anticommunist" joined the strike. But Lorwin was considering the top CGT and Federation of Miners' leaders at the national level, most of whom opposed the Communists. In the mining areas, however, the Communists had obtained a great deal of popular support. Val Lorwin, *The French Labor Movement* (Cambridge, Mass., 1954), 82–83.

88. *La Tribune des mineurs*, 14 and 21 October 1939.

89. Ibid., 27 January and 11 May 1940.

90. Writing with the benefit of hindsight in 1955, E. Drexel Godfrey made the following observation: "The communists were systematically expelled from the CGT, but in many places they were replaced by less efficient and less experienced union officials. The door remained open for the return of these organizers when the Communists were welcomed back into the fold." E. Drexel Godfrey, *The Fate of the Non-Communist Left in France* (New York, 1955), 36.

CHAPTER 2: COAL POLITICS FROM WAR TO LIBERATION, 1940–1945

1. France, *Journal officiel, état français, lois et décrets*, 18 August 1940, 4731–33, and Hoover Institution, *France During the German Occupation, 1940–1944* (Stanford, Calif., 1959), 149–54.

2. On the organization committees see Henri Rousso, "L'Organisation industrielle de Vichy," *Revue d'histoire de la deuxième guerre mondiale* 116 (1979): 27–44; Richard Kuisel, *Capitalism and the State in Modern France: Renovation and Economic Management in the Twentieth Century* (Cambridge, England, 1981), 134–44; and Henry Ehrmann, *Organized Business in France* (Princeton, N.J., 1957), 82–83, 87.

3. Olivier Kourchid, *Production industrielle et travail sous l'occupation: Les mines de Lens et les mineurs, 1940–1944* (Paris, 1985), 154.

4. Charbonnages de France, *Note sur le comité des houillères* (Paris,

1962), 6. The Charbonnages de France noted: "Fabre, who had served as secretary general of the Coal Mines Committee since 1931, held the same position in the Organization Committee until November 1944 and the same pattern held for most of the other personnel." Ibid.

5. Kourchid, *Production industrielle*, 162, 200, 212.

6. Source material in the archives of the organization committees, which was not available until recently, is either not usable or has disappeared. See Rousso, "L'Organisation industrielle," 28. However, I found some of the records of the Coal Mines Organization Committee in the archives located in the offices of the Charbonnages de France in Paris. Hereafter, these documents are referred to as Comité d'Organisation des Houillères, or COH.

7. Ehrmann, *Organized Business*, 63.

8. J. G. Merigot, *Essai sur les comités d'organisations professionelles* (Paris, 1943), 541–42.

9. Étienne Dejonghe, "Les Ingénieurs et societé dans les houillères du Nord–Pas-de-Calais de la Belle Époque à nos jours," in *Ingénieur dans la societé française*, ed., André Thépot (Paris, 1985), 181.

10. On the reintroduction of the Bedaux system see Étienne Dejonghe and Daniel Laurent, *Libération du Nord et du Pas-de-Calais* (Paris, 1974), 231, and Kourchid, *Production industrielle*, 252–62.

11. COH, Memorandums of 2, 25 February, and 1 March 1943, all published in *Revue de l'industrie minérale* (May 1943), 5. The problem of German demands for labor are treated in detail by Étienne Dejonghe, "Pénurie charbonnière et répartition en France, 1940–1944," *Revue d'histoire de la deuxième guerre mondiale* 102 (1976): 21–55. See also Alan S. Milward, *The New Order and the French Economy* (Oxford, 1970), 181–209.

12. COH, *Sur la politique charbonniére depuis l'armistice*, 6, Carton 26. See also Commission d'Études des Problèmes d'Après-Guerre (hereafter referred to as CEPAG), "Situation de l'industrie houillère," report of 21 January 1943, 9. André Théret described how the mines were flooded by these raw, young workers who were considered by the miners to be "city boys." Interview with André Théret, August 1977.

13. Dejonghe and Laurent, *Libération*, 233.

14. CEPAG, "Situation," 9.

15. COH, "Lettre du Schensky aux compagnies minières," 15 November 1943.

16. Robert O. Paxton, *Vichy France: Old Guard and the New Order 1940–1944* (New York, 1972), 355.

17. Kuisel, *Capitalism and the State*, 131.

18. Ibid., 135.

19. Rousso, "L'Organisation industrielle," 30, 34.

20. CEPAG, "*Situation*," 6. See also Richard Kuisel, "Vichy et planisme," *Le Mouvement social* 98 (1977).

21. CEPAG, "*Situation*," 5.

22. Richard Kuisel, "Vichy et les origines de la planification économique, 1940–1946," *Le Mouvement social* 98 (1977), 88.

23. Ibid., 84, and Paxton, *Vichy France*, 219.

24. COH, "Circulaire," 19 March 1943.

25. CEPAG, "*Situation*," 5.

26. Aimé Leperq, captured by the Germans in 1940, was appointed president of the COH in 1941. *Voix du Nord* claimed that he disagreed with the Vichy policy of sending dissident miners to Germany. *Voix du Nord*, 11 November 1944. Ehrmann points out that the Civil and Military Organization was particularly strong in northern France and had created cells inside the organization committees and established an alliance with the Resistance group "Libération-Nord." Ehrmann, *Organized Business*, 97.

27. See Guy Bouthillier, *La Nationalisation du gaz et de l'électricité* (Paris, 1968), 185.

28. This is a key point made frequently in Paxton, *Vichy France*, and also by Kuisel, *Capitalism and the State*. Most of the staff of the Ministry of Industrial Production continued in the posts they had held after the liberation. A large part of the General Delegation of National Equipment (DGEN), the planning agency created in 1940, formed the cadre in the Ministry of National Economy in November 1944. J. A. Rabier, "Une Expérience à planification," *Le Plan Monnet* (Paris, 1950).

29. Rousso, "L'Organisation industrielle," 43.

30. B. R. Mitchell, *European Historical Statistics, 1750–1970* (London, 1978), 189, 236.

31. Several examples of economic planning by Resistance groupings are included in Henri Michel and B. Mirkine-Guetzevitch, *Les Idées politiques et sociales de la Résistance* (Paris, 1954), 359–79. Analyses of various Resistance plans to restructure the postwar economy are discussed by Gaetan Pirou, "Le Problème des trois secteurs," *Revue d'économie politique* 4–6 (1940–1944): 447–66. Kuisel makes the important point that "Vichy and the resistance can be treated as parallel, yet antagonistic, historical forces. In their common rejection of the Third Republic both led France toward a new economic configuration." Kuisel, *Capitalism and the State*, 128.

32. France, *Annuaire statistique: Résumé rétrospectif* (1966), 388, 425.

33. Dejonghe and Laurent, *Libération*, 190.

34. Yasmine Chudzinski and Jacques Renard, *Paroles et mémoires du bassin houiller du Nord–Pas-de-Calais* (Lille, 1981), 120.

35. Ibid., 120, 90.

36. Ibid., 138.

37. Étienne Dejonghe, "Les Communistes dans le Nord–Pas-de-Calais de juin 1940 à la veille de la grève des mineurs," *Revue du Nord* 270 (1986): 709, 701.

38. Ibid., 688.

39. Chudzinski and Renard, *Paroles*, 123.

40. Dejonghe, "Les Communistes," 691.

41. Chudzinski and Renard, *Paroles*, 138.

42. Dejonghe, "Les Communistes," 690.

43. Ibid., 707, 711.

44. Leaflet circulated by striking miners in May 1941. Copy in author's possession.

45. Chudzinski and Renard, *Paroles*, 124.

46. Irwin Wall, *French Communism in the Era of Stalin: The Quest for Unity and Integration, 1945–1962* (Westport, Conn., 1983), 23.

47. Chudzinski and Renard, *Paroles*, 123–25.

48. Étienne Dejonghe, "Chronique de la grève des mineurs du Nord–Pas-de-Calais (27 mai–6 juin 1941)," *Revue du Nord* 273 (1987): 326.

49. Ibid., 327.

50. Ibid., 324.

51. Ibid., 333–34.

52. Chudzinski and Renard, *Paroles*, 133–36.

53. Archives Départementales Pas-de-Calais (Arras), "Lettre du 6 juin 1941," SC 481, cited in Dejonghe, "Chronique," 335.

54. Ibid., 338.

55. Roger Pannequin, *Ami si tu tombes: Les années sans suite, 1* (Paris, 1976), 103–5.

56. Kourchid, *Production industrielle*, 334.

57. Ibid., 334, 373–75, 379–81.

58. Ibid., 9–10, and Milward, *The New Order*, 207.

59. Henri Krasucki et al., *Le Mouvement syndical dans la Résistance* (Paris, 1975), 210.

60. Kourchid, *Production industrielle*, 381–82, 386, 383.

61. COH, "Strikes of November 3, 1943," Carton 78, Dossier 5.

62. The COH compiled some reports on the strikes in the northern basin in October 1943. German authorities complained that the French officials were too lenient with the strikers. The leader in Lille, Bertrand, complained: "In some cases because of energetic action the miners returned to work. But they were not tough enough with the strikers, probably because they did not want to arouse the anger of the French population. And even though this strike movement has been going on for several days, they have not told me who the ringleaders are. Nor have they arrested anyone yet." COH, Letter from Bertrand to M. Carles (regional prefect in Lille), 17 October 1943, Carton 78, Dossier 5.

63. Kourchid, *Production industrielle*, 389, 232, 389.

64. Institut National de la Statistique et des Études Économiques (INSEE), *Mouvement économique en France de 1938 à 1948* (Paris, 1950), 218.

65. Krasucki, *Le Mouvement syndical*, 210.

66. "The Resistance organizations, the three major parties, several smaller parties, and the labor federations were energetically supporting a broad program of nationalization of key industries and credit. Even General de Gaulle himself endorsed their demands. Only a small group of conservatives dared to oppose openly so popular a reform, and they were powerless to stop the momentum of the movement." David Pinckney, "The French Experiment in Nationalization, 1944–1950," in *Modern France*, ed. Edward Mead Earle (New York, 1964), 354. On the regional press, see Natalie Dumez, *Le Mensonge reculera*, (Lille, 1946), and Dejonghe and Laurent, *Libération*, 145–48.

67. The members of the Nord Liberation Committee appeared in *Nord-Matin* on 5 September 1944. On the committees, see Dejonghe and Laurent, *Libération*, 68.

68. Ibid., 78. See also Charles Foulon, *Les Commissaires de la République* (Paris, 1974), 222. Foulon notes that in Pas-de-Calais, out of 906 councils, 633 were relieved, and 283 were modified.

69. *Voix du Nord*, 22 November 1944. *Voix du Nord* reported that "the conflict of authority is very great" and editorialized against the situation in Mauberg where large crowds demanded the deaths of various collaborators.

70. Ibid.

71. *Nord-Matin*, 7 October 1944; *Liberté*, 12 and 21 September 1944.

72. R. Dujardin-Thoumin, "Le Parti démocrate populaire dans le Nord, 1925–1939," *Revue du Nord* (1974): 289.

73. Parti Communiste Français (PCF), *Vie régionale (internal bulletin)*, June 1943. Portions of this document are found in Alain Segond, *La Presse clandestine communiste, juin 1941–août 1944* (Lille, 1973).

74. Membership figures from PCF, *Rapports du comité central*, Tenth and Eleventh Party Congresses, cited in J. P. Hirsch, "La Seule Voie possible: Remarques sur les communistes du Nord et du Pas-de-Calais de la libération aux grèves de novembre 1947," *Revue du Nord* 227 (1975): 578.

75. Ibid., 569.

76. Pierre Mauroy, *Héritiers de l'avenir* (Paris, 1977), 29.

77. See *L'Espoir*, 21 January and 18 February 1945.

CHAPTER 3: NATIONALIZING COAL, ORGANIZING LABOR

1. Bruno Mattei, "Après la guerre . . . la bataille (1945–1947)," in *La Foi des charbonniers: Les mineurs dans la bataille du charbon 1945–1947*, ed. Évelyne Desbois et al. (Paris, 1986), 20.

2. Key sections of the National Council of the Resistance Charter charter appear in Alexander Werth, *France, 1940–1955* (London, 1956), 222–23.

3. *Nord-Matin, Liberté, Voix du Nord*, and other newspapers, 13 September and 2 October 1944. Although all the northern newspapers reported that de Gaulle supported nationalization, his speech was actually quite vague. De Gaulle did not favor a "punitive nationalization," a fact that was applauded by *Voix du Nord*. On the other hand, *Liberté* highlighted these words from the general: "Today we can no longer allow these concentrations of power that people refer to as the trusts to continue." De Gaulle was also quite vague with regard to the internal regime of the nationalized mines, supporting "collaboration of all personnel" but noting that their relationship might change later. *Liberté*, 3 October 1944.

4. On the nationalizations see Claire Andrieu, Lucette Le Van, Antoine Prost, eds., *Les Nationalisations à la libération: De l'utopie au compromis* (Fondation nationale des sciences politiques, Paris, 1987). Also, see several papers presented at the colloquium entitled *La France en voie de modernisation, 1944–1952* (Fondation nationale des sciences politiques, Paris, December 1981): Patrick Fridenson, "La Puissance publique et les nationalisations"; Jean-Paul

Thullier, "Les Houillères du Nord–Pas-de-Calais: Nationalisation et planification d'un secteur en déclin"; Claire Andrieu, "Nationalisations et participation ouvrière en France"; Michel Launay, "La CFTC et les nationalisations"; and Annie Lacroix-Riz, "L'État face aux nationalisations." On nationalization of the electricity industry, see Robert Frost, "La Technocratie au pouvoir . . . avec le consentement des syndicats: La technologie, les syndicats et la direction à l'électricité de France (1946–1968)," *Le Mouvement social* 130 (1985): 81–96. For a comparative examination of the nationalizations in western Europe, see the special edition of *Le Mouvement social* entitled "Les Nationalisations d'après guerre en Europe occidentale," 134 (1986).

5. M. Makuchzak, *Réalisations économiques et sociales des charbonnages de France* (Paris, 1957), 36.

6. *Liberté*, 12 September 1944.

7. This was a big issue for two reasons. First, the reinstatement of some of these workers, dismissed mainly because of political organizing or for strike activity, coincided with attacks on some of the management personnel who had played a role in those dismissals. Second, the issue touched on the question of union stewards and the replacement of Communist stewards by anti-Communist stewards in 1939. In November, Henri Martel and other CGT leaders met with the "committee of five," five provisional administrators representing the companies. Martel's main complaint concerned the fact that management personnel remained virtually intact. Already couching the union's demands within the framework of the "battle of production," Martel asserted that in pits with new management, production had increased from 25 percent to 50 percent. *Le Peuple*, 25 November 1944.

8. Étienne Dejonghe and Daniel Laurent, *Libération du Nord et du Pas-de-Calais* (Paris, 1974), 241. Cadel, who became president of the Charbonnages de France in the early 1950s, stated: "In the confusion of the liberation period, most of the leaders of the mining companies had abandoned their functions." R. Cadel, *Dix Ans de nationalisation des charbonnages de France* (Brussels, 1956), 11.

9. COH, "Note de la ministère de la production industrielle," 20 September 1944, Carton 26. The COH reported that Lacoste had removed the authority of the COH, received the resignation of its president M. Crussard, and appointed Duhameau to assume the committee's powers.

10. COH, "Rétablissement de la légalité républicaine," 9 October 1944, Carton 26.

11. COH, "Note d'information sur la réforme des comités d'organisation," 25 October 1944, Carton 26.

12. "XXX," "La Nationalisation des houilléres du Nord et du Pas-de-Calais, *Droit social* (April 1945): 126.

13. The relatively small role for mining personnel in the provisional nationalization was a glaringly obvious weakness from the miners' point of view. The defenders of nationalization were hard pressed to explain it. The Socialists in the north were embarrassed by this aspect and they expressed that opinion in their newspapers. See *Nord-Matin*, 23 January 1944.

14. *Journal officiel*, 4 December 1944, 1876–79.

15. From the beginning, the state reserved for itself the role of arbiter between two poles of power in the mines: the general director and the representational body, in this case the consultative committee. A critic of the nationalization (probably Robert Fabre), who wrote under the name of "XXX," was quick to focus on the inevitable tension between the general director and the consultative committee, implying that representational administrators would impede professionalism and efficiency. "XXX," "La Nationalisation," 124–26.

16. Ibid., 126. Duhameau, reflecting Lacoste's view, did not want control of the nationalization restricted by financial controllers, particularly at that early date. The existence of such a check on the financial operations remained intact but was not really implemented until 1948, when a parliamentary body produced its first report on the nationalized industries.

17. *La Vie ouvrière*, 5 October 1944. Frachon's blunt assault on the mine owners, while conforming to a good deal of public sentiment, obscured the Communist party's confusion on the question of nationalization. Thus, in his speech, Frachon quibbled with the differences between "confiscation" and "requisition" and displayed an uneasiness as to what kind of nationalization might emerge. Traditionally, at least since the 1930s, the PCF had always opposed nationalization and economic planning, seeing "fascism in the guise of social-democracy" in these schemes. See "Sur le plan de Man," *Cahiers du communisme*, 15 March 1934. Even after they accepted nationalization, the Communists always went to great lengths to indicate that nationalization was not socialism or even a "structural reform" but a positive reform under some circumstances. See "Apropos à la nationalisation," *Servir la France*, April 1945. Guy Bouthillier is probably correct when he claims that the Communists supported the nationalization because they were patriotic and productionist. Guy Bouthillier, *La Nationalisation du gaz et de l'électricité* (Paris, 1968), 112. Once committed, however, the Communists became the most active proponents of nationalization. The CGT generally followed this trajectory. Two non-Communist CGT leaders, Jean Duret and Pierre Lebrun, wrote frequently on the subject. See *Le Peuple*: 18 November, 2 and 16 December, 1944; 6, 27 January, 10, 24 February, 3, 10 March, 2 June, 8 September, 24 November, and 1 December 1945; 9 and 10 March 1946.

18. *L'Humanité*, 6 December 1944, and *La Vie ouvrière*, 30 November 1944.

19. Jules Moch, *Guerre aux trusts, solutions socialistes* (Paris, 1945), 86–87. Moch, like his comrades André Philip and Robert Lacoste, was a long-time proponent of nationalization and economic planning. During the war the three men had undertaken a further study of the subject. See Jules Moch, *Confrontations* (Paris, 1952), preface. Moch saw nationalization as anticapitalist because it "weakens capitalism by removing key sectors from it and provides a shelter for democracy against the pressures of the big banks." Ibid., 222. At their congress of November 1944 the Socialists attached "socialization" to nationalization, seeing it as an "intermediary stage of the state in transition." In Roubaix, Léon Blum used this argument, saying that the old bourgeoisie had abandoned its role as a ruling class. *Le Populaire*, 16 October 1945. Socialist theory on

nationalization, however, should be seen against other statements such as Robert Lacoste's comment to *Figaro* in the turbulent months of the liberation: "A wide free sector remains the fundamental condition of French activity and economic recovery." *Figaro*, 17 October 1944.

20. *L'Humanité* and *Le Populaire*, 3 March 1945.

21. COH, "Lettre de Cheradame au directeur," 4 December 1944.

22. Lacoste wrote: "Every day my attention is attracted to the particular cases of small stockholders who have a pressing need to make use of these stocks which they have bought (but) who currently find themselves deprived of this source." Ministère des Finances (MF), "Lettre de Lacoste à Lochard," 20 December 1944, Carton 9805.

23. MF, Commission chargée d'étudier l'indemnisation des propriétaires des houillères nationalisées, *Procès verbaux*, meetings of 9 January and 15 February 1945, Carton 9805.

24. MF, Inspecteur générale des finances, "Rapport à M. le chef du gouvernement sur l'ordonnance modifiant l'ordonnance du 13 décembre 1944," 25 July 1945, Carton 9805.

25. Ibid.

26. Most newspapers, 3 March 1945.

27. R. Fabre, "Les Houillères du Nord et du Pas-de-Calais," *Droit social*, April 1945.

28. Henry Ehrmann, *Organized Business in France* (Princeton, N.J., 1957), 348–49.

29. This was evident in the party and trade union press as the various political groups attempted to define what they favored and assess the steps that had already been taken. Some miners thought nationalization meant some type of workers' control, but the CGT and the Communists polemicized against the old slogan "the mine to the miners." Socialists, especially left Socialists in Pas-de-Calais, wrote about "socialization," but their ideas were left unheeded and flatly contradicted Lacoste's actions. In January, *Nord-Matin* analyzed the nationalization and the situation in the mines. Socialist writers criticized the lack of worker representation and the retention of old management personnel. See *Nord-Matin*, 23 January 1945. A survey circulated by the government in January 1946 showed certain popular misgivings about the real value of nationalization. See Institut Français d'Opinion Publique, *L'Opinion du monde du travail sur les conditions de vie économique et sociale* (Paris, 1946), 52.

30. *La Tribune des mineurs*, 13 January 1945.

31. Ibid., 23 June 1945.

32. COH, "Mines du Nord et du Pas-de-Calais: La situation au poste du matin," 11 September 1944, Carton 78, Dossier 2.

33. Dejonghe and Laurent, "*Libération*," 238. As a commissar of the republic, Closon represented the highest authority of the French state in the two departments of the north. A Gaullist and a conservative resistant, Closon kept in close contact with the general about the situation in the north. Closon's estimate of the situation is revealing. He noted the collapse of public order, the gaping chasm between the old ruling figures and the mass of working people who were

angry, relatively organized, and armed. Some of Closon's reports were used by Raymond Aron in his history of the purges, and sections of Closon's reports have also appeared in *Revue du Nord* 227 (1975), 671–75. Dejonghe and Laurent, *Libération*, 239.

34. *La Tribune des mineurs*, 7 November 1944.

35. Dejonghe and Laurent, *Libération*, 239–40.

36. *Liberté*, 13 October 1944.

37. F. Closon, "Sur le problème social des mines du Nord et du Pas-de-Calais, mai 1945," *Revue du Nord* 102 (1975): 672.

38. *La Tribune des mineurs*, 7 November 1944.

39. *Voix du Nord*, 7 December 1944.

40. Letters to *La Tribune des mineurs* in the winter of 1944 and the spring of 1945 regularly expressed these sentiments.

41. Closon, "Sur le problème social," 673.

42. Dejonghe and Laurent, *Libération*, 239.

43. Ibid., 191, 194.

44. *Voix du Nord*, 15 December 1947. The company was placed under the control of the unions in December 1944. *Liberté*, 16 December 1944. The union, however, had already begun to distribute food to the miners through the company. *L'Espoir*, 11 February 1945.

45. *La Tribune des mineurs*, 30 December 1944, 27 January 1945.

46. Mattei, "Après la guerre," 31.

47. Office Professionel des Houillères (OPH), "Situation des grèves dans le Nord et Pas-de-Calais," 16 May 1945, Carton 78, Dossier 5.

48. *Nord-Éclair*, 15 and 16 May 1945.

49. *La Tribune des mineurs*, 12 May 1945.

50. *Le Monde*, 17 May 1945.

51. OPH, "Arrêt du ministère de la production industrielle et du ministére du travail," 6 June 1945, Carton 3, Dossier 1.

52. MF, "Rapport au chef du gouvernement provisoire," 27 August 1945, Carton 9805.

53. Dejonghe and Laurent, *Libération*, 236.

54. Closon, "Sur le problème social," 672. Closon wrote: "Some uninformed observers have expressed views that the use of force and authority by the state will suffice to restore order. But public opinion is against such an idea. The *milieu* of the mine is one of social and political agitation, and many of the workers are armed. A police operation would cause exchanges of gunfire, death, and a battle that would spread to all the mines and then to the other industries of the region. In such a situation, the workers' unions would immediately pass into the opposition and would lead a violent struggle." Ibid., 673.

55. The mine directors' report stated: "The incidents of May, strikes and other work stoppages, show that, in nearly all the mines, factors beyond our control can counteract all our efforts to improve production." OPH, Directors' meeting, 14 June 1945, Carton 3, Dossier 1.

56. Closon, "Sur le problème social," 673–74; *Voix du Nord*, 16 March 1945; and *Le Monde*, 23 May 1945.

57. *La Tribune des mineurs*, 16 June 1945.

58. Ibid., 21 July and 25 August 1945.

59. Marcel Gillet, "La Bataille du charbon," *L'Histoire* 99 (1987): 44; *Liberté*, 19 July 1945; Maurice Thorez, "Produire: Faire du charbon," speech at Waziers (Nord), 22 July 1945.

60. Philippe Robrieux, *Maurice Thorez: Vie secrète et vie publique* (Paris, 1975), 292.

61. Auguste Lecoeur, *Le Partisan* (Paris, 1963): 216.

62. Roger Pannequin, *Adieu, camarades* (Paris, 1977): 54–58.

63. J. P. Hirsch, "La Seule Voie possible: Remarques sur les communistes du Nord et du Pas-de-Calais de la libération aux grèves de novembre 1947," *Revue du Nord* 227 (1975): 573.

64. Jacques Fauvet, *Histoire du PCF*, vol. 2 (Paris, 1965): 160.

65. Mattei, "Après la guerre," 35.

66. Lecoeur, *Le Partisan*, 216.

67. *Le Monde*, 15 September 1945; *Voix du Nord*, 13 September 1945.

68. Werth, *France*, 267.

69. *L'Espoir*, 26 August 1945.

70. Ibid., 5 and 19 August 1945; *Nord-Éclair*, 13 September 1945.

71. *Nord-Éclair*, 13 September 1945.

72. *La Tribune des mineurs*, 15 and 22 September 1945.

73. But the Socialists gained little, as a writer in *L'Espoir* revealed: "Now that the strikes are over, we can discuss the issue. Of course the Socialist party was blamed for the strikes. The Communists ordered the miners back to work before the union decided anything. It should be the union members who decide for themselves what should be done. . . . Paul Sion, vice president of the union, was chosen to represent the miners in Paris. But that same day the union issued communiqués that criticized the strike. The experience demonstrates once more that the Communists control the miners' union in Pas-de-Calais." *L'Espoir*, 30 September 1945.

74. Étienne Dejonghe, "Les Houillères à l'épreuve, 1944–1947," *Revue du Nord* 227 (1975): 651. Henri Martel was responding to this sentiment when he issued a rather conciliatory appeal on the second day of the strike: "We know quite well that the strikers are not saboteurs but are moved by anger and indignation." *Liberté*, 14 September 1945.

75. André Théret, *Mineurs en lutte, 1944–1948* (Paris, 1974), 13; *Le Monde*, 20 September 1945.

76. *La Tribune des mineurs*, 22 September 1945.

77. OPH, "Procès-verbal de la réunion de la commission paritaire provisoire," 2 August 1945.

78. Werth, *France*, 263.

CHAPTER 4: THE BATTLE OF PRODUCTION IN THE MINES

1. The "battle for coal" in 1944–1947 is analyzed by Rolande Trempé in *Les Trois Batailles du charbon, 1936–1947* (Paris, 1989). See also Évelyne

Desbois, Yves Jeanneau, and Bruno Mattei, *La Foi des charbonniers: Les mineurs dans la bataille du charbon, 1945–1947* (Paris, 1986).

2. Mattei, "Après la guerre . . . la bataille (1945–1947)," in *La Foi des charbonniers*, 18.

3. Interview with André Théret by the author, 3 August 1977.

4. Benoit Frachon, "Rapport aux cadres syndicaux de la région parisienne," in *La Bataille de la production* (Paris, 1946), 40; *Le Peuple*, 28 September 1944.

5. *La Tribune des mineurs*, 6 January 1945, 30 December 1944. The Foulon article provoked some miners to question whether this kind of slogan belonged in a union paper. Foulon attempted to clarify his meaning in the next issue. Work stoppages were not to be permitted, although demands could always be raised. But demands could not be "demagogic." The union referred to this approach as "constructive unionism." The PCF's theoretical journal listed the acceptable tactics: "delegations, petitions, meetings with public officials, distribution of leaflets explaining demands, well-organized demonstrations, etc." Eugène Hénaff, "Les Revendications et les moyens de les faire aboutir," *Cahiers du communisme*, January 1946. See also Jacques Duclos, "Notre Politique," *Cahiers du communisme*, June–July 1945, and Jean Laffitte, "Le Problème des prix et de la production," *Cahiers du communisme*, February 1946.

6. *La Vie ouvrière*, 30 November 1944; *La Tribune des mineurs*, 6 January 1945.

7. B. Frachon, "Fabriquer des armes pour nos soldats," radio speech of 2 December 1944. See Frachon, *La Bataille de la production*, 107.

8. *La Vie ouvrière*, 30 November 1944.

9. Ibid., 11 November 1944.

10. Benoit Frachon, "Rapport au comité national de la CGT," 27 March 1945, in Benoit Frachon, *Au rhyme des jours*, vol. 1 (Paris, 1973), 76.

11. J. P. Hirsch, "La Seule Voie possible: Remarques sur les communistes du Nord et du Pas-de-Calais de la libération aux grèves de novembre 1947," *Revue du Nord* 227 (1975): 571.

12. Office Professionel des Houilléres (OPH), "Comparaison des salaires mines et métalurgiques," Meeting of 18 October 1945, Carton 3, Dossier 1. See also COH, "Procès-verbal de la réunion au COH 5 juillet 1945," 26 July 1945.

13. Mattei, "Après la guerre," 29.

14. OPH, "Procés-verbal de la réunion de la commission paritaire provisoire," 2 August 1945, 2.

15. The Socialists were quick to point out that individual payment was not popular with the miners. The Communists were compelled to defend the practice on several occasions, including Thorez in the Waziers speech and Lecoeur, as late as April 1947. *La Tribune des mineurs*, 12 April 1947. See also Mattei, "Après la guerre," 29.

16. Houillères du Bassin Nord–Pas-de-Calais (HBNPC), Directors' meeting, 25 September 1945.

17. The response to Frachon's speech is described in [André Théret], *Mineurs en lutte, 1944–1948* (Paris, 1974), 12–13.

18. HBNPC, Directors' meeting, 23, 30 October, and 6 November 1945.

19. Ibid., 23 October 1945.

20. *La Tribune des mineurs*, 19 May 1945.

21. HBNPC, Directors' meeting, 20 November 1945.

22. Étienne Dejonghe, "Les Houillères à l'épreuve, 1944–1947," *Revue du Nord* 227 (1975): 658.

23. The fullest treatment of this aspect of the battle of production is found in Yves Jeanneau, "Les Murs de l'histoire," in Desbois et al., *La Foi des charbonniers*, 69.

24. *Liberté*, 10 November 1945, 7 February 1946.

25. *Voix du Nord*, 16 August 1945.

26. *Liberté*, 1 March 1946, and Desbois et al., *La Foi des charbonniers*, 30.

27. Jeanneau, "Les Murs," 75–77, and *Liberté*, 8 March 1946.

28. *Liberté*, 5 March 1946.

29. *Le Peuple*, 12 January 1946; *La Tribune des mineurs*, 12 February 1946.

30. See issues of the monthly journal *Mineurs* in 1947. Also, see the interview with Léon Delfosse in Dejonghe, "Les Houillères," 653.

31. Roger Pannequin, *Adieu, camarades* (Paris, 1977), 57. "Rapports des renseignments généraux," September 1945, Archives Départementales du Pas-de-Calais (ADPC): ADPC M 778 and ADPC M 403, cited in Mattei, "Après la guerre," 35, 38.

32. Mattei, "Après la guerre," 39–44.

33. Jeanneau, "Les Murs," 63–70 and 81.

34. André Ribaud, *Essai sur la France contemporaine* (Paris, 1949), 160.

35. The best discussions of the role of mining management are Étienne Dejonghe, "Ingénieurs et société dans les houillères du Nord–Pas-de-Calais de la Belle Époque à nos jours"; Jean-Paul Thullier, "Les Images de l'ingénieur depuis 1945 dans la région du Nord"; and Diane Cooper-Richet, "Les Ingénieurs des mines vus d'en bas" in *L'Ingénieur dans la société française*, ed. André Thépot (Paris, 1985). See also Évelyne Desbois, "Des ingénieurs perdus," in Desbois et al., *La Foi des charbonniers*, 105–26.

36. Dejonghe, "Ingénieurs et société," 175.

37. On the education of mining engineers, see Thépot, *L'Ingénieur*, especially Étienne Dejonghe, "L'Ingénieur exploitant dans les houillères du Nord–Pas-de-Calais et sa formation," 141–46.

38. Dejonghe, "Ingénieurs et société," 181.

39. Étienne Dejonghe and Daniel Laurent, *Libération du Nord et du Pas-de-Calais* (Paris, 1974), 240.

40. Desbois, "Des ingénieurs perdus," 105–6.

41. Dejonghe, "Ingénieurs et société," 182.

42. Desbois, "Des ingénieurs perdus," 121.

43. Ibid., 123.

44. In 1936, thousands of cadres enrolled in various unions, the largest of which was affiliated with the CGT, and signed the Accords of Matignon. André Malterre, *La Confédération Générale des Cadres* (Paris, 1972), 14–15. In 1937,

the Fédération des Techniciens-CGT had grown from 1,000 members to 80,000. In 1939 the union claimed a membership of 66,000. D. Kerchelievitch, *Le Syndicalisme des techniciens* (Paris, 1940), 113.

45. *Le Peuple,* 30 December 1944.

46. Frachon, "Rapport au comité national de la CGT," 27 March 1945. See Frachon, *Au rhythme des jours,* 75–90.

47. *Le Peuple,* 17 February and 9 June 1945.

48. Desbois, "Des ingénieurs perdus," 124.

49. Ibid., 125.

50. *La Tribune des mineurs,* 15 December 1945, 23 March 1946.

51. *Nord-Industriel,* 19 October 1946.

52. HBNPC, Directors' meeting, 2 October 1945.

53. *Le Peuple,* 24 March 1945; *La Tribune des mineurs,* 16 June 1945.

54. A flyer summarizing Frachon's speech in Lens is reproduced in Théret, *Mineurs en lutte,* 19–20.

55. Author's interview with André Théret, 3 August 1977.

56. HBNPC, Directors' meetings, 11 September 1945 and 8 January 1946.

57. Auguste Lecoeur, *L'Autocritique attendu* (Paris, 1955), 222–23.

58. Jacques Fauvet, *Histoire du PCF,* vol. 1 (Paris, 1965), 162, and Irwin Wall, *French Communism in the Era of Stalin: The Quest for Unity and Integration, 1945–1962* (Westport, Conn., 1983), 247–48. See also Lecoeur's books: *L'Autocritique attendu*; *Le Partisan* (Paris, 1963); and *La Croix de guerre pour une grève* (Paris, 1970).

59. *Liberté,* 5 February 1946.

60. Ibid., 12 February 1946.

61. Ibid., and *La Tribune des mineurs,* 2 February 1946.

62. INSEE, *Mouvement économique en France de 1938 à 1948* (Paris, 1950), 217.

63. *La Tribune des mineurs,* 2 March 1946. *Liberté* continued: "Now a miner, our comrade Léon Delfosse, secretary of the CGT miners' union of the Pas-de-Calais, has been named as a director along with an engineer who is a militant unionist. Clearly a new phase in the battle of production has begun." *Liberté,* 27 February 1946.

64. *Nord-Matin,* 8 March 1946.

65. Ibid., 13 March 1946; *Liberté,* 7 March 1946, and *La Tribune des mineurs,* 9 March 1946.

66. *La Tribune des mineurs,* 20 March 1946; letter from Lecoeur to Duhameau, 25 March 1946, in the possession of Léon Delfosse.

67. *Liberté,* 24–25 March 1946.

68. *L'Année politique: 1946* (Paris, 1947), 92.

69. France, *Journal officiel,* 18 May 1946, 4272–76.

70. Frederick Meyers, *European Coal-Mining Unions: Structure and Function* (Los Angeles, 1965), 50–51.

71. *Mineurs,* February 1947.

72. Mattei, "Après la guerre," 29, and Trempé, *Les Trois Batailles,* 240. Trempé also makes the important point that many of the features of the statute,

including the length of the work week, overtime rules, social security, and the retirement system, were actually items that had already been won or were regained after losing them.

73. Yasmine Chudzinski and Jacques Renard, *Paroles et mémoires du bassin houiller du Nord–Pas-de-Calais* (Lille, 1981), 95.

74. Dejonghe, "Les Houillères," 646.

75. *Nord-Éclair*, 31 May 1946; *L'Écho des mines*, August 1946.

76. Dejonghe, "Les Houillères," 646.

77. *La Tribune des mineurs*, 22 June 1946.

78. Ibid., and other articles in April, June, and August.

79. *Nord-Industriel*, 10 August 1946, and *Liberté*, 29 May 1946.

80. *La Tribune des mineurs*, 10 August 1946.

81. *Liberté*, 1–2 September 1946.

82. *La Tribune des mineurs*, 17 August and 7 September 1946.

83. *L'Espoir*, 24 March 1946; *Nord-Matin*, 18 September and 3 October 1946.

84. *Liberté*, 25 September 1946; *L'Écho des mines*, August 1946; *Nord-Industriel*, 5 October 1946.

85. HBNPC, "Procès-verbaux du conseil d'administration," 30 August and 26 September 1946.

86. INSEE, *Mouvement économique*, 218, 311.

87. Charbonnages de France, *Rapport de gestion* (Paris, 1946), 13.

88. INSEE, *Mouvement économique*, 308.

89. HBNPC, *Rapport de gestion, 1946*, (Paris, 1947), 4.

90. HBNPC, Directors' meeting, 16 April 1946.

91. *Nord-Matin*, 6 December 1946.

92. *Nord-Industriel*, 14 June 1947.

93. See Thiébault's report in *Nord-Industriel* 41 (1947): 1136–39.

94. HBNPC, *Rapport de gestion, 1948* (Paris, 1949), 13.

95. *La Tribune des mineurs*, 31 May 1947.

96. *Nord-Matin*, 14 October 1946.

97. In fact, members of the pit committees could not be paid for time spent on union business. HBNPC, Directors' meeting, 19 February 1946. Also, all CGT cards and stamps had to be distributed and collected outside the mines. *Ibid.*, Directors' meeting, 15 May 1946.

98. *L'Écho des mines*, August 1946.

99. Lecoeur's speech in Douai, 30 August 1946, was reprinted in *Mineurs*, January 1947.

100. Wall, *French Communism*, 42–43.

101. *Nord-Matin*, 22 December 1946.

102. *La Tribune des mineurs*, 11 January 1947.

103. Préfecture du Pas-de-Calais, *Enquête sur le ravataillement*, August 1946, in Dejonghe, "Les Houillères," 663.

104. *L'Écho des mines*, April 1947.

105. *La Tribune des mineurs*, 2 May 1947.

106. Lampin, a Socialist and FO member, wrote the article for *La Tribune*

that criticized the strikes. He urged the miners to "wait for the union." *La Tribune des mineurs*, 31 May 1947.

CHAPTER 5: COAL POLITICS AND THE COLD WAR

1. Alexander Werth, *France: 1940–1955* (Boston, 1966), 253–58.

2. Letter from Monnet to Assistant Secretary of State William Clayton, 10 July 1945, National Archives–Diplomatic Papers (hereafter cited as NA-DP) (851.6362/7–1045).

3. Letter from Durand Smith to M. Merchant, 20 August 1946, NA-DP (851.6362/802045).

4. Telegram from Caffrey to Secretary of State, 8 January 1946, NA-DP (851.6362/1–846).

5. Telegram from Clay to Secretary of State, 25 April 1946, NA-DP (851.6362/4–2546).

6. See report on "Possibility of Polish or Russian coal being sent to France," written by Wayne G. Johnson for the Department of State, 26 February 1947, NA-DP (851.6362/2–2647).

7. Memorandum from J. K. Galbraith to Clayton, 26 April 1946, NA-DP (851.6362/4–2646).

8. Werth, *France*, 310.

9. Telegram from James Byrnes to American Embassy in Paris, 11 January 1947, NA-DP (851.6362/1–1147).

10. Note from Clay to War Department and American Embassy in Paris, 10 March 1947, NA-DP (851.504/4–2847).

11. Werth, *France*, 309.

12. Telegram from Caffrey to Secretary of State, 11 March 1947, NA-DP (851.50/3–1147).

13. John Gimbel, *The Origins of the Marshall Plan* (Stanford, Calif., 1976), 200.

14. Ibid., 215–17.

15. Val Lorwin, "Nationalization of Industry Not an Issue in U.S. Aid," 21 July 1947, NA-DP (851.504/7–2347).

16. INSEE, *Mouvement économique en France de 1938 à 1948* (Paris, 1950), 219.

17. Telegram from Caffrey to Secretary of State, 14 October 1948, NA-DP (851.6362/10–1448).

18. Werth, *France*, 351.

19. Raymond Aron, *Combat*, 25 January 1947; François Goguel, *L'Esprit*, May 1947.

20. Letter from Caffrey to Secretary of State, 25 June 1945, NA-DP (851.6362/6–2845).

21. H. Freeman Matthews to Secretary of State, Undersecretary, and Lovett, 25 June 1947, NA-DP (851.00/6–2447).

22. Memorandum of conversation from Thorp to Hickerson and Galbraith, 25 June 1946, NA-DP (851.63632/6–2546).

23. Jean Monnet, *Memoirs* (Garden City, N.Y., 1978), 251–52.

24. Report from Caffrey to Secretary of State, 21 April 1947, NA-DP (851.50/4–2147). Several months later Monick and Schuman arranged a luncheon meeting with Will Clayton and Ivan White in order to press for emergency interim aid for France. Attempting to impress upon the Americans the gravity of the situation in France, Schuman and Monick took the American officials to a restaurant in the Montparnasse area that served black bread and no meat. The Americans viewed it as a ruse, but the tactic may have helped, and the conversation resulted in the granting of aid. See Columbia Oral History Project Papers, "The Marshall Plan," Columbia University Manuscript Collection, New York. Also, see Joseph Alsop's column in the *New York Herald Tribune* on 2 September 1947 entitled "The Clayton Cable."

25. Gimbel, *The Origins*, 200.

26. *L'Espoir*, 22 September 1946.

27. HBNPC, Director's Meeting, 14 January 1947.

28. *Journal officiel, lois et décrets* (Paris, 17 January 1947), 64–51.

29. *La Tribune des mineurs*, 2 March 1945.

30. Charbonnages de France, *Composition des conseils d'administration des houillères de bassin depuis leur créations* (Paris, no date).

31. Several sources have been used to determine that many of the top administrators from the interwar period and the Vichy period were reinstalled after 1947. Annual reports of the *Comité des Houillères*, available at the offices of the Charbonnages de France in Paris, include lists of administrators and officers for the period up to 1939. During the Vichy period the comité was transformed into the Coal Mines Organization Committee. The composition of the organization committee and other officers of that organization can be found in dossiers at the offices of the Charbonnages de France.

32. Some had argued that a nationalized industry could produce coal more cheaply than a privately owned industry. Commercial interests, especially the steel industry and other large coal consumers, generally opposed price hikes in coal. Henry Ehrmann, *Organized Business in France* (Princeton, N.J., 1957), 352; France, *Rapport Mendés-France, 1953* (Paris, 1953), 48–49; Harold Lubell, *The French Investment Program: A Defense of the Monnet Plan* (Paris, 1951), 194. In 1946 the steel industry strongly opposed an increase in the sale price of coal. *Nord-Industriel*, 7 December 1946. Marcel Ventenat wrote: "Must we increase the price of coal in order to balance the budget in the mines, thus hindering industry's ability to hold down production costs and compete with foreign competitors?" Marcel Ventenat, *L'Expérience des nationalisations: Premier bilan* (Paris, 1947), 151.

33. The Jules Moch solution was agreed upon. Vincent Auriol, *Journal du septennat*, vol. 1, 1947 (Paris, 1970), 514–15. For a description of the government's decision to fix the price of coal, see the footnote in Auriol, 814–15.

34. For a critique of this unusual agreement, see Ventenat, *L'Expérience*, 150–51; Ehrmann, *Organized Business*, 299–30; and *Nord-Industriel*, 5 October 1946. The annual report of the HBNPC for 1946 suggests that other factors caused price increases, especially the cost of the Miners' Statute and increases in family allowances.

35. *Nord-Industriel* initially withheld its criticism but doubted Lecoeur's

statement that the wage hikes would not precipitate price hikes. *Nord-Industriel,* 27 July and 10 August 1946. Lecoeur had argued that the wage increases could be financed by compressing the profit margins and by a 10 percent increase in productivity. *Liberté,* 1–2 September 1946.

36. The Audibert commission was initiated by Marcel Paul in reponse to criticisms of the industry. The purpose of the commission was to determine the proper price for coal. As Paul pointed out, the commission was needed because the administrative councils of the Nord–Pas-de-Calais and other basins had not been fully installed. *Nord-Industriel,* 5 October 1946. The commission found that without a subsidy from the state the sale price of coal would have to be increased. *Nord-Industriel,* 7 December 1946.

37. The commission included four inspectors-general from Finance, National Economy, and Mines. *Journal officiel,* 21 January 1947. Ventenat claimed that the real purpose of the commission was to report on the Charbonnages de France. Ventenat, *L'Expérience,* 152. See also Didier Philippe, *Les Charbonnages français nationalisés: Organisation du pouvoir; résultats économiques* (Paris, no date), 15–16.

38. *Nord-Industriel,* 31 May 1947.

39. The Wahl commission included Wahl, an engineer from the Ministry of Bridges; Lorain, an inspector-general from National Economy; Guirard, undersecretary from Finance; Fayet, a civil administrator; and Jenn, a mining engineer. *Journal officiel,* 16 November 1947. The results of the investigation remained classified, although *Nord-Industriel* and *Creusot des cadres,* the newspaper of the CGC, received portions of the report. CGT leaders charged that the results were suppressed because the findings supported the recommendations that had been made by CGT representatives in the administrative councils.

40. The Belgian Senate Committee report is reprinted in an appendix to Ventenat's book.

41. Ventenat, *L'Expérience,* 151.

42. Charbonnages de France, *La Situation des houillères nationalisées,* 30 May 1947, report from Duguet and Lacoste.

43. France, Assemblé National, *Débats* (Paris, 5 June 1947), 1906.

44. Ibid., 13 June 1947, 2096–97, 2100–103.

45. *Nord-Industriel,* 22 February 1947; Charles Rist, "The French Financial Dilemma," *Foreign Affairs* (April 1947): 460.

46. Mario Einaudi, Maurice Byé, and Ernesto Rossi, *Nationalization in France and Italy* (Ithaca, N.Y., 1955), 179–80.

47. SNIM included 750 engineers, cadres, and foremen in September 1946, according to an FO leader of the CGT Federation of Miners. The writer estimated that 60 percent of the cadres belonged to the CGT, but the estimate is probably too high. According to the Charbonnages de France, 1,906 engineers and managers were employed in the mines in 1946. In 1947 the number increased to 2,034. Charbonnages de France, *Rapport de gestion, 1947,* 12.

48. Étienne Dejonghe, "Ingénieurs et société dans les houillères du Nord–Pas-de-Calais de la Belle Époque à nos jours," in André Thépot, ed., *L'Ingénieur dans la société française* (Paris, 1985), 177–78, 183.

49. According to *Nord-Industriel*, 5 July 1947, elections for administrators of the retirement funds for Nord, Pas-de-Calais, Moselle, Loire, Bouches-du-Rhône, Cévennes, l'Aquitaine, Bourgogne, and Dauphine yielded the following results:

SIHN (CGC)	1,304 (five representatives elected)
SNIM (CGT)	781 (three representatives elected).

50. *L'Écho des mines*, August 1946; *L'Espoir*, 23 November 1947; Étienne Dejonghe, "Les Houillères à l'épreuve, 1944–1947," *Revue du Nord* 227 (1975): 661–62.

51. Several articles in the local Socialist press hinted of opportunism among certain engineers who worked closely with the Communists after the liberation. The Socialists used this as an election issue in the October 1946 elections. Ventenat and others incorrectly accused Armanet of being a Communist and some Socialists apparently agreed. Armanet said he was a Socialist. He refrained from criticizing the Communists publicly until the spring of 1947.

52. Auguste Lecoeur, "Hola, planistes!" *Mineurs*, February 1947; Léon Delfosse, "L'Homme, précieux capital," *Mineurs*, March 1947.

53. *La Tribune des mineurs*, 10 May 1947.

54. "Onzième congrès national du SNIM," *Mineurs*, March 1947.

55. Dejonghe, "Les Houillères," 662.

56. *La Tribune des mineurs*, 3 May 1947.

57. Lecoeur asked: "Why did the General Director [Armanet] tell the engineers to stay away from the UNITEC meeting?" *La Tribune des mineurs*, 5 April 1947.

58. *Nord-Industriel*, 5 April 1947.

59. HBNPC, "Procès-verbaux du conseil d'administration," 13 March 1947.

60. Frederick Meyers, *European Coal-Mining Unions: Structure and Function* (Los Angeles, 1959), 51–52; Val Lorwin, *The French Labor Movement* (Cambridge, Mass., 1954), 255–56.

61. Meanwhile underground miners complained that the number of cadres increased too rapidly, reflecting management's need for more supervisors. A miner wrote: "At number two Marles we used to have one head engineer. Now we have two and the second brought three new engineers with him. Two years ago, we had two engineers. Now we have eight." *La Tribune des mineurs*, 1 March 1947. A writer criticized overstaffing of engineers, foremen, and supervisors in *Force ouvrière*, 2 January 1947. According to the Charbonnages de France, the number of managerial staff increased as follows:

	1946	1947
Managers/Engineers	1,906	2,034
Foremen/Technicians	13,502	15,195

62. "Plan Mort-ne? Non!" *Mineurs*, March 1947.

63. Marc Wolf, "Les Fédérations socialistes face aux difficultés de l'unité ouvrière," *Revue du Nord* 227 (1975): 579–93.

64. One miner wrote: "When will the next congress of the miners' union be held? It has been thirteen months since the last meeting in December 1944 when the hard-liners used the purge to take control of the union." *L'Espoir*, 27 January 1946. The congress was finally held in February 1946, but the results disappointed the Socialists. According to *L'Espoir*, "The meeting took place in a small hall in order to avoid any problems. Only designated delegates could attend. Some union locals did not even meet before the congress to discuss resolutions." *L'Espoir*, 7 April 1946.

65. *Liberté* criticized a Socialist member of the union, Émile Raux, who had made "demagogic" speeches at the CGT congress demanding that workers receive wage increases regardless of the level of production. *Liberté*, 19 April 1946. The Socialists defended Raux a few days later. *Nord-Matin*, 25 April 1946.

66. *L'Espoir*, 30 June, 2 September, and 17 November 1946.

67. *Force ouvrière*, 14 February, 4 July, 24 April 1946, 16 January 1947, and 12 September 1946.

68. Eleven FO members initiated Friends of FO but claimed that in doing so they were subjected to "violent attacks" from the Communists. *Force ouvrière*, 23 January 1947.

69. Ibid., 29 August 1946.

70. Ibid., 14 February and 6 March 1947.

71. Mériaux was described as a *chartiste* by *La Tribune des mineurs*. He had been a member of the confederated wing of the CGT and had been removed from a union position in December 1944. See *Force ouvrière*, 6 and 27 March 1947, and *La Tribune des mineurs*, 22 February, 8 and 15 March 1947.

72. This "euphoria" led some Socialist activists in Pas-de-Calais to suggest again that the Socialists were "more left than the Communists." *L'Espoir*, 12 January 1947. A year earlier, Lechantre claimed that the Socialists were the real revolutionaries because the Communists and the MRP "do not know what their final goal is." *Nord-Matin*, 7 December 1945. The Left Socialists of Pas-de-Calais expressed some of their views in *L'Espoir* between January and March 1946: "We are the only party that has really maintained our doctrine. We are the most Left and the most revolutionary. We have not flirted with the MRP and we did not hide behind the 'antifascist slate' like the Communists did." The Left Socialists encouraged their comrades in the government to resign, but they also feared unity of action with the Communists for fear of being absorbed by the Communist Party. *L'Espoir*, 24 February 1946. Jean Piat wrote: "The Socialist party is the only real representative of the extreme left. We have no one to our left. We sing the *Internationale*." *L'Espoir*, 10 March 1946. The Communists' steady criticism of the Socialists in the Communist press had also subsided, contributing to Socialist desires to maintain amicable relations with the Communists. *L'Espoir*, 12 March 1946.

73. *Force ouvrière*, 12, 19 December 1946, and 2, 16 January 1947.

74. Ibid., 13 March 1947.

75. Ibid., 20 March, 17 and 24 April 1947.

76. Sinot and other veteran Socialist union officials saw the problem in the mines as more complex than the fact that Communists dominated the union. As a Socialist group reported in mid-May: "In the mines we see a certain effervescence, a sharpening of conflicts, and a situation where the stewards are bypassed and not listened to by the miners. The stewards say they are helpless before this movement. At first glance, it seems that political passions are prompting the miners to strike, but anyone who lives and works with the miners knows that the situation is worse than the leaders of the union understand. The Bedaux system and individual payment are unpopular. There are too many cadres in the mines. Who is to blame for it all? The Communist leaders of the union. They brought the reaction into the administrative councils of the mines and imposed the Bedaux system and individual payment on us. What should we do? Under the current circumstances, strikes are a crime. But the miners should push for new meetings and replace the Communist delegates." *L'Espoir*, 18 May 1947.

77. *Force ouvrière*, 12 June 1947.

78. Ibid., 26 June 1947.

79. Ibid., 5, 19 June, 14 May, and 3 July 1947; also *L'Espoir*, 18 May 1947.

80. *Force ouvrière*, 26 July 1947.

81. Ibid., 3 July 1947.

82. Most of the early discussions of the "grandes grèves" written in the 1950s by writers such as Georges Lefranc (*Les Expériences syndicales en France de 1939 à 1950* [Paris, 1950]), Val Lorwin (*The French Labor Movement*), Herbert Luethy (*France Against Herself* [New York, 1955]), and David Schoenbrun (*As France Goes* [New York, 1957]) focused on the strikes as proof that the Communists sought to use the strikes to undercut the economy and weaken the influence of the Marshall Plan in France. These authors viewed the strikes as products of the cold war. Other writers, in closer contact with the labor movement, recognized the cold war as a key element, but not necessarily the main element, in the big strikes of 1947 and 1948. Alexander Werth (*France*) saw the causes for the strikes in economic deterioration and the fact that hopes for a new society seemed frustrated. Writers for newspapers of the Center and Left (*Combat, Franc-Tireur, L'Esprit*) tended to be critical of the Communists and the government for intransigence on both sides. Dominique Desanti, a journalist and former Communist writer, spent eight weeks in the northern mining basin in 1948. She considered the miners' demands justified and believed that the government welcomed the strikes in order to physically defeat the miners' movement. Desanti also raised criticisms of some of the tactics used by the strikers, as well as the decision by top leaders to continue the 1948 strike long after many miners were unwilling to remain off the job. Insiders who were close to union decision making generally conclude that the purpose of the 1947 strike was to allow the Communists back into the government. This includes CGT leaders Roger Pannequin (*Adieu, camarades* [Paris, 1977]), André Barjonet (*La CGT* [Paris, 1968]), and André Théret (*Mineurs en lutte, 1944–1948* [Paris, 1974]). Socialists have usually avoided the strikes. An exception is Jules Moch, whose memoirs

(*Une Vie si longue*) maintain that the leaders of the Cominform were responsible for calling the 1947 and 1948 strikes. In this view, it was necessary to defeat the strikes in order to defend the Fourth Republic from both the Communists and the Gaullists. Roger Quilliot (*La SFIO et l'exercice du pouvoir: 1944–1958* [Paris, 1972]), a Socialist writer who has written articles on the miners for the party's former journal *La Revue socialiste*, sidesteps the strikes. Although Socialist leaders and rank-and-file activists played important roles in the strikes, Quilliot devotes only a few lines to them in his book. The CGT and PCF produced several articles on the strikes when they occurred, but little systematic analysis has been made. In 1954 and 1971 Communist writers pointed to sectarian errors made during the strikes. The offices of the mines have published no materials on the strikes. Their officials claim that little information was ever gathered by their offices. Government and intelligence reports, along with regional police materials, are not yet available. Some memoirs are starting to appear from individuals who were involved in the strikes.

83. Yasmine Chudzinski and Jacques Renard, *Paroles et mémoires du bassin houiller du Nord–Pas-de-Calais* (Lille, 1981), 99.

84. Irwin Wall, *French Communism in the Era of Stalin: The Quest for Unity and Integration, 1945–1962* (Westport, Conn., 1983), 57, 58.

85. George Ross, *Workers and Communists in France: From Popular Front to Eurocommunism* (Berkeley, Calif., 1982), 51.

86. Lorwin, *French Labor*, 198.

87. Dejonghe, "Les Houillères," 665.

88. Ibid.

89. *Franc-Tireur*, 18 November 1947.

90. *Le Populaire*, 18 November 1947; *Nord-Matin*, 18 and 20 November 1947.

91. *L'Espoir*, 23 November and 30 November 1947.

92. Werth, *France*, 380; Vincent Auriol, *Mon Septennat*, vol. 1 (Paris, 1970), 712–14.

93. Françoise Salion, *Les Socialistes et les grèves du Nord et du Pas-de-Calais, 1947–1948* (Lille, 1971), 41–42.

94. R. Goetz-Girey, *Le Mouvement des grèves en France* (Paris, 1965), 38.

95. *Combat*, 22 November 1947.

96. Auriol, *Mon Septennat*, 568.

97. Lorwin, *French Labor*, 120.

98. Auriol, *Mon Septennat*, 558–59.

99. Ibid., 712–13.

100. *Force ouvrière* and *Combat*, 20 November 1947.

101. *Nord-Matin*, 16 November 1947.

102. *Combat*, 29 November 1947.

103. Ibid., 21 and 22 November 1947.

104. Ibid., 25 November 1947.

105. Ibid.

106. Ibid., 2 and 3 December 1947; *La Vie ouvrière*, 3 December 1947; *Combat*, 4 December 1947; *La Vie ouvrière*, 3 December 1947; *Combat*, 5 December 1947.

107. *L'Humanité*, 6 December 1947; Roger Pannequin, *Adieu, camarades*, 94–97.

108. Wall, *French Communism*, 68; *Combat*, 6 December 1947; *Le Peuple*, 6 December 1947.

109. *Combat*, 6 December 1947.

110. *L'Espoir*, 21 November 1947; Lorwin, *French Labor*, 126; and E. Godfrey Drexel, *The Fate of the Non-Communist Left in France* (New York, 1955), 51.

111. *Combat*, 14 December 1947.

112. Chudzinski and Renard, *Paroles*, 99.

113. Werth, *France*, 384.

CHAPTER 6: THE MINERS' STRIKE OF 1948

1. Françoise Salion, *Les Socialistes et les grèves du Nord et du Pas-de-Calais, 1947–1948* (Lille, 1971), 89–90.

2. Jules Moch, *Rencontres avec Léon Blum* (Paris, 1970), 323, 321.

3. *L'Espoir*, 21 August 1948.

4. *La Tribune des mineurs*, 6, 13, and 20 March 1948.

5. Ibid., 12 February 1948.

6. *Nord-Matin*, 13 March 1948.

7. *L'Espoir*, 21 March 1948.

8. *Force ouvrière*, 25 March 1948.

9. Salion, *Les Socialistes*, 69–71.

10. *La Tribune des mineurs*, 21 February 1948.

11. *Le Travailleur du sous-sol*, March–April 1948.

12. *Liberté*, 11 and 12 September 1948.

13. *La Vie française*, 8 October 1948.

14. *La Tribune des mineurs*, 18 September 1948.

15. Ibid.

16. *Le Peuple*, 20 May 1948.

17. *Creusot des cadres*, 15 September 1948.

18. *Nord-Industriel*, 12 June 1948.

19. Ibid., 19 June 1948.

20. Ibid., 12, 26 June, 11, 18, and 26 September 1948.

21. *La Vie française*, 8 October 1948.

22. Benoit Frachon, "La Grève des mineurs français," in *Servir la France*, January 1949.

23. Didier Philippe, *Les Charbonnages français nationalisés: Organisation du pouvoir; résultats économiques* (Paris, no date), 109.

24. *L'Espoir*, 8 August 1948.

25. André Théret, *Mineurs en lutte, 1944–1948* (Paris, no date), 22.

26. *Le Patriote de St Étienne*, 26 September 1948.

27. *Travaux de l'action populaire*, February 1949, 108.

28. Georges Lefranc, *Les Expériences syndicales en France de 1939 à 1950* (Paris, 1950), 215.

29. *Travaux de l'action populaire*, February 1949, 108.

30. *Le Patriote de St. Étienne*, 25 September 1948.

31. *Travaux de l'action populaire*, February 1949, 109.

32. *Voix du Nord*, 21 October 1948.

33. *Paroles françaises*, 15 October 1948.

34. *Travaux de l'action populaire*, February 1949, 108.

35. *L'Humanité*, 3, 7 July, and 8 September 1948.

36. *Le Peuple*, 26 August 1948.

37. *L'Ouvrier des mines*, 21 March and 29 July 1948.

38. Ibid., 29 August 1948.

39. *Syndicalisme*, 26 August, 9 and 15 September 1948.

40. *Liberté*, 25 September 1948.

41. *L'Ouvrier des mines*, 3 October 1948.

42. Lefranc, *Les Expériences syndicales*, 216.

43. *Nord-Éclair*, 5 October 1948, and *Liberté*, 3 October 1948.

44. C. Angelli and P. Gillet, *La Police dans la politique* (Paris, 1967), 214.

45. Georgette Elgey, *La République des illusions, 1945–1951* (Paris, 1965), 399.

46. *Libération*, 4 October 1948.

47. *Liberté*, 2 October 1948.

48. *Franc-Tireur*, 5 October 1948.

49. *Nord-Matin*, 4 October 1948; *L'Ouvrier des mines*, 10 October 1948; *Le Populaire*, 4 October 1948.

50. *Franc-Tireur*, 6 October 1948.

51. Lefranc, *Les Expériences syndicales*, 216.

52. United States, Department of State, *Foreign Relations of the United States, 1948*, vol. 3, *Western Europe*, 663.

53. *L'Ouvrier des mines*, 17 October 1948.

54. *Combat*, 5 October 1948.

55. *L'Ouvrier des mines*, 17 October 1948.

56. *Combat*, 5 October 1948.

57. *Liberté*, 5 October 1948.

58. *Force ouvrière*, 7 October 1948; *Combat*, 6 October 1948; *Voix du Nord*, 7 October 1948.

59. *Combat*, 7 October 1948.

60. *Nord-Matin*, 8 October 1948.

61. *Franc-Tireur*, 8 October 1948.

62. *Nord-Éclair*, 13 October 1948; *Combat*, 12 October 1948.

63. *Combat*, 8, 9–10, and 12 October 1948.

64. *La Gauche*, October 1948.

65. Vincent Auriol, *Mon Septennat*, vol. 2 (Paris, 1970), 475.

66. *Combat*, 13 October 1948.

67. Ibid.

68. *Nord-Éclair*, 13 October 1948.

69. *Combat*, 13 October 1948.

70. *Nord-Éclair*, 13 and 16 October 1948.

71. *Liberté*, 5 October 1948.

72. *Combat*, 18 October 1948.

73. *Force ouvrière*, 16 October 1948.

74. Auriol, *Mon Septennat*, 491.

75. *Combat*, 18 October 1948.

76. Angelli and Gillet, *La Police*, 215.

77. *Combat*, 20 October 1948.

78. *La Dépêche démocratique* (St Etienne), 20 October 1948.

79. Fédération Nationale des Travailleurs du Sous-sol, *Communiqué*, 16 October 1948.

80. *Nord-Éclair*, 19 October 1948.

81. *Voix du Nord*, 19 October 1948.

82. Ibid., 20 October 1948.

83. *Combat*, 20 October 1948.

84. *Liberté*, 23 October 1948.

85. *Combat*, 22 October 1948.

86. *Nord-Matin*, 21 October 1948.

87. *Combat*, 21 October 1948.

88. Auriol, *Mon Septennat*, 493.

89. Moch, *Rencontres*, 334–35.

90. *Voix du Nord*, 23 October 1948.

91. *Combat*, 26 October 1948.

92. Moch, *Rencontres*, 335.

93. République française, *Ordre de requisition individuelle*, 20 October 1948.

94. *Combat*, 2 November 1948.

95. Fédération Nationale des Travailleurs du Sous-sol, *Communiqué*, 6 November 1948.

96. *Croix du Nord*, 26 October 1948.

97. *Voix du Nord*, 28 October 1948.

98. *Nord-Éclair*, 27 October 1948.

99. *La Bataille socialiste*, 27 October 1948.

100. Roger Pannequin, *Adieu, camarades* (Paris, 1977), 108.

101. Dominique Desanti, *Les Staliniens* (Paris, 1975), 126.

102. Lefranc, *Les Expériences syndicales*, 217.

103. Desanti, *Les Staliniens*, 126.

104. *Nord-Éclair*, 29 and 28 October 1948.

105. *Combat*, 23–24 October 1948.

106. Pannequin, *Adieu, camarades*, 108–9.

107. *Combat*, 3 November 1948.

108. Lefranc, *Les Expériences syndicales*, 218, and Léon Delfosse, *Personal Papers*.

109. Delfosse, *Personal Papers*.

110. Lefranc, *Les Expériences syndicales*, 218. See also *L'Humanité* and *Liberté* during the period of the strike.

111. Lefranc, *Les Expériences syndicales*, 217.

112. *Voix du Nord*, 29 October 1948.

113. *Nord-Éclair*, 29 October 1948.

114. Pannequin, *Adieu, camarades*, 113.

115. CGT, *Communiqué*, 30 October 1948.

116. *La Bataille socialiste*, 29 October 1948.

117. *L'Humanité*, 6 November 1948.

118. Pannequin, *Adieu, camarades*, 113.

119. Fédération Nationale des Travailleurs du Sous-sol, *Communiqué*, 6 November 1948.

120. Louis Couturier, Les *"Grandes Affaires" du parti communiste français* (Paris, 1972), 58–65.

121. PCF, *L'Histoire du parti communiste (manuel)* (Paris, 1962).

122. Roger Grimaud, "Nous avons payé trop cher: Étude sur les rapports du PCF et du SFIO, 1943–1956" (unpublished, 1971).

123. *Le Rassemblement ouvrier*, 23 and 30 October 1948.

124. *Croix du Nord*, 28 October 1948.

125. Desanti, *Les Staliniens*, 130.

126. Louis Lengrand and Maria Craipeau, *Louis Lengrand, mineur du Nord* (Paris, 1974), 94–98.

127. *Force ouvrière*, 22 November 1948, and *Syndicalisme*, 25 November and 1 December 1948.

128. Théret, *Mineurs en lutte*, 30–31.

129. HBNPC, *Procès-verbaux de la réunion du conseil d'administration*, 25 November 1948.

130. Rolande Trempé, *Les Trois Batailles du charbon, 1936–1947* (Paris, 1989), 245.

131. Moch, *Rencontres*, 341, and Delfosse, *Personal Papers*.

132. Théret, *Mineurs en lutte*, 49, 50.

133. Pannequin, *Adieu, camarades*, 114.

134. *Esprit*, January 1949, 123–24.

135. Théret, *Mineurs en lutte*, 49.

136. Herbert Luethy, *France Against Herself* (New York, 1955), 152–53.

137. David Schoenbrun, *As France Goes* (New York, 1957), 85–86.

138. Alexander Werth, *France, 1940–1955* (Boston, 1966), 403.

139. *Combat*, 4 September 1948.

140. Desanti, *Les Staliniens*, 131.

CHAPTER 7: ECONOMIC INTEGRATION AND THE RETREAT FROM COAL

1. Alexander Werth, *France, 1940–1955* (Boston, 1966), 402–5.

2. Richard F. Kuisel, *Capitalism and the State in Modern France: Renovation and Economic Management in the Twentieth Century* (Cambridge, England, 1981), 250.

3. Pierre Gerbet, "La Genèse du plan Schuman: Des origines à la déclaration du 9 mai 1950," *Revue française de la science politique* 6, 3 (1956): 548.

4. Richard Mayne, *The Recovery of Europe, 1945–1973* (Garden City, N.Y., 1973), 216–30.

5. Jean Monnet, *Memoirs* (Garden City, N.Y., 1978), 292.

6. François Caron, *An Economic History of Modern France* (New York, 1979), 325.

7. Derek C. Bok, *The First Three Years of the Schuman Plan* (Princeton, N.J., 1955), 10.

8. William Chaikin, "Notes on French Economic Plans," 8 January 1946, National Archives–Diplomatic Papers (hereafter cited as NA-DP) (851.50/1-1046).

9. See the European Cooperation Administration (ECA), *Thirteenth Report*, in Hadley Arkes, *Bureaucracy, the Marshall Plan and the National State* (Princeton, N.J., 1972), 238.

10. Charbonnages de France, *La Modernisation des houillères françaises* (Paris, 1950).

11. Arkes, *Bureaucracy*, 363.

12. European Cooperation Administration (Marshall Plan)–Office of the Special Representative (hereafter cited as ECA-OSR), "U.S. Coal Prices in Europe," 18 August 1949.

13. ECA-OSR, "Statement Presented by U.S. Delegate at ECA Coal Committee," 27 August 1949, RG 286, Box 95.

14. ECA-OSR, "The Bissell Reports," 6 March 1950, RG 286, Box 97.

15. ECA-OSR, "Critical Sectors of French Investment Program," 20 October 1949, RG 286, Box 95.

16. ECA-OSR, "The Bissell Reports," April 1950, RG 286, Box 97.

17. Hoffman is quoted in William Brown and Redvers Opie, *American Foreign Assistance* (Washington, D.C., 1953), 271, and Gabriel and Joyce Kolko, *The Limits of Power* (New York, 1972), 465–66.

18. United States, Department of State, *Foreign Relations of the United States* (hereafter cited as US-FR), 1949, vol. 4, 485–88.

19. Werth, *France*, 481.

20. René Roux, "The Position of Labour under the Schuman Plan," *International Labour Review* 65, 3 (1952): 290. On social policy in general terms, see Doreen Collins, *The European Communities: The Social Policy of the First Phase*, vol. 1: *The European Coal and Steel Community, 1951–1970* (London, 1975).

21. Telegram from Harriman, special representative in Europe, to Secretary of State, US-FR, 20 May 1950, vol. 3, 703.

22. US-FR, 12 May 1950, vol. 3, 698–99.

23. *Le Monde*, 25 May 1950.

24. PCF, "Le Plan Schuman: Plan de désastre national, plan de guerre mondiale" (Paris, 1951).

25. *L'Humanité*, 20 June 1950.

26. Telegram from High Commissioner for Germany, McCloy, to Secretary of State, US-FR, 23 May 1950, vol. 3, 707.

27. Roux, "The Position of Labor under the Schuman Plan," 292.

28. See Bernard Lavergne, *Le Plan Schuman* (Paris, 1951).

29. Werth, *France*, 481.

30. Jean-Pierre Rioux, *The Fourth Republic, 1944–1958* (Cambridge, Mass., 1987), 32.

31. W. G. Jensen, *Energy in Europe, 1945–1970* (London, 1980), 28.

32. Henry Ehrmann, *Organized Business in France* (Princeton, N.J., 1957), 344–45.

33. Alfred Sauvy, "La Situation économique française," *Revue française de l'énergie*, October 1950, 30.

34. Commissariat Général du Plan, *Two Years of Execution of the Plan of Modernisation and Equipment* (Paris, 1949), 24.

35. Commission de Vérification des Comptes des Entreprises Publiques (CVCEP), *Rapport d'ensemble*, 21 August 1949, 26 January 1951, and 3 October 1952.

36. Charbonnages de France, *Rapport sur les aspects économiques du plan de modernisation des houillères* (Paris, 1949).

37. Charbonnages de France, *La Modernisation des houillères françaises: Le programme d'ensemble, l'intervention du plan Marshall* (Paris, 1949).

38. Commissariat Général du Plan, *Two Years*, 58.

39. R. Cadel, *Dix Ans de nationalisation des charbonnages de France* (Brussels, 1956), 18, and Henri Claude, *Les Monopoles contre la nation* (Paris, 1956), 202.

40. Commissariat Général du Plan, *Two Years*, 24.

41. Ministére des Finances, INSEE, *Mouvement économique en France de 1938 à 1948* (Paris, 1950). 218.

42. See André Barjonet, *La CGT* (Paris, 1968), 93–94.

43. Michel Toromanoff, *Le Déclin du charbon et les problèmes de fermeture des mines* (Paris, no date), 34.

44. Mario Einaudi, Maurice Byé, and Ernesto Rossi, *Nationalization in France and Italy* (Ithaca, N.Y., 1955), 161.

45. J. Grondien, "Les Houillères en France et l'Angleterre," *Revue française de l'énergie* (March 1950): 252.

46. *Le Monde*, 10 June 1953.

47. Quoted in Yasmine Chudzinski and Jacques Renard, *Paroles et mémoires du bassin houiller du Nord–Pas-de-Calais, 1914–1980* (Lille, 1981), 188.

48. Donald Reid describes how miners in the Aubin mining basin confronted the threat of deindustrialization in his *The Miners of Decazeville: A Genealogy of Deindustrialization* (Cambridge, Mass., 1985), 194–200.

49. Auguste Lecoeur, "Pour empêcher que nos riches départements du Nord et du Pas-de-Calais soient transformés en désert." Speech delivered at the Congress of the CGT Federation of Miners, Waziers, June 1950.

50. Alain Touraine, "L'Évolution de la conscience et de l'action ouvrières dans les charbonnages," in Louis Trenant, ed., *Le Charbon et sciences humaines* (Paris, 1964), 253–56.

51. Serge Moscovici, "Les Mineurs jugent la nationalisation," *Sociologie du travail* 2 (1960): 219–25.

52. Juliette Minces, *Le Nord* (Paris, 1967), 82–83.

53. Achilles Blondeau, "La Productivité dans les mines," *Économie et politique* (March 1956): 246.

54. Minces, *Le Nord*, 83.

55. Louis Courturier, *Les "Grandes Affaires" du parti communiste français* (Paris, 1972), 58–65, and Irwin Wall, *French Communism in the Era of Stalin: The Quest for Unity and Integration, 1945–1962* (Westport, Conn., 1983), 247–48.

56. Blondeau, "La Productivité," 242.

57. *L'Humanité*, 26 October 1950.

58. Charbonnages de France, *Rapport de gestion, 1955* (Paris, 1956).

59. Jean-Jacques Carré, Edmond Malinvaud, and Paul Dubois, *French Economic Growth* (Stanford, Calif., 1975), 487.

60. Bok, *The First Three Years*, 10.

61. Louis Lister, *Europe's Coal and Steel Community* (New York, 1960), 114.

62. Charbonnages de France, *Rapport de gestion*, 1947 and 1948, and Jocelyne Moniez, *L'Industrie charbonnière française depuis 1946* (Lille, 1959), 259.

63. M. Hincker, "Énergie en Europe et en France," *Économie et politique*, November 1959.

64. Dominique Saumon and Louis Puiseux, "Actors and Decisions in French Energy Policy," in *The Energy Syndrome*, ed. Leon Lindberg (Lexington, Mass., 1977), 139.

65. René Oizon, *L'Évolution récente de la production énergique française* (Paris, 1973), 353.

Selected Bibliography

MANUSCRIPTS AND COLLECTIONS

Primary sources and manuscript materials for this study were drawn from a wide range of archives, institutions, organizations, and individuals in France and the United States.

In France, government documentation from the postwar period is not readily available. Gradually, however, some materials are beginning to appear. On the coal industry, the archives of the Charbonnages de France (the national coal board) proved very useful and quite accessible. Their documentation extends from the days of the private coal-mining firms into the nationalized era. The regionally based coal board, the Houillères du Bassin, Nord and Pas-de-Calais, also has documentation on the mining industry. Documentation at the regional level comes from the departmental archives in Nord (Lille) and Pas-de-Calais (Arras). In Paris, the Ministry of Finance has material on the nationalized coal mines, especially on the issue of compensating the mining firms.

In the United States, primary documentation was obtained from the voluminous U.S. State Department records in Washington, D.C. Also useful were the manuscript collections at the George C. Marshall Library in Lexington, Virginia, the State Historical Society of Wisconsin, and the Walter Reuther Archives in Detroit.

Several research centers and libraries in the Paris region offered useful materials, including the Archives Nationales and Bibliothéque Nationale, the Bibliothéque de Documentation Internationale Contemporaine in Nanterre, the Centre de Documentation de l'Institut Français d'Histoire Sociale, the Musée Social, and the Centre de Recherches d'Histoire des Mouvements Sociaux et du Syndicalisme. Primary source materials on the war years can be found at the archives of the Comité d'Histoire de la Deuxième Guerre Mondiale in Paris. A wide range of graduate student research papers on coal mining and regional politics in the northern region are housed in a special library at the Université de Lille III.

FRENCH GOVERNMENT PUBLICATIONS

Charbonnages de France. *Bulletin d'information technique*. Paris, 1949.
———. *La Modernisation des houillères françaises: Le programme d'ensemble, l'intervention du plan Marshall*. Paris, 1949.

————. *Note sur le comité des houillères*. Paris, 1972.

————. *Rapport de gestion*. Paris, 1946–1954.

————. *Rapport sur les aspects économiques du plan de modernisation des houillères*. Paris, 1949.

————. *Régions minières: Groupe des charbonnages de France—Nord–Pas-de-Calais*. Paris, 1970.

Comité d'Études Régionales Économiques et Sociales. *Inventaire des productions charbonnières et sidérugiques dans les départements du Nord et du Pas-de-Calais*. Lille, July 1955.

Commissariat Général du Plan. *Quatre Ans d'exécution du plan de modernisation et d'équipement de l'union française: Réalisations, 1947–1950, et programme, 1951*. Paris, 1951.

————. *Rapport du Commissaire Général sur le plan de modernisation d'équipement de l'union française: Réalisations, 1947–1949, et objectifs, 1950–1952*. Paris, December 1949.

————. *Rapport général sur le premier plan de modernisation et d'équipement*. Paris, November, 1946.

————. *Rapport sur la réalisation du plan de modernisation et d'équipement de l'union française: Année 1952*. Paris, 1953.

————. *Two Years of Execution of the Plan of Modernization and Equipment*. Paris, 1948.

Commission d'Études des Problèmes d'Après-Guerre (CEPAG). *La Situation de l'industrie houillère*. London, 1943.

Commission de Vérification des Comptes des Entreprises Publiques. *Rapport d'ensemble*. 21 August 1949. *Journal officiel, annexe administrative*. Paris, 1949. Additional reports: 1951, 1952, and 1953.

Conseil de la République. *Rapport annuel au nom de la sous-commission du Conseil de la République chargée de suivre la gestion des entreprises nationalisées*. Document 824, Paris, 1950.

Conseil Économique. *Revenu national et conjoncture économique*. Paris, 1952.

Houillères du Bassin du Nord et du Pas-de-Calais (HBNPC), conseil d'administration. *Procès-verbaux des réunions du conseil d'administration*. Douai, 1946–1947.

————. *Documents économiques et sociaux*. Douai, April 1947.

————. *L'Histoire et l'avenir du bassin minier*. Douai, 1976.

————. *Rapport de gestion*. Douai, 1946–1949.

————. *Réconstruction, équipement, modernisation*. Douai, September 1948.

Institut National de la Statistique et des Études Économiques (INSEE). *Bulletin de la statistique générale de la France (mensuel)*. 1945–1954.

————. *Mouvement économique en France de 1938 à 1948*. Paris, 1950.

————. *Mouvement économique en France de 1944 à 1957*. Paris, 1958.

Ministère des Finances. *Inventaire de la situation financière, 1913–1946*. Paris, 1946.

————. *Inventaire de la situation financière*, Paris, 1951.

————. *La Nationalisation des houillères du Nord et du Pas-de-Calais* (dossier). Paris, 1944–1949.

Ministère d'Information. *Les Nationalisations en France*. Paris, 1945.

UNITED STATES GOVERNMENT PUBLICATIONS

Central Intelligence Agency. *Memoranda for the President from R. H. Hellenkoetter, Director of Central Intelligence.* 10 October 1947.

————. *Opposition to E.C.A. in Participating Countries.* 2 February 1949.

Department of State. *Foreign Relations of the United States, 1947.* Vol. 3, *Western Europe.* 1974.

————. *Foreign Relations of the United States, 1948.* Vol. 3, *Western Europe.* 1974.

————. Office of Intelligence and Research. *Bibliography.* 1950.

————. Office of Intelligence and Research. *European Reconstruction Survey: France, Preliminary Draft.* 19 August 1946.

————. Office of Intelligence and Research. *French Economic Outlook and Commodity Trade.* Washington, D.C. 18 March 1946.

————. Office of Intelligence and Research. *The Monnet Four-Year Plan for the French Economy.* 28 February 1947.

House of Representatives. *Council on Foreign Affairs.* 1947–1949.

Office of Strategic Services, Research and Analysis Branch. *A Selected Who's Who in Vichy France.* 24 October 1944.

Senate. *Council on Foreign Affairs.* 1947–1949.

OTHER REPORTS AND PUBLICATIONS

Bulletin de l'Association des Porteurs de Valeurs des Charbonnages. *La Première Nationalisation.* Paris, July 1945.

Confédération Générale du Travail (CGT). *Congrès national, 1946: Compte rendu.* Paris, 1946.

————. *Congrès national, 1948: Compte rendu.* Paris, 1948.

————. Cour d'Appel de Douai. *Les Mines et la région du Nord.* Douai, 1972.

————. Fédération Nationale des Travailleurs du Sous-sol (CGT). *Unité du corps minier contre le plan Schuman: Rapport de la troisième congrès de la fédération des mineurs du Nord et du Pas-de-Calais.* Paris, 1953.

Hoover Institute. *France During the German Occupation, 1940–1944.* Stanford, Calif., 1959.

International Labor Organization. The Coal Mines Committee. Session Two: *The Origins of the European Coal Organization.* Geneva, 1947.

————. The Coal Mines Committee. *International Relations.* Geneva, 1948.

————. The Coal Mines Committee. *Third Session.* Pittsburgh, 1949.

————. *Studies and Reports.* Series B: *The World Coal-Mining Industry.* Geneva, 1938.

————. *Labour-Management Cooperation in France.* Geneva, 1950.

Organization for European Economic Cooperation. *Coal and European Economic Expansion.* Paris, 1952.

————. *Coal Production and Supplies for Western Europe in 1952 and 1953.* Paris, 1953.

————. *Economic Conditions in France.* United Nations. Paris, 1954.

————. *Economic Commission for Europe: Coal Division.* Geneva, 1948.

————. *Postwar Shortages of Food and Coal.* Washington, D.C., 1948.

Sénat de la Belgique. *Rapport sur les charbonnages de France.* Brussels, April 1947.

SPEECHES AND MEMOIRS

Auriol, Vincent. *Journal du septennat.* 2 vols. (1947–1948). Paris, 1970.

Billoux, François. *Quand nous étions ministres.* Paris, 1972.

Frachon, Benoit. *Au rythme des jours.* Vol. 1. Paris, 1973.

Lecoeur, Auguste. *L'Autocritique attendu.* Paris, 1955.

————. *Avec les masses, éléver notre travail d'organisation.* Twelfth National Congress of the PCF at Grenevilliers. 2–6 April 1950.

————. *Croix de guerre pour une grève.* Paris, 1971.

————. *Le Partisan.* Paris, 1963.

————. *La PCF et la lutte pour la paix.* Paris, 1951.

————. *La PCF et la Résistance.* Paris, 1968.

————. *Pour empêcher que nos riches départements du Nord et du Pas-de-Calais soient transformés en désert.* Paris, 1950.

————. *La Vérité sur la grève des mineurs.* Paris, 1948.

Moch, Jules. *Le Communisme et la France.* Assemblée nationale, Paris, 16 November 1948.

————. *Rencontres avec Léon Blum.* Paris, 1970.

Monnet, Jean. *Memoirs.* Garden City, N.Y., 1978.

Pannequin, Roger. *Adieu, camarades.* 2 vols. Paris, 1977.

Roucate, G. *La Guerre de Moche contre les mineurs.* Assemblée nationale, 17 November 1948.

[Théret, André]. *Mineurs en lutte, 1944–1948.* Paris, 1974.

————. *Parole d'ouvrier.* Paris, 1978.

Thorez, Maurice. *Courage et confiance pour gagner des nouvelles batailles.* Montceau-les-mines, 17 February 1946.

————. *Il faut gagner la bataille du charbon.* Waziers, 1945.

UNPUBLISHED MANUSCRIPTS AND PAPERS

Bethouart, Bruno. "Histoire du mouvement républicain populaire dans l'arrondissement du Lille." Lille, 1972.

Bouzon, J.-P. "Enquête sur le probléme politique de l'épuration dans le Nord, 1944–1946." Lille, 1970.

Brionval, Léon. "Les Délégués et la sécurité des ouvriers mineurs." Lille, 1950.

Cienkansi, Pierre. "Les Élections municipales dans cinq villes du bassin houiller du Pas-de-Calais de 1947 à 1971." Lille, 1972.

Fine, Martin. "Toward Corporatism: The Movement for Capital-Labor Collaboration in France, 1914–1936." Ph.D. dissertation. Madison, Wis., 1971.

Gordon, Richard. "Coal Pricing and the Energy Problem in the European Countries." Cambridge, Mass., 1960.

Grimaud, Roger. "Nous avons payé trop cher: Étude sur les rapports du PCF et du SFIO, 1943–1956." Paris, 1971.

Hadjo-Lazaro, Jean-Pierre. "Étude de la grève des mineurs du Nord et du Pas-de-Calais, 1941." Lille, no date.

Laurent, Daniel. "Statistique de la répression des faits de collaboration dans le département du Nord, 1940–1948." Lille, 1971.

Lubell, Harold. "The French Investment Plan: A Defense of the Monnet Plan." Cambridge, Mass., 1951.

Mendelson, Jean. "Recherches sur la vie intérieure du PCF de 1944 à 1952." Paris, 1971.

Peterson, W. C. "Economic Recovery in France, 1946–1952." Ann Arbor, Mich., 1953.

Salion, Françoise. "Les Socialistes et les grèves du Nord et du Pas-de- Calais, 1947–1948." Lille, 1971.

Segond, Alain. "La Presse clandestine communiste, 1941–1944." Lille, 1973.

Windmuller, John F. "America's Role in the International Labor Movement, 1945–1950." Ithaca, N.Y., 1951.

BOOKS

Adam, Gérard. *La CFTC, 1940–1958*. Paris, 1964.

Adam, William J., and Christian Stoffaes, eds. *French Industrial Policy*. Washington, D.C., 1986.

Allais, Maurice. *La Gestion des houillères nationalisées et la théorie économique*. Paris, 1953.

Andrieu, Claire, Lucette Le Van, and Antoine Prost, eds. *Les Nationalisations de la libération: De l'utopie au compromis*. Paris, 1987.

Angelli, C., and P. Gillet. *La Police dans la politique*. Paris, 1967.

Aragon, Louis. *Le Pays des mines*. Lens, 1949.

Ardagh, John. *The New French Revolution*. New York, 1968.

Ariés, Philippe. *Histoire des populations françaises*. Paris, 1948.

Aron, Raymond. *Les Conséquences sociales de la guerre*. Paris, 1945.

———. *Histoire de l'épuration*. Paris, 1974.

Audibert, Étienne. *Cinq Ans de la nationalisation*. Paris, 1951.

Babichon, G., and Serge Moscovici. *Modernisation des mines, conversion des mineurs*. Paris, 1962.

Barjonet, André. *La CGT*. Paris, 1968.

———. *Les Nationalisations: La sécurité sociale*. Paris, 1950.

Barron, Richard. *Parties and Politics in Modern France*. Washington, D.C., 1959.

Barton, Paul. *Misère et révolte de l'ouvrier polonais*. Douai, 1961.

Baudot, Pierre. *La Planification française: Quinze ans d'expérience*. Paris, 1963.

Baum, Warren C. *The French Economy and the State*. Princeton, N.J., 1958.

Bergounioux, Alain. *Force ouvrière*. Paris, 1975.

Berthomieu, Charles. *La Gestion des entreprises nationalisées*. Paris, 1970.

Bettelheim, Charles. *Problèmes théoriques et pratiques de la planification*. Paris, 1951.

Blum, Léon. *L'Oeuvre de Léon Blum, naissance de la Quatrième République, la vie du parti et la doctrine socialiste*. Paris, 1958.

Bok, Derek C. *The First Three Years of the Schuman Plan*. Princeton, N.J., 1955.

Bouthillier, Guy. *La Nationalisation du gaz et de l'électricité*. Paris, 1968.

Brachet, Philippe. *L'État-patron: Théories et réalités*. Paris, 1974.

Branciard, M. *Société française et lutte de classes, 1914–1967*. Paris, 1968.

Brown, Irving. *Les Syndicats européens et americains unis pour le plan Marshall*. Brussels, 1948.

Brown, William, and Redvers Opie. *American Foreign Assistance*. Washington, D.C., 1953.

Byé, Maurice, and L. Juillot de la Marandiére. *Les Nationalisations en France et à l'étranger*. Paris, 1948.

Caron, François. *An Economic History of Modern France*. New York, 1979.

Carré, Jean-Jacques, Paul Dubois, and Edmond Malinvaud. *French Economic Growth*. Stanford, Calif., 1975.

Chabert, Alexandre. *Les Salaires dans l'industrie française: Les charbonnages*. Paris, 1957.

Chardonnet, Jean. *Crise du charbon en France*. Paris, 1945.

Chenot, Bernard. *Les Enterprises nationalisées*. Paris, 1956.

Chudzinski, Yasmine, and Jacques Renard. *Paroles et mémoires du bassin houiller du Nord–Pas-de-Calais*. Lille, 1981.

Claude, Henri. *Les Monopoles contre la nation*. Paris, 1956.

Claudin, Fernando. *The Communist Movement: From Comintern to Cominform*. Part 2. New York, 1975.

Collinet, Michel. *Essai sur la condition ouvrière française*. Paris, 1951.

———. *L'Ouvrier français, esprit du syndicalisme*. Paris, 1952.

Copin, Auguste. *L'Aurore s'élève du pays noir*. Paris, 1966.

Courturier, Louis. *Les "Grandes Affaires" du parti communiste français*. Paris, 1972.

Cross, Gary. *Immigrant Workers in Industrial France: The Making of a New Laboring Class*. Philadelphia, 1983.

Debergh, François. *La Mine en colère*. Paris, 1971.

Dehove, Gérard. *Le Mouvement ouvrier et la politique de 1939 à 1946*. Paris, 1948.

Dejonghe, Étienne, and Daniel Laurent. *Libération du Nord et du Pas-de-Calais*. Paris, 1974.

Delouvrier, P., and R. Nathan. *Politique économique de la France*. Paris, 1953.

Delwiche, Michel, and Francis Groff. *Les Gueules noires*. Brussels, 1985.

Dépreux, Édouard. *Souvenirs d'un militant*. Paris, 1972.

Desanti, Dominique. *Les Staliniens*. Paris, 1974.

Desbois, Évelyne, Yves Jeanneau, and Bruno Mattei. *La Foi des charbonniers: Les mineurs dans la bataille du charbon, 1945–1947*. Paris, 1986.

Dolléans, Édouard. *Histoire du mouvement ouvrier*. Paris, 1967.

Drexel, E. Godfrey. *The Fate of the Non-Communist Left in France*. New York, 1955.

Dubois, Pierre. *Mort de l'état-patron*. Paris, 1974.

Dumez, Natalie. *Le Mensonge reculera*. Lille, 1946.

Dupeux, Georges. *La France de 1945 à 1969*. Paris, 1972.

Duverger, Maurice. *Les Partis politiques*. Paris, 1951.

Ehrmann, Henry. *Organized Business in France*. Princeton, N.J., 1957.

————. *La Politique du patronat français, 1936–1955*. Paris, 1959.

Einaudi, Mario, Maurice Byé, and Ernesto Rossi. *Nationalization in France and Italy*. Ithaca, N.Y., 1955.

Elgey, Georgette. *La République des illusions, 1945–1951*. Paris, 1965.

Fabre, Robert. *La France manquée du charbon*. Paris, 1945.

Fauvet, Jacques. *Les Forces politiques en France*. Paris, 1951.

————. *Histoire du PCF*. Paris, 1965.

Fougeron, J. *La Mort du mineur*. Paris, 1950.

Foulon, C.-L. *Le Pouvoir en Provence à la libération*. Paris, 1975.

Frachon, Benoit. *La Bataille de la production*. Paris, 1946.

Gaucher, Roland. *Histoire secrète du PCF, 1920–1974*. Paris, 1975.

Geiger, Reed. *The Anzin Coal Company: Big Business in the Early Stages of the French Industrial Revolution*. Newark, Del., 1974.

Gendarme, René. *La Région du Nord*. Paris, 1954.

Gillet, Marcel. *Les Charbonnages du nord de la France au XIXe siècle*. Paris, 1973.

Gillet, Marcel, et al. *La Qualité de la vie dans la région du Nord et du Pas-de-Calais*. Paris, 1976.

Gimbel, John. *The Origins of the Marshall Plan*. Stanford, Calif., 1976.

Godson, Roy. *American Labor and European Politics: The AFL as a Transnational Force*. New York, 1974.

Goetz-Girey, Robert. *Le Mouvement des grèves en France, 1919–1962*. Paris, 1965.

Hamilton, Richard F. *Affluence and the French Worker in the Fourth Republic*. Princeton, N.J., 1967.

Hoffmann, Stanley, and Charles S. Maier. *The Marshall Plan: A Retrospective*. Boulder, Colo., 1984.

Holland, Stuart. *The State as Entrepreneur*. London, 1972.

Houdart, René. *Enquête sur le comportement des ouvriers mineurs du Nord et du Pas-de-Calais*. Lille, 1952.

Jensen, W. G. *Energy in Europe, 1945–1980*. London, 1980.

Jouhax, Leon. *Le Syndicat et la CGT*. Paris, 1948.

Kerchelievitch, D. *Le Syndicalisme des techniciens*. Paris, 1940.

Kolko, Gabriel, and Joyce Kolko. *The Limits of Power*. New York, 1972.

Kourchid, Olivier. *Production industrielle et travail sous l'occupation: Les mines de Lens et les mineurs, 1940–1944*. Paris, 1985.

Krasucki, Henri. *Le Mouvement syndical dans la Résistance*. Paris, 1975.

Kriegel, Annie. *Communisme au miroir français*. Paris, 1974.

————. *The French Communists: Profile of a People*. London, 1972.

Kuisel, Richard F. *Capitalism and the State in Modern France: Renovation and Economic Management in the Twentieth Century*. Cambridge, England, 1981.

Lacoste, Robert. *Devant la fermeture des marchés étrangers*. Paris, 1951.

Lacroix-Riz, Annie. *La CGT de la libération à la scission*. Paris, 1983.

————. *Le Choix de Marianne: Les relations franco-américaines de la libération aux débuts du plan Marshall, 1944–1948*. Paris, 1985.

Lafitte-Laplace, Robert. *L'Économie charbonnière de la France*. Paris, 1933.

Lavergne, Bernard. *Le Plan Schuman*. Paris, 1951.

————. *Le Problème des nationalisations*. Paris, 1946.

Lefranc, Georges. *Essais sur les problèmes socialistes et syndicaux*. Paris, 1970.

————. *Les Expériences syndicales en France de 1939 à 1950*. Paris, 1950.

Lengrand, Louis, and Maria Craipeau. *Louis Lengrand, mineur du Nord*. Paris, 1974.

Lister, Louis. *Europe's Coal and Steel Community*. New York, 1960.

Lorwin, Val R. *The French Labor Movement*. Cambridge, Mass., 1954.

Luethy, Herbert. *France Against Herself*. New York, 1955.

Maillet-Chassagne, Monique. *Influence de la nationalisation sur la gestion des entreprises publiques*. Paris, 1956.

Makuchzak, M. *Réalisations économiques et sociales des charbonnages de France*. Paris, 1957.

Malterre, André. *La Confédération générale des cadres*. Paris, 1972.

Marabuto, Paul. *Les Partis politiques et les mouvements sociaux sous la IVe République*. Paris, 1948.

Maspero, F., ed. *Les Mineurs accusent*. Paris, 1970.

Mauroy, Pierre. *Héritiers de l'avenir*. Paris, 1977.

Mayer, Daniel. *Pour une histoire de la gauche*. Paris, 1969.

————. *Les Socialistes dans la Résistance*. Paris, 1968.

Mayne, Richard. *The Recovery of Europe, 1945–1973*. Garden City, N.Y., 1973.

Merigot, J. G. *Essai sur les comités d'organisations professionelles*. Paris, 1943.

Meyers, Frederick. *European Coal-Mining Unions: Structure and Function*. Los Angeles, 1959.

Michel, Henri. *Les Courants de pensée de la Résistance*. Paris, 1962.

Michel, Henri, and B. Mirkine-Guetzevitch. *Les Idées politiques et sociales de la Résistance*. Paris, 1954.

Milward, Alan S. *The New Order and the French Economy*. Oxford, 1970.

Minces, Juliette. *Le Nord*. Paris, 1967.

Moch, Jules. *Confrontations*. Paris, 1952.

————. *Guerre aux trusts, solutions socialistes*. Paris, 1945.

Monatte, Pierre. *Où va la CGT?* Paris, 1947.

Moniez, Jocelyn. *L'Industrie charbonnière française depuis 1946*. Lille, 1959.

Novel, Paul. *Le Charbon et l'énergie en France*. Paris, 1970.

Novick, Peter. *The Resistance versus Vichy*. New York, 1968.

Oizon, René. *L'Évolution récente de la production énergique française*. Paris, 1973.

Paxton, Robert O. *Vichy France: Old Guard and New Order, 1940–1944*. New York, 1972.

Pellenc, Marcel. *Le Bilan de six ans d'erreurs*. Paris, 1950.

Perrot, Michelle, and Jean Louis Gugliemi. *Salaires et revendications sociales en France, 1944–1952*. Paris, 1953.

Perroux, François. *Les Nationalisations*. Paris, 1946.

Philip, André. *Les Socialistes*. Paris, 1967.

Philippe, Didier. *Les Charbonnages français nationalisés: Organisation du pouvoir; résultats économiques*. Paris, no date.

Poulantzas, Nicos. *Pouvoir politique et classes sociales*. Paris, 1975.

Price, H. B. *The Marshall Plan and Its Meaning*. Ithaca, N.Y., 1955.

Quilliot, Roger. *La SFIO et l'exercice du pouvoir, 1944–1958*. Paris, 1972.

Reiber, Alfred J. *Stalin and the French Communist Party*. New York, 1962.

Reid, Donald. *The Miners of Decazeville: A Genealogy of Deindustrialization*. Cambridge, Mass., 1985.

Reynaud, Jean-Daniel. *Les Syndicats en France*. Paris, 1975.

Ribard, André. *Essai sur la France contemporaine*. Paris, 1949.

Rioux, Jean-Pierre. *The Fourth Republic, 1944–1958*. Cambridge, Mass., 1987.

Rivero, Jean. *Le Régime des nationalisations*. Paris, 1948.

Robrieux, Philippe. *Histoire intérieure du parti communiste*. Vol. 2. Paris, 1981.

―――. *Maurice Thorez: Vie secrète et vie publique*. Paris, 1975.

Roger, Jean-Pierre. *Bully-les-Mines: 2000 ans d'histoire*. Lievin, 1971.

Romeuf, Jean. *Le Charbon*. Paris, 1949.

Ross, George. *Workers and Communists in France: From Popular Front to Eurocommunism*. Berkeley, 1982.

Rossi, A. *Physiologie du parti communiste français*. Paris, 1949.

Sauvy, Alfred. *La Vie économique des français de 1939 à 1945*. Paris, 1978.

Schoenbrun, David. *As France Goes*. New York, 1957.

Schonfield, Andrew. *Modern Capitalism: The Changing Balance of Public and Private Power*. London, 1970.

Shorter, Edward, and Charles Tilly. *Strikes in France, 1830–1968*. London, 1974.

Stil, André. *Le Mot mineur, camarades*. Paris, 1949.

Sturmthal, Adolph. *Left of Center: European Labor Since World War II*. Urbana, Ill., 1983.

Taix, Gabriel. *Le Plan Monnet: Est-il une réussite?* Paris, 1953.

Téreul-Mania, Pierre. *Du léninisme au panzer-communisme*. Paris, 1971.

Tiersky, Ronald. *French Communism, 1920–1972*. New York, 1974.

Tiffon, Georges. *Le Charbon*. Paris, 1983.

Toromanoff, Michel. *Le Déclin du charbon et les problèmes de fermeture des mines*. Paris, no date.

Trempé, Rolande. *Les Mineurs de Carmaux, 1848–1914*. Paris, 1971.

―――. *Les Trois Batailles du charbon, 1936–1947*. Paris, 1989.

Valier, Jacques. *Le Parti communiste français et le capitalisme monopolistique d'état*. Paris, 1976.

Veillard, Raymond. *Le Plan de la CGT*. Paris, 1938.

Ventenat, Marcel. *L'Expérience des nationalisations: Premier bilan*. Paris, 1947.

Vidalenc, Georges. *Les Scissions syndicales*. Paris, 1956.

Vilain, Michel. *La Politique de l'énergie en France.* Paris, 1969.

Wall, Irwin. *French Communism in the Era of Stalin: The Quest for Unity and Integration, 1945–1962.* Westport, Conn., 1983.

Werth, Alexander. *France, 1940–1955.* Boston, 1966.

Williams, Philip. *Politics in Modern France.* London, 1955.

Williard, Claude. *Socialisme et communisme français.* Paris, 1967.

ARTICLES

Andrieu, Claire. "La France à la gauche de l'Europe." *Le Mouvement social* 134 (1986).

Arum, Peter. "Du syndicalisme révolutionnaire au réformisme: Georges Dumoulin." *Le Mouvement social* 87 (1974).

Bouvier, Jean. "Mouvement ouvrier et conjonctures économiques." *Le Mouvement social* 48 (1964).

Brochard, P. "Le Syndicalisme ouvrier et les nationalisations." *Travaux de l'action populaire* (September–October 1948).

Closon, F. "Sur le probléme social des mines du Nord et du Pas-de-Calais, mai 1945." *Revue du Nord* 102 (1975).

Dejonghe, Étienne. "Chronique de la grève des mineurs du Nord–Pas-de-Calais (27 mai–6 juin 1941)." *Revue du Nord* 273 (1987).

———. "Les Communistes dans le Nord–Pas-de-Calais de juin 1940 à la veille de la grève des mineurs." *Revue du Nord* 270 (1986).

———. "Les Houillères à l'épreuve, 1944–1947." *Revue du Nord* 227 (1975).

———. "Ingénieurs et société dans les houillères du Nord–Pas-de-Calais de la Belle Époque à nos jours." In *L'Ingénieur dans la société française*, edited by André Thépot. Paris, 1985.

———. "Pénurie charbonnière et répartition en France, 1940–1944." *Revue d'histoire de la deuxième guerre mondiale* 102 (1976).

———. "Les Problèmes sociaux dans les enterprises houillères du Nord et du Pas-de-Calais durant la seconde guerre mondiale." *Revue d'histoire moderne et contemporaine* 18 (1971).

Domenach, J.-M. "Une Grève des mineurs." *Esprit* (January 1949).

Duguet, Victorin. "La Modernisation des houilléres." *Notes documentaires et études* 551 (18 February 1947).

Dumontier, J. "Réflexions sur la grève des houillères." *La Vie intellectuelle* (December 1948).

Dupuis, Jean. "La Nationalisation des houillères et la politique de l'énergie." *Économie et humanisme* (September–October 1953).

Ehrmann, Henry. "French Labor Goes Left." *Foreign Affairs* (April 1947).

Frost, Robert. "La Technocratie au pouvoir . . . avec le consentement des syndicats: La technologie, les syndicats et la direction à l'électricité de France, 1946–1968." *Le Mouvement social* 130 (1985).

Gerbet, Pierre. "La Genèse du plan Schuman. Des origines à la déclaration du 9 mai 1950." *Revue française de la science politique* 6, 3 (1956).

Gillet, Marcel. "La Bataille du charbon." *L'Histoire* 99 (1987).

————. "The Coal Age and the Rise of the Coalfields in the North and the Pas-de-Calais." In *Essays in European Economic History*, edited by François Crouzet. London, 1969.

Granez, André. "Aspects économiques de la région d'Auchel." *Revue du Nord* 159 (1958).

Goetz-Girey, Robert. "Problèmes actuels." *Politique* (June 1949).

Hainsworth, Raymond. "Les Grèves de 1936 dans les mines du Nord–Pas-de-Calais." *Le Mouvement social* 96 (1976).

Hardy-Hemery, Odette. "Permanences et mouvements dans un pôle industriel: Les Valenciennes de septembre 1944 à 1947." *Revue de la deuxième guerre mondiale* 102 (1976).

————. "Rationalisation technique et rationalisation du travail à la Compagnie des Mines d'Anzin, 1927–1938." *Le Mouvement social* 72 (1970).

Hirsch, J. P. "La Seule Voie possible: Remarques sur les communistes du Nord et du Pas-de-Calais de la libération aux grèves de novembre 1947." *Revue du Nord* 227 (1975).

Holter, Darryl. "Labour Leadership and Left Politics in Northern France, 1929–1949." *Studies in History and Politics* 5 (1986).

————. "Mineworkers and Nationalization in France: Insights into Concepts of State Theory." *Politics and Society* 11 (1982).

————. "Nationalization Reconsidered in France." *French Politics and Society* 14 (1986).

————. "Politique charbonnière et guerre froide." *Le Mouvement social* 130 (1985).

Julliard, Jacques. "Jeune et vieux syndicat chez les mineurs du Pas-de-Calais." *Le Mouvement social* 47 (1964).

Lacroix-Riz, Annie. "Majorité et minorité de la CGT de la libération au XXVIe congrès confédéral." *Revue historique* 266, 2 (1981).

Lavau, Georges. "The PCF, the State, and the Revolution: An Analysis of Party Policies, Communications, and Popular Culture." In *Communism in Italy and France*, edited by Donald L. M. Blackmer and Sidney Tarrow. Princeton, N.J., 1975.

Le Maner, Yves. "Les Communistes du Nord et du Pas-de-Calais de l'agonie du front populaire à la guerre." *Revue du Nord* 277 (1988).

Lorwin, Val. "Communist Strategy and Tactics in Western European Movements." *Industrial and Labor Relations Review* 6, 3 (1953).

Michel, Joël. "L'Échec de la grève générale des mineurs européens avant 1914." *Revue d'histoire moderne et contemporaine* 29 (1982).

————. "Mineurs, tullistes, métalurgistes: Le Nord dans le métropole, 1919–1939." In *La Qualité de la vie dans la région Nord–Pas-de-Calais au 20e siècle*. Paris, 1975.

————. "Syndicalisme minier et politique dans le Nord–Pas-de-Calais: Le cas Basly (1880–1914)." *Le Mouvement social* 87 (1974).

Moscovici, Serge. "Les Mineurs jugent la nationalisation." *Sociologie du travail* 2 (1960).

Moutet, Aimée. "La Rationalisation dans les mines du Nord à l'épreuve du front populaire: Étude d'après les sources imprimées." *Le Mouvement social* 135 (1986).

Peyret, Henry. "La Modernisation des charbonnages français—ses résultats et ses objectifs." *L'Économie* (14 March 1953).

Pinckney, David. "The French Experiment in Nationalization, 1944–1950." In *Modern France*, edited by Edward Mead Earle. New York, 1964.

Quilliot, Roger. "Dix Ans de nationalisations des houillères." *La Revue socialiste* (November 1956).

———. "La Mentalité du mineur." *La Revue socialiste* (February 1947).

Rogliano, Marie-France. "L'Anticommunisme dans la CGT: 'Syndicats.'" *Le Mouvement social* 87 (1974).

Rousso, Henri. "L'Organisation industrielle de Vichy." *Revue d'histoire de la deuxième guerre mondiale* 116 (1979).

Roux, René. "The Position of Labour under the Schuman Plan." *International Labour Review* 65 (1952).

Saumon, Dominique, and Louis Puiseux. "Actors and Decisions in French Energy Policy." In *The Energy Syndrome*, edited by Leon Lindberg. Lexington, Mass., 1977.

Sauvy, Alfred. "La Situation économique française." *Revue française de l'énergie* (October 1950).

Théret, André. "Les Mineurs contre le fascisme." *Les Temps modernes* (1972).

Tilly, Charles. "The Shape of Strikes in France, 1830–1960." *Comparative Studies in Society and History* 13 (1971).

Touraine, Alain. "L'Évolution de la conscience et de l'action ouvrières dans les charbonnages." In *Le Charbon et sciences humaines*, edited by Louis Trenant. Paris, 1964.

Uri, Pierre. "La Querelle des nationalisations." *Les Temps modernes* 5 (1949).

Vigne, Pierre. "Quelques types de psychologie ouvrière: Le mineur." *Droit social* 7 (1950).

Wolf, Marc. "Les Fédérations socialistes face aux difficultés de l'unité ouvrière." *Revue du Nord* 227 (1975).

Index